# Henry VI and Ma

## A Marriage

# Henry VI and Margaret of Anjou:

## A Marriage of Unequals

Amy Licence

PEN & SWORD
HISTORY

AN IMPRINT OF PEN & SWORD BOOKS LTD.
YORKSHIRE – PHILADELPHIA

First published in Great Britain in 2018 by
Pen & Sword History
An imprint of
Pen & Sword Books Ltd
Yorkshire - Philadelphia

ISBN 9781526709752

A CIP catalogue record for this book is available from the British Library.

Typeset in Ehrhardt MT 11/13.6 by SRJ Info Jnana System Pvt Ltd

Printed and bound in the UK by TJ International

Pen & Sword Books Ltd incorporates the Imprints of Pen & Sword Books
Archaeology, Atlas, Aviation, Battleground, Discovery, Family History,
History, Maritime, Military, Naval, Politics, Railways, Select, Transport, True
Crime, Fiction, Frontline Books, Leo Cooper, Praetorian Press, Seaforth
Publishing, Wharncliffe and White Owl.

For a complete list of Pen & Sword titles please contact

PEN & SWORD BOOKS LIMITED
47 Church Street, Barnsley, South Yorkshire, S70 2AS, England
E-mail: enquiries@pen-and-sword.co.uk
Website: www.pen-and-sword.co.uk

or

PEN AND SWORD BOOKS
1950 Lawrence Rd, Havertown, PA 19083, USA
E-mail: Uspen-and-sword@casematepublishers.com
Website: www.penandswordbooks.com

# Contents

For Tom, Rufus and Robin

# Introduction

O n 21 May every year, a small crowd gathers at the Tower of London. They are not the usual tourists, waiting to hear the lurid tales about escapes, executions and jewels, before heading off to take photographs and buy souvenirs. This group has the look of connoisseurs as it makes for the southern section of the Tower of London, close where the Thames rushes under Traitor's Gate, and enters the squat, circular Wakefield Tower. Students from Eton School and King's College, Cambridge, come forward to place lilies from Eton and roses from King's on the floor in remembrance of their founder. Huddled inside an octagonal room, off which an ornate little painted chapel stands, the choir sings as the last rays of the sun slant in through the large windows. The annual Ceremony of the Lilies and Roses is a small, gentle, but defiant, act of remembrance for the Lancastrian, Henry VI, who was murdered there on that date in 1471, or very soon afterwards. The first ceremony was held in 1923, when a plaque commemorating the king was placed in the floor and marked with a bunch of lilies. The roses followed in 1947. Symbolic of his inheritance, of the struggle between two countries and of his marriage, the flowers lying together on the tiles give little indication of the turbulent relationship between England and France, or the union between its representatives, Henry and Margaret of Anjou. It is a suitable, fitting memorial for a king whose gentle, pious character was at odds with the military and merciless demands of medieval kingship, who struggled to model strong leadership with differing degrees of success, plagued by the little-understood issues of poor mental health.

Henry VI has been described by modern historians in ways as damning as a nadir of the English monarchy or 'an incompetent innocent'.[1] He has inspired frustration and sympathy in equal measure as a man uniquely unsuited to the role into which he was born, a role which was inescapable, a role which gave him responsibility for the smooth running of the country and the welfare of his people. Bernard Wolffe has delivered the hard-hitting truths that Henry mismanaged the economy and was a capricious, bad decision-maker, whose character proved key to his own failure,[2] but this approach has not met with widespread approval, being rejected by Christine Carpenter as being 'almost deliberately provocative'.[3] R. A. Griffiths and James Ross take a gentler, more empathetic approach, with the latter asserting that it is hard not to feel sympathy for Henry, a man who was admired as pious by his subjects, but who had very different priorities and who only occasionally engaged in politics.

However, not all Henry's subjects were so admiring; Abbot John Whethampsted described Henry as 'his mother's stupid offspring, not his father's, a son greatly degenerated from the father, who did not cultivate the art of war',[4] and John Neville repeatedly calling him a 'puppet'. John Watts presents a Henry who was unable to assert his individual kingship for the benefit of his people, but his is a broadly sympathetic picture of a passive figure, a vacuum at the heart of government, while the most recent study of the king, by David Grummitt, explores a complex figure whose longevity and hold on power continues to fascinate.

In the decades after his death, a cult sprung up around Henry, as he reputedly cured the sick, rescued those in danger and even brought the dead back to life. The efforts of his nephew, Henry VII, to get him canonised may have owed more to politics than faith, but his reputation at that time speaks volumes about the affection in which he was held, and implies recognition of the discrepancy between his nature and the demands of kingship. Although he may have mismanaged events, the suffering he endured during his reign was interpreted as divine will, a test of adversity in order to prove his faith. Henry's was essentially a localised cult, centered upon his bones at Chertsey Abbey, then at Windsor, with pilgrim badges being made in the city over a span of around three decades. Only Canterbury produced more surviving pilgrims' badges, yet that represents the output of three centuries, and in the last years of the fifteenth century, Henry rivalled Thomas Becket as the nation's favoured saint. Yet there were representations of the unfortunate king all round the country, in East Anglia, Devon, Hampshire, Northumberland, and a notable surviving portrait on the rood screen at St Michael's, at Barton Turf in Norfolk. Historian John W. McKenna asserts that the cult is not plausible because Henry was considered unkingly by his contemporaries; his reputation was manipulated later by others whom it suited politically. Simon Walker agrees on the political nature of the cult, but considered Henry a saint, who died because of the opposing ruling faction; their use of his saintliness helped to restore balance afterwards, and make a degree of reparations for the turbulence of the Wars of the Roses.

Historians are equally polarised when it comes to Henry's wife, Margaret of Anjou, but for very different reasons. When Margaret came to England to be married, in 1445, she was 15, French, and female; three things that immediately posed a challenge in a xenophobic country, making her an alien, an enemy and a figure to be managed by those in charge of the young king rather than to be given a voice. Raised in a country torn apart by dynastic struggles, she already understood the nature of factional politics and the importance of strong women who were able to step into their husband's shoes and rule, campaign, or even fight, during their illness or absence. Just as mid-fifteenth century England was unprepared for a king who modelled a different kind of masculinity, neither was it ready for a queen who refused to conform to the expected back-seat ideal of passive, fertile mercy. A contemporary addressed the unusual character–gender division in the marriage with the quip that all would have been well if only Margaret had been king and Henry had been queen. But their world was only of inflexible boundaries, unable to accept the fluidity of such a solution. After Shakespeare's depiction of Margaret as a she-wolf, the resulting attitude of blame and derision towards the French queen became entrenched, as it was repeated by historian after historian. The familiar vision of her as 'foreigner, white devil, shrew, virago, vengeful fury',[5] upon which were compounded images of extreme cruelty and barbarism, have obstructed more balanced interpretations. Until relatively recently, there has been little recognition that she deserved 'credit for taking on an impossible job', as Christine Carpenter commented.

Margaret's contemporaries were in no doubt about her strength and influence. Gregory's chronicle states that all the lords knew that 'all the workings that were done grew by her' because she was 'far wittier [cleverer] than the king'. The Milanese ambassador considered her 'wise and charitable', Louis XI saw her as 'bold' and, most famously, is John Bocking's comment that she was a 'great and strong laboured woman' who spared 'no pain to [pur]sue her things to an intent and conclusion to her power'. In the generation following her death, Margaret was considered by Polydore Vergil to be 'a young lady exceeding others of her time' but who displayed 'manly qualities' in her determination to 'take upon herself' the governance of the realm. This was echoed by Edward Hall, who initially considered her 'a manly woman', unwilling to be governed by others – meaning men – progressing to insults such as 'cankered crocodile and subtle serpent'. The *History of the Memorable and Extraordinary Calamities of Margaret of Anjou*, written by Michel Baudier in the early seventeenth century and published in London in 1773, establishes a tone of doom before the text starts, swiftly followed by the introduction of 'the miseries of life' and the great height from which royalty may fall. Despite the interference of hindsight, Baudier allows Margaret to have been possessed of admirable qualities, including 'an excellent understanding, sagacity and prudence', consideration, diligence and beauty. Late Victorian sympathy for Margaret is evident in the romanticised version of her life written by Mary Ann Hookham and that of Jacob Abbott, who described her as a heroine, not of romance and fiction, but of 'stern and terrible reality', and J. Bagley's 1948 account presents her as a 'brave and determined champion' but lacking in wisdom and understanding of her situation. More recently, Anne Crawford has emphasised the female models from Margaret's childhood, Patricia-Ann Lee has deconstructed the

Tudor male gaze when it comes to Margaret's reputation and Diana Dunn has unpicked the effects of Tudor propaganda upon her queenship prior to 1453. Helen E. Maurer's study of 2003 presents a more balanced picture of the queen, recognising the complications of nationality and gender as she tried to provide the country with the stability her husband could not offer.

Little attention has been given to Henry and Margaret as a pair, in terms of their marriage, their life together and their joint rule. This is partly because less evidence survives about their intimate relationship, leading it to be reduced to a few simple anecdotes about Margaret being already a woman at the time of her marriage and Henry's reputed prudery. For all the efforts of their enemies to discredit the couple, nothing suggests there were any instances of disharmony between them or lack of respect, other than the typical slurs about Margaret conceiving Prince Edward in adultery, which was the usual weapon of choice against aristocratic women and their heirs. Contemporary and subsequent historians have exploited a far more subtle relationship dynamic to undermine Henry and Margaret as individuals, as a couple and as rulers, by playing on fifteenth-century gender expectations. With qualities of action, ambition and political influence considered to be 'masculine', and mercy, gentleness and peace classed as 'feminine', the reversal of these attributes created a confusion of identities that gave the Lancastrian's enemies rich food for criticism. Thus, Margaret was a 'masculine' woman and Henry, as a man displaying 'feminine' qualities, attracted accusations of weakness, passivity and being easily controlled. Almost six hundred years after Henry's birth, the time is right for a reappraisal of their lives and marriage, which has no need to adhere to strict cultural codes about gender, but can use them as a starting point to deconstruct the identities of two atypical individuals.

Amy Licence
Canterbury, October 2017

# Prologue

In the summer of 1422, farmers across France were hoping for good weather. From the lush green fields of Champagne to the meadows of the Auvergne and the warm, fertile rolling hills of Provence, it was time to make hay and begin the harvest. They shaded their eyes and looked into the distance, watching the horizon for the shadows that would foretell the arrival of rain, or the ripple of marching men in an approaching army. There was both comfort and struggle in the cycle of the year. Along with the church calendar summoning them to pray and observe the feasts of saints, the agricultural routine urged farmers to action; to plough and sow, to winnow and reap. Survival that winter might depend upon the harvest, and 1422 had proved to be a particularly hot, dry summer.[1] Monstrelet's chronicle reminds us of the plight 'of the poor commonality and labourers of France', who declared that 'no corn in our granary is stored' and that, in contrast with the wine on the tables of the rich, 'no vintage cheers our heavy hearts'.[2] As August gave way to September, as the crops were being cut and gathered, those who farmed along the Seine between Paris and Rouen, or near the stretch of land that hugged the coast north up to Calais, paused their labours to watch as the most extraordinary procession passed along the dry roads, between the poplar trees and the waving wheat.

The King of England was dead. Having made a searing impact upon France by driving its archers into the mud at Agincourt, Henry V had laid siege to Dreux, then to Meaux, bombarding their walls with cannon and undermining them with tunnels. Just three months earlier, he had been banqueting in the Louvre Palace, 'gorgeously apparelled' and crowned in his 'most precious diadems', which the whole of Paris had turned out to see. At his side was his young wife Catherine, the beautiful princess of France, whose marriage was set to unite the two countries and put an end to their decades of war. By the treaty of Troyes, Henry was named as the heir to the Valois king, Charles VI, instead of his son, the dauphin Charles, then a rebellious youth of 17. Yet Meaux had proved to be a pyrrhic victory. Even while Henry was feasting at the Louvre, in anticipation of his French inheritance, the deadly bacteria were spreading through his intestines. On 31 August, between 2 and 3 in the morning, he died an agonising death from dysentery, contracted among the terrible conditions at Meaux. The chronicler Thomas Basin saw the hand of justice in this event, claiming that Henry had been struck down by the illness known as 'St Fiacre's evil' because he had allowed his troops to sack a chapel near Meaux dedicated to the saint. Yet this faith in divine retribution could not interfere with the signatures made at Troyes. According to the terms of the treaty, the crowns of France and England passed to Henry's son, a 10-month-old baby left behind in England, whom Henry had never seen.

The body of Henry V was prepared in line with contemporary practice. He was the first English king to die outside his country since Richard I in 1199, and he had to return home. In preparation for the long journey back to Westminster, the king's entrails were removed and buried at the church of Saint-Maur-des-Fossés, and the flesh was separated from his bones, in order for the remains to survive. One source, though, suggests that Henry's body was already so consumed by disease that he required little more than to be embalmed, wrapped, encased in lead and placed in a wooden coffin, which was then put in a larger one of lead.[3] The coffin was taken 'in great funeral pomp', attended by English princes, Henry's household and a 'multitude of other people', on a journey of five miles from Vincennes into the centre of Paris. The coffin was placed within a car drawn by four horses, and was topped by a life-sized effigy of Henry, made of boiled leather, painted to appear lifelike, wearing a gold crown and carrying an orb and sceptre. At the Cathedral of Nôtre-Dame, where the English and French nobility had gathered, a solemn service was performed, and Catherine of Valois was brought 'in great state' from the countryside, where she had been 'kept in ignorance [of] how dangerously ill the king was' and 'knew not of his death' until after the event.[4]

From Paris, the body was carried through the countryside to Rouen. Farmers working the fields of the Loire valley and Normandy witnessed the passing of a long, slow cavalcade of mourners. In their midst, the effigy stared up at the heavens, and the autumn sunshine might have caught the vermilion covering on which it lay, interwoven with beaten gold. Whenever the procession passed through a town, a canopy of silk was carried above the king and the flags of St George, France and England flew amid the Norman fields. Mass was celebrated in each church in which they stopped along the route. At Rouen, the coffin rested in the cathedral, surrounded by torches, awaiting the arrival of Queen Catherine, who reached the city on 24 September, accompanied by eighteen carts of Henry's possessions and four of her own, draped in black. The entourage remained there until 8 October, before moving on seventy miles north-east to Abbeville, where the body was placed in the church of St Ulfran (Wulfram) and rows of priests on either side of his body sung masses for Henry's soul from dawn until noon. From there, they travelled on to Hesdin, before veering sharp west to Montreuil and Boulogne, thus avoiding the famous field of Agincourt, with the queen and her 'numerous attendants' going at a slower pace, about a league behind the corpse. They must have arrived at Calais around the time of

Catherine's twenty-first birthday, which fell on 27 October. A fleet of English ships awaited them.

The ship carrying Henry's body sailed into port at Dover on 31 October 1422. The first of a series of hearses was awaiting him, to transport him to Canterbury, Ospringe, Rochester, Dartford and, finally, into London. On 5 November, the bishops, abbots, clergymen, mayor and aldermen came out to meet the procession as it passed over London Bridge, through the freshly cleaned streets, the civic dignitaries dressed in black, and the guildsmen all clad in white, bearing burning torches. The coffin rested in St Paul's overnight before making its final journey to Westminster Abbey. The king was interred on 7 November, with his coffin drawn up to the nave by four horses and 'greater pomp and expenses were made than had been done for two hundred years at the interment of any king of England'.[5] Thus Henry V, Prince Hal, the survivor of Shrewsbury, victor of Agincourt, conqueror and heir to the throne of France, was laid to rest at the age of 35, long before he had had an opportunity to fulfil his potential. As his story came to an end, another was beginning. The new king of England was a baby, unable to feed or dress itself, even to speak yet, perhaps not even to survive the dangers of infancy. The future, which had seemed so certain, was now called into question.

*Chapter One*

# Henry 1421–1444

## I

The most famous of all medieval illuminations was created just a few years before the birth of Henry VI. Depicting the labours of the months of the year, the *Très Riches Heures de Duc de Berri* was illustrated between 1412 and 1416, in dazzlingly bright blues, reds and golds on calfskin, all watched over by the twelve zodiac signs moving through the arc of the heavens. January represents a splendid feast, where the duke in flowing robes sits behind a table laden with food; in March, a golden dragon flies above the white-walled Chateau, while April is devoted to the pursuits of love. In May, young aristocrats dress in the latest fashions to ride to the sound of trumpets, they hunt with falcons in August and chase the boar to its death in December. Reproduced on modern calendars and postcards, their gothic castles and stylised scenes represent an idealised glimpse into the romance of medieval life, six centuries ago, a simulacrum that fuels fiction, a misleading idyll, a fairy tale.

And yet, the labours of the months depicts a second narrative too. In the depths of the February snow, one peasant chops wood while another drives an ass to market; in March they sow the fields; in the summer months they harvest and shear the sheep; September sees them picking the grapes; in October they plough and till, while November has them watching the pigs, fattening them with acorns ahead of the traditional Martinmas slaughter. But the pigs don't die in the pretty woodland scene, with its exquisite clump of trees, each leaf lovingly delineated. They will be slaughtered elsewhere, in order to furnish the duke's table. The *Très Riches Heures* is a reminder that the world in 1421 encompassed extremes of wealth and poverty, of dazzling castles full of cupboards of gold plate and wooden hovels where clothes hang from the walls to dry. There are labourers in plain, torn garments, giving a bawdy glimpse of the thigh or the buttocks, and women in immaculate white wimples, trailing gold ornament. A golden-haired lady with feathers in her hat receives a ring from a lover while a heavily pregnant grape-picker pauses for a moment amid her work. Rich and poor live side by side, both dependent upon the land, both certain of their place in the world and the relative freshness of their linen.

Perhaps the most significant aspect of medieval life is conspicuously absent from the labours of the months. However, the Catholic faith suffuses the rest of the *Très Riches Heures*, implicit in its very name. The labours comprise only a small percentage of the text, while the remainder is made up of prayers and reflections, intended to be read at times of the canonical hours, which were the daily times designated by the church for worship. Containing psalms, readings, prayers and masses, the theme of the manuscript is the powerful faith that provided the framework for the secular lives of all classes, from castle-dwellers to the field-workers. The churches of England and France were the largest landowners after the crown and wielded significant political influence. Religious belief and practices were never far away, underpinning the structure of each day and the thinking of Henry and his contemporaries. Thus, life in the 1420s, when Henry was born, was defined by religion and duty, leisure and pleasure, within the context of the social hierarchy and the church.

In demographic terms, 1420 was a year of transition. England and France had been through a devastating period of plague, revolt and famine, decimating the population and emptying villages. Estimates at population have offered figures for England of 3 million and France of 14 million in 1400, which were equal, or less, to what they had been a century before.[1] By the time of Henry's birth however, the tide was starting to turn. His father's successes in France had contributed to a sense of national identity and pride, the flourishing wool industry created new wealth and population began to climb. Less than a fifth of English people lived in a town, perhaps even as few as only ten per cent, but the country's infrastructure began to grow following the investment of a new gentry class. New churches sprung up across Suffolk and Norfolk, decorated in the gothic style, dwarfing the scattering of households they were intended to serve. Fortunes were made in trade and money lending, with perhaps the most famous example being London's mayor, Richard 'Dick' Whittington, who served his fourth and final term in 1419–20. He founded a library at London's Guildhall, a hospital for illegitimate births, fresh public drinking fountains and public toilets, before leaving the equivalent of £3 million in his will to charity. London's livery companies flourished, raised imposing new buildings in which to conduct their business and received royal charters. Although many of the old dangers still lurked on the horizon, a cautious new sense of optimism began to be felt in the corridors of Westminster Palace and among the farmers' ridges and furrows.

Henry VI was born at Windsor Castle on 6 December 1421. Built of sturdy grey stone, it had been remodelled by Edward III, using money from his success in the wars against France. He had created three courts, new gateways, a chapel and hall with large windows, luxurious royal apartments and a mechanical clock, totalling over £50,000[2] of work over two decades prior to Edward's death in 1377, more than was spent on any other building by any medieval king.[3] Further work and modernisation had taken place under his son, Richard II, making Windsor the most advanced, comfortable castle of its age. Catherine of Valois, who was used to the Parisian splendour of the Louvre and Hôtel St Pol, chose it as her residence and delivered her son there.

Henry arrived on the feast day of St Nicholas, a date associated with gift-giving and the election of 'boy-bishops', when a child was chosen from among the choristers to enact a parody of real ecclesiastical duties, inverting the usual order of age and experience. Yet this was not just a humorous custom. By association, Henry's birthdate marked both generosity and the exaltation of the humble and meek over the mighty. John Capgrave, the Norfolk historian, who was a teacher of 28 in 1421, saw a divine significance in the day of Henry's arrival, considering that it was 'not without a reason that certain great men have herded together on certain days of greater desert than others'. He added that it was also the month in which the 'Blessed Virgin was conceived' and 'the Saviour of the World was born', drawing the conclusion that 'he who is born at a holy season may imitate His holy life'. Capgrave also commented that Henry had taken after St Nicholas, as both men lived restrained, abstemious lives and had remained dignified when raised to power.[4] Henry was probably christened in the chapel at Windsor, with his uncles Henry Beaufort, Bishop of Winchester and John, Duke of Bedford as godfathers and his aunt by marriage, Jacqueline, Duchess of Hainault, as godmother. Only the fourth godparent, Henry Chichele, Archbishop of Canterbury, was unrelated to the baby.[5]

Henry was quickly established in his own nursery, independent of his mother. Payments recorded in the Patent Rolls tell us that his main nurse was a Joan Astley, or Asteley, whose husband Thomas was also in royal service. As the recipient of £20 a year, Joan was clearly more important than Matilda Foebroke, his day-nurse who received £10, or Agnes Jakeman and Margaret Brotherham, both described as 'chamberer and laundress', at salaries of 100s a year.[6] Henry remained in the care of his nurses until the end of April 1423, by which time he was 16 months old, and probably beginning to walk. The following month he was reported to be 'in perfect health'[7] and when Joan Asteley relinquished her role, her annuity doubled to £40 as a reward.[8] Her place in the boy's household was taken by a Dame Alice Butler, or Botiller, an expert on 'courtesy and nature', who would have been Henry's first teacher and advised on the spending of his household's budget.[9] By the end of 1426, at the time of Henry's fifth birthday, her role came to an end, and she was granted 50 marks a year for life.[10]

In a significant move that marked the end of Henry's babyhood, Alice Butler's replacement was male. On 1 June 1428, Richard Beauchamp, Earl of Warwick, was appointed as the young king's guardian, at a salary of 250 marks. Beauchamp was then aged 46 and already had years of distinguished royal service behind him. His father, Thomas, had been governor to the boy-king Richard II, a relationship that influenced the choice of the king as young Beauchamp's godfather, back in 1382. As a young man, he had fought alongside the future Henry V at the decisive Battle of Shrewsbury, defeating the Welsh and being created a Knight of the Garter. He had continued to serve Henry after his accession as king in 1413, acting as Lord High Steward at his coronation, serving on the royal council, fighting alongside Henry in French sieges, becoming Captain of Calais and Master of the Horse. There was also a deeply devout side to Beauchamp, who had undertaken a lengthy pilgrimage to the Holy Lands. He had been present at the death of Henry V at Vincennes, where the dying king named him as the man to oversee his young son's education.

When it came to the infant king of England, it was not merely a question of raising the boy and furnishing him with a suitable education. The country also needed to be run until he came of suitable age to play a more active role in government. Beauchamp had been part of the minority council established in 1422 when the political transition from father to son had been surprisingly smooth. On the unexpected early death of Henry V, which provoked an outpouring of national grief, it would appear that the country, personified by its leading nobles and prelates, wanted England to be ruled by Henry V's son. There was no question about the boy's legitimacy, or health, and no challenge was mounted to his accession. This shows just how far the Lancastrian dynasty had secured its position in the space of three generations, since Henry IV had usurped his cousin, Richard II. Just twenty-three years after that event, the baby Lancastrian grandson was considered the legitimate heir in spite of the existence of Edmund Mortimer, a fully-grown man of 31, whose line had been nominated by the childless Richard II as his heirs. Mortimer had the advantage of birth and maturity, but in 1422, no one championed his cause over that of the infant Henry VI. In fact, Mortimer was one of the seventeen men appointed to the Regency Council and the following year, he was appointed to be Lieutenant of Ireland at an annual salary of 5,000 marks; a further quarrel with the king's uncle, Humphrey of Gloucester, neatly removed him from the picture before his early death from plague.[11] The Council had come together by September that year, being formally sworn into their duties on 9 December, to 'assist' in the government of the realm 'during the tender age' of the king.[12] They were charged to remain impartial, honest, confidential and loyal, under the rule of the two men whose influence upon the infant Henry was due to their relation to him.

Henry V had been survived by two of his three brothers. As the king's uncles, it was perhaps inevitable that two such experienced, ambitious men would not wield or relinquish power easily. John of Lancaster, Duke of Bedford, was one of the most wealthy, cultured men of his age, who had been appointed Lieutenant of England during Henry V's French campaigns. He had proved an effective, efficient ruler, acting swiftly to repel enemies, whether it was the Scots or traitors within government, and had commanded a fleet to lift the blockade of Harfleur harbour, an essential port for English access to France. Until 1422, John would have been a natural choice as protector during a royal minority, with Lancastrian possessions across the Channel being governed by their elder brother, Thomas. But Thomas's death in 1421 led Henry V to name Bedford as regent of France, with the guardianship of the young king being given to their youngest brother Humphrey, Duke of Gloucester. This was a reversal of their former roles, which had established England as Bedford's sphere of influence, while Gloucester had been Thomas's deputy in France, and was to create a degree of tension between the brothers that was never satisfactorily resolved.

The other most significant influence during Henry's childhood years was his mother, Catherine of Valois. The codicil Henry V added to his will in August 1422, bequeathed ships and jewellery to be sold in order to pay for the upbringing of his son, who was expected to remain with his mother. In spite of her nationality and youth, coupled with her diminished status as a widow, Catherine's right to remain with her son was never challenged. Nor, does it seem, did she ever seriously consider returning to her native France. Her dower payment was generously settled by Parliament at 40,000 crowns, a larger sum than that which had been specified by the Treaty of Troyes. Henry had also left her income from his Lancastrian estates, including those of the de Bohun line, which he inherited from his mother, so she was well provided for. Still very young and relatively new to queenship, Catherine's character remains elusive beyond her reputation for beauty and that which has been extrapolated by historians regarding her supposed 'romantic' tendencies and love of pleasure. She wielded little political influence over her son or the course of his early reign, but neither she, nor the council, would have expected her to play a role in statescraft; her influence was essentially of the nurturing, domestic kind.

The first official record of Henry and his mother together dates from 1423, when he was approaching his second birthday. The *London Chronicle* records that upon Saturday 13 November, Catherine brought her son from Windsor, in order to be present at the second Parliament of his reign, which had assembled in October under the speaker Sir John Russell. They spent Saturday night at Staines, seven miles from Windsor and around twenty miles to the south-west of their destination of Westminster Palace, but on the Sunday morning, as

Henry was carried to his mother's 'chare,' or chariot, he 'schriked and cryed and sprang, and wolde nought be caryed forthere'. He was carried back into the inn, where he remained all day, appearing happy to travel again on Monday. That day they went as far as Kingston, reached Kennington on Tuesday and arrived in Westminster on Wednesday, where Henry was carried in his mother's arms 'with a glad sembland and mery chere'.[13] This incident was cast in a religious light by some of Henry's contemporaries, and hinted at in the chronicle, as an innate sign of the infant's piety that he would not travel upon a Sunday.

On 16 November, Henry and Catherine left Windsor and travelled to Waltham, 'a certen tyme there were abiding'.[14] They would have stayed at the manor house of Great Waltham, which had been part of the dowager's de Bohun legacy, favoured by the royal family for its proximity to the forest and the opportunities for hunting. Founded in the twelfth century on the site of an existing church, the nearby Abbey was one of the largest churches in England and, as Henry's reign coincided with a surge in pilgrimage, it would have been busy as visitors flocked to see its primary relic, the Holy Cross. From there, they travelled the twelve miles north to Catherine's other property, Hertford Castle, where Henry was to spend significant periods of his childhood. Once the possession of his paternal great-grandfather, John of Gaunt, it had also provided a home to Catherine's elder sister Isabella, the young bride of Richard II in the 1390s. They stayed at Hertford for the Christmas season, where they were joined by another young man who knew the house well and for a few years was like another member of the family, perhaps even providing a role model for the infant king.

The uncrowned King James I of Scotland, a handsome, poetic, romantic figure, was 29 years old by the time he celebrated Christmas with the King of England and the dowager queen. Following the murder of his elder brother, he had been smuggled out of Scotland to escape his enemies, but his ship had been seized by the English and he became a prisoner of Henry IV in 1406. Just weeks later, his father died, and the 12-year-old captive became king. Since then, he had been treated like a king in exile; educated, entertained, provided for and invited to play an active role in court life. As part of the household of Henry V, James had accompanied the king to France and been knighted in 1421; he had sat at Catherine's side during her coronation banquet and accompanied her back to England after her husband's death. He was Catherine's only friend at court who was of an equal status, as well as understanding the difficulties of being a foreigner in England. The evidence suggests that their similarities led to the development of a close, sympathetic connection, that provided mutual support to them both. If there were ever any deeper feelings involved, no record survives of it, and the resulting complexities of a potential union between the two, which would have made the King of Scots stepfather to the King of England, might make a romantic story, but there would have been a contemporary understanding that this would create a political minefield. The Regency Council would never have agreed to such a match.

However, James remained a close family friend. He was still living at Windsor Castle in the first half of 1423, at the same time as Henry and Catherine, where he was described as 'extra hospitium regis', or lodging outside the king's hospital. His status was that of an important guest, although in reality he did not yet have his liberty. That June, James received £100, which 'the present Lord the King, with the advice and assent of his council, ordered to be paid to the said James of his gift, for his private expenses', while in July and October, further expenses were granted to cover such costs as 'provisions purchased, carriage, portage, boatage, freightage and other necessary costs and charges whatsoever'.[15] Yet 1423 was to be the Scottish King's final Christmas in England. Negotiations were already well underway for his release and marriage to a second cousin of Henry's, Joan Beaufort. It is likely that Catherine and Henry attended their wedding on 12 February 1424, taking the opportunity to bid their friend goodbye. Henry's relationship with his fellow king would continue for another fourteen years, but the pair would never meet again.

The question of Queen Catherine's private life caused concern and discussion in the council. She may not have entered into a relationship with James Stewart, but there were rumours circulating by 1427 that she was engaged to be married to Henry V's cousin, Edmund Beaufort, 2nd Duke of Somerset. Five years Catherine's junior, Beaufort headed one of the greatest families in England and was a direct descendant of Edward III, albeit through a line that was legitimised retrospectively.

In 1427–8, Parliament passed a bill forbidding the queen dowager to remarry without the consent of the king. If she did so, her bridegroom would forfeit all lands and titles in his possession. In addition, Henry was only deemed able to give his consent if he was of age, so given that he was 6 or 7 at the time of the bill, this meant a whole decade would elapse before Catherine could remarry. The council thought they had tied her hands. Catherine, however, was not prepared to wait. To circumvent the clause about the confiscation of her husband's lands, she simply chose a man who did not have any. Owen Tudor was the keeper of her wardrobe, a handsome Welshman who reputedly fell into her lap while he was dancing. Whatever the truth of their romance, Catherine was able to keep the relationship secret up to a point. She fled into seclusion at Much Hadham in Hertfordshire to deliver her second child, a son named Edmund, in 1430, and then bore a third, Jasper, at Hatfield in 1431. Two or three other children may have been born to the couple. Henry had been in his mother's care until

1428 but his seventh birthday marked an important rite of passage in medieval boyhood, after which his household was restructured to create a masculine influence. It has been suggested that his removal was a sign of disapproval at Catherine's conduct but there is no evidence for this, and it is far more likely that the dowager queen's new role, taking a backseat in her son's life, was the catalyst for her seeking out new ties. Exactly how much Henry knew about his mother's second family during these early years is unclear.

## II

Life at court continued, in education, ceremony and administration. While Henry would later become an ascetic and humble adult, his infancy was certainly spent in a degree of luxury. In November 1423, his goldsmith William Randolf of London was paid £85 11s 4¾d for a large silver spice plate, three silver salt cellars, and three silver gilt candlesticks 'for the use of the said Lord the King' and the 'divers jewels and vessels of gold and silver' given away by Henry V as guarantee against his loans, had been returned to the treasury 'for the King's use'.[16] In May 1425, a John Stout was paid 108 shillings for making a dozen 'quysshons', or cushions, and five 'banquers' worked with tapestry bearing the arms of England and France, for use of the Regency Council sitting in the Star Chamber, presumably for Henry's third parliament which assembled on 30 April. New carving knives were purchased for the king at a price of £13 4d and two gold cups, 'garnished with pearls and precious stones', were brought from the Duke of Exeter at a cost of £702, to be given as a gift to Peter, son of the King of Portugal, 'lately arrived in England'.[17] Peter, Duke of Coimbra, was a son of Philippa of Lancaster, making him a grandson of John of Gaunt and a cousin of Henry, so the cups made a suitably magnificent gift to mark his visit in 1425. Two years later, Peter was admitted as a Knight of the Garter at the traditional April ceremony at Windsor.

In the coming years, Catherine was to remain a constant in her son's life while his paternal uncles came and went. In 1425, Humphrey, Duke of Gloucester, travelled to Hainault in pursuit of his wife's claims, along with titles and lands in Holland and Zealand. According to the *Short English Chronicle*, Gloucester 'was at the fyrst worsshupfully resseyved, but after they sett nott by him, and so came home and lefte his lady at Moynys in Henaude'.[18] The king was more sympathetic to the plight of his aunt, who was imprisoned in Ghent by the cousin who held her lands. Late in 1427, Henry's council approved a loan of 9,000 marks 'to be applied in aid and relief of the Duchess of Gloucester, his wife, the king's kinswoman, then in Holland in great trouble, distress and adversity'.[19] Henry's elder uncle, John, Duke of Bedford, remained in England initially, and was responsible for knighting the young king at Leicester at Whitsun 1426, along with a group of thirty-four young aristocratic men, in order to establish ties of affinity to the Lancastrian line.[20] Many of them were to play significant roles in Henry's future. The following February, though, John and his wife returned to France.

Henry's coronation had been delayed due to his age, but in 1429, as he approached his eighth birthday, the plans were drawn up and the ceremony went ahead. No strict rule governed the timing of this formal anointing but, when it came to young children, precedents had been set by Henry III, who had received his crown at the age of 9 and Richard II, who had been through the process at the age of 10. Otherwise it was a question of judging the child's ability to withstand the demands of the occasion. In Henry's case though, the decision may have been hastened by the developing situation in France, as the influence of the young peasant girl Joan of Arc forced the English armies to abandon the siege of Orléans, weakening Henry's control over his French territories. The deciding factor was probably the coronation of his Valois rival and brother-in-law, as Charles VII, that July. A show of power was required, as a precursor to the king crossing the Channel.

On Saturday 5 November, Henry was at the Tower of London to create thirty-two new Knights of the Bath in the traditional pre-coronation ritual;[21] sadly their names have not survived. The following day, Henry was dressed in scarlet robes lined with ermine and processed from the Tower, through the decorated London streets to Westminster. It was one of the rare opportunities for his subjects to see their king, who did not often appear in public. He had visited Woodstock in 1425, and Leicester in 1426, where his parliament was held, but otherwise his early years had been passed close to home, between Windsor, Westminster and his mother's properties in the home counties. Henry was carried the final distance to the Abbey by his tutor, Richard Beauchamp, Earl of Warwick who then placed the boy on his feet, carrying the royal train as the boy entered. Proceeded by prelates carrying relics, Henry was led onto a scaffold that had been erected between the high altar and choir, covered in the traditional say cloth, where he took his seat 'beholding the people all about sadly and wisely'.[22] The Archbishop of Canterbury, Henry Chichele, proclaimed the boy to the crowd, after which Henry prostrated himself before the altar, 'long tyme lyyng stylle'. Afterwards, his clothing was removed so that he sat in his shirt, which was unlaced to expose his chest. He was anointed on the breast, chest, back, shoulders, elbows and the palms of his hands, with oil that was to remain in place for eight days.[23] Then he was dressed again in scarlet and resumed his seat to receive the sceptre and sword, before St Edward's crown was placed briefly upon his head, although it proved 'over heavy for him as he was of tender age'.[24] He received the sacrament of bread and wine, before being led out of the Abbey into the great hall of Westminster Palace for his coronation feast.

Henry sat in state between his half great-uncle, Cardinal Henry Beaufort, Bishop of Winchester on one side, and the Chancellor, John Kemp, Archbishop of York, along with the Bishop of France on the other. The king's champion, Sir Philip Dymmock, rode into the hall dressed as St George, with all the heralds about him, proclaiming the king to all the quarters of the place. Then the food was served and it was, indeed, a feast fit for a king. The first course comprised a boar's head set amid the arms of a royal castle, frumenty with venison, gilded meats, swan, capon, heron and pike, a red pudding decorated with a crowned lion, custard with a fleur de lys set in gold, fritters like the sun, set with more fleur de lys and a subtlety of marzipan, depicting St Louis and St Edward, carrying the young king in their arms. The verse attached to the king's coat of arms read:

> Lo here be ij kyngys ryght profitabylle and ryght goode,
> Holy Synt Edwarde and Synt Lowys.
> Also the branche borne of hyr blode,
> Lyvynge amonge Crystyn moste soverayne of price,
> Inheritor to the flowre de lysse.
> God graunte he may throughe grace of Cryste Jesu
> The vj[te] Harry to raygne, and be as wyse,
> And hym resemble in kynghood and vertu.[25]

The second and third courses contained similar delicacies, dressed and gilded, along with subtleties depicting The Holy Roman Emperor Sigismund and Henry V, followed by Our Lady, with the baby Jesus on her lap, flanked by St George and St Denis. The corresponding verses lauded the strength and actions of the emperor and king, and asked Mary and the saints to shine their light upon the new king, who was 'born by descent and title of right, justly to rule in England and in France'.[26] It was his rights in the second of these kingdoms that were next to come into focus.

In December 1430, Henry travelled to France, accompanied by a large retinue of his court. Earlier that year, Joan of Arc had been captured by the Burgundians and handed over to the English. Held by the Duke of Bedford at Rouen, she would be tried, condemned for heresy and burned at the stake on 30 May 1431. It had been intended to crown Henry at Reims, as a symbolic undoing of the recent ceremony of Charles VII, but this proved impossible, so Paris was selected instead. The city had been recently attacked by Charles, so it now put on a display for his enemy, decking itself out decorations and pageantry, with clerics standing before their churches holding holy water and relics for the king to kiss. Monstrelet's chronicle describes how a company of Parisian dignitaries met Henry outside the gates, dressed in scarlet and crimson with blue hoods, and he was presented with three red hearts, which released small birds and flowers to be thrown over him. At the bridge of St Denis, he was welcomed by a pageant of three savages and a woman engaged in combat, a fountain of hippocras wine with three mermaids swimming in it, and more pageants of the Holy Virgin and St Denis, 'which was much admired by the English'.[27]

Outside the Church of the Innocents, on the Rue St Denis, an artificial forest had been created in the street with horsemen and hounds pursuing a stag to Henry's feet, upon which he granted the animal its life. Before the stronghold of the Châtelet, the king himself was depicted by a boy of the same age, crowned and seated on a platform beneath the crowns and arms of England and France. Greeted by lords of both nations, he was conducted to the Hôtel de Tournelles, where his aunt Anne, Duchess of Bedford awaited him and acted as hostess. After the meal, he met his maternal grandmother, Queen Isabeau at the Hôtel St Pol, before retiring to the Chateau de Vincennes. On 17 December, he returned to the city centre and the Cathedral of Notre Dame, where he mounted an 8ft platform covered in azure blue decorated with gold fleur de lys. Some controversy was caused when he was crowned by the Bishop of Winchester, instead of the Bishop of Paris 'who said that office belonged to him'.[28] After hearing mass, he was conducted to a marble table in the nearby palace, to dine, listen to music and watch four more pageants. After a few more days in Paris, he departed for Rouen and the coast. Henry VI embarked at Calais and soon arrived back in England; the London-based Gregory's chronicle claims he landed on 29 January, while poet John Lydgate cites 9 February. He would never return to France.

Further pageantry awaited his return. Riding up from Dover, through Canterbury, Faversham, Ospringe, Sittingbourne, Rochester, Dartford and Eltham, Henry entered London on either 14 or 21 February. Not to be outdone by their Parisian rivals, the citizens had prepared a mighty giant to stand guard upon London Bridge, with its sword drawn, and verses proclaiming its intention to defeat all the king's enemies and make him mighty. At the drawbridge, a tower of silk and arras had been erected, housing three crowned ladies in gold, representing Nature, Grace and Fortune, who were surrounded by virgins in white. These girls endowed the king with the seven gifts of the Holy Ghost (wisdom, intelligence, good counsel, strength, cunning, pity and fear of God) and the seven gifts of Grace (crown of glory, sceptre of cleanliness, sword of victory, mantle of prudence, shield of faith, helmet of health and the girdle of love and peace). Then he proceeded to Cornhill, to hear a speech delivered by the figure of Clemency, then on to the Conduit at Cheap, where ladies administered water from the wells of Mercy, Grace and Pity, surrounded by trees flourishing with fruit, including rare imported oranges, lemons, dates, almonds, peaches, pomegranates and quinces alongside the home-grown apples, pears and plums, in a pageant named 'Paradise'. Further on, temporary towers displayed the king's ancestral descent, as well as that of St Edward and St Louis by a jasper-green castle, and a personification of the Holy Trinity related verses of welcome. The king's journey culminated at St Paul's Cathedral where he made an offering at the shrine of Edward the Confessor. To a 10-year-old boy, who had been king as long as he could remember, the coronations, welcomes and pageantry confirmed the unshakeable truth that he was king of England and France in the sight of God. The following year, a blazing comet appeared in the south-west,[29] which must have seemed to Henry and his subjects as if the heavens had been observing events.

In September 1435, bad news arrived from France. The unexpected death of John, Duke of Bedford, at the age of 46 left a vacuum of power that would not be so easily filled. A few weeks later, the Burgundians, formerly England's allies, defected to the French, signing the Treaty of Arras to the effect that Paris should be returned to Charles VII. Gradually, the French started to claw back some of the English territories, taking Dieppe, Arques and Harfleur by the end of that year. In response, around 1,770 men were dispatched to the Norman coast to reinforce the English powerbase at Rouen, followed by a further 2,000 in February 1436 and 5,000 in May. That July, the Burgundians lay siege to Calais but the English troops repelled them, with Gloucester pursuing them into Flanders and spending eleven days on a campaign of arson and destruction. The threat was averted for the time being but the retention of his father's territories across the Channel would always be of significance for Henry.

Henry had been crowned twice, but the next milestone would be his coming-of-age, his assumption of rule in his own right. In December 1434, the arrival of the king's thirteenth birthday marked a significant moment but the council advised him that he was not yet ready to assume the reins of power. He attended a meeting of the council for the first time on 1 October 1435, overseeing the appointment of a new lieutenant of Calais. Another important rite of passage was Warwick's resignation as Protector in May 1436, deeming that the king no longer required his services. That July, Henry signed his first official paperwork on a warrant issued to Cardinal Beaufort at Canterbury, on the occasion that Humphrey, Duke of Gloucester was on his way to Dover to embark for Calais. At this point, something of the young king's character emerges as he favoured peace in France, supported by Beaufort and Suffolk, while Gloucester and his ally, the Duke of York, wanted to continue the war. Another event soon after the king's birthday in December also marked a milestone in his independence and maturity, although it came at a cost.

Late in 1436, Queen dowager Catherine retired to Bermondsey Abbey, situated on the south bank of the Thames opposite the Tower of London. At 35 she may have sought seclusion because of an illness, a scandal, or as the result of another pregnancy. Victorian historian Agnes Strickland believed that her retirement was at the command of the Duke of Gloucester, who had recently discovered her illicit union with Tudor and banished her from court. However, the will she made on 31 December refers to a 'long, grievous malady', and appears to confirm that she had been suffering from a serious affliction that caused her to believe her days to be numbered. She named her 16-year-old son as her executor, so it is very likely that the king was aware of the severity of her condition. That New Year, Henry sent her the gift of a gold tablet decorated with pearls and sapphires, an ornate item of worship that combined her religious devotion with her royal status. Two days later, Catherine died. Henry heard the news while staying at Eltham Palace. Gregory's chronicle relates how her funeral took place on 9 February, 1437 as she was carried from St Katherine's by the Tower, to St Paul's and on to Westminster Abbey, with her coffin topped by the wooden effigy that has survived and remains in the Abbey today.

Any lingering ignorance Henry experienced regarding his mother's second marriage must have been dispelled on Catherine's death. Within days he had summoned his stepfather, Owen Tudor, to his presence, although what passed between them went unrecorded. At the instigation of the Duke of Gloucester, Tudor was brought before the council and required to defend his conduct in defiance of Parliament's bill. He was formally acquitted on that occasion and allowed to leave, but Gloucester was not content to let him go unpunished, and ordered his arrest and incarceration as Tudor attempted to return home to Wales. For the time being, Henry's two young half-brothers, Edmund and Jasper Tudor, lived with the Duke of Suffolk, with the king as a distant presence in their lives. Henry's rule was affirmed when he sat in state, crowned, presiding over his court at Merton Priory in early November 1437.[30] Shortly after this, a new council was created, redefining the roles of those involved in his regency so that they were no longer able to act independently from the king in important matters, taking merely an advisory role or dealing with issues that Henry chose to refer to them. From this point, Henry was issuing grants and exercising his will independently, with Cardinal Beaufort commenting that the king had now reached a point that the Cardinal 'may the better absente him', or increasingly take a back seat.[31]

The young Henry was displaying promise as a new king. Although he was not of the martial calibre of his father or grandfather, he knew his own mind, was charitable and pious and favoured peace with France. Most of the criticisms of his weakness, inability and ill-health date from later in his reign. Little survives about Henry's personality at this point, as the exercise of his individual will is difficult to disentangle from the little that is known about his kingship. Perhaps this in itself is significant; it was a long, slow process by which Henry gained power and few records suggest any sense of assertion or any acts that would allow him to be more clearly defined. Having been a king since he was a baby, Henry never had to fight for his position or aspire to the power that he had symbolised since 1422: he had no one to overthrow, as in the case of his grandfather Henry IV, nor a live, reigning father against whom to define himself, as the rebellious Henry V had done in his youth. There was no rush for Henry to emerge as king and he took his time. He made concessions to the gestures of kingship. In 1440, he founded Eton School to provide a free education for seventy poor boys who would then proceed to King's College, Cambridge which Henry established the following year. Yet Henry had little contact with the school afterwards, staying there once, on the night of 15 April, 1443. He also maintained a busy itinerary, keeping on the move among the home counties and branching out to the east and south coasts, but he did not really travel further north than Kenilworth and Leicester, did not venture into the west or the Welsh borders and did not return to France. In a typical year, he moved roughly every two weeks, often less, occasionally more, dividing his time between his favourite palaces of Eltham, Windsor, Sheen and Westminster. In 1437, he went on summer progress into the midlands; in 1438 into Essex and Wiltshire before returning to Kenilworth for Christmas; in 1439 he travelled through north Kent, which he repeated early in 1440, 1441 and 1442, staying close to home in 1443 and venturing down into Hampshire in 1444. On the whole, geographically, Henry's early kingship was low-key, quiet, slow and safe.

Yet there was one aspect of his life in which Henry stood firm. When it came to the punishment of heretics, he embraced his role as the instrument of God's justice. On 14 May 1438, he wrote to the Sheriffs of London laying out his mandate for the burning of John Bismire, alias John Chandyrer, of the parish of St Mary at Axe, 'who had fallen back into the heresy which he held'. Henry described himself as 'zealous for justice and revering the catholic faith and willing to uphold and defend Holy Church', and commanded the Sheriffs 'with all strictness possible' that John should be 'committed to flames in some public and open place ... by way of an abomination of a crime of this kind, and as an open example to others'. Nor was this a one-off. Henry had written to his uncle the Duke of Burgundy in 1431 concerning the 'superstitious sorceress and ... diabolical blasphemeress' Joan of Arc, whose 'perilous and inflamed spirit of pride and outrageous presumption' led her to be 'delivered to the secular power, the which condemned her to be burnt, and consumed her in the fire'. The same year Henry wrote twice to the Abbot of St Edmundsbury, urging him to resist the Lollards, the heretics following the teachings of John Wycliffe, with 'all the power and might that ye can, [to] chastise and subdue the damnable malice and enterprise of God's said traitors'. He ordered the Abbot to seek out any individuals who had recently left their trades and places, as well as any strangers, 'such as any matter of suspicion may reasonably be felt in' and to 'arrest, search and examine them in the straightest' of ways.[32] What force the young Henry may have lacked in the council chamber, he certainly made up for in the pursuit of religious anomalies.

Gloucester's influence at court had been growing since the death of his brother John in 1435 and the resignation of Warwick the following year, but soon the rising stars of Suffolk, Somerset and Beaufort were to eclipse him. In 1441, a scandal broke regarding his second wife, Eleanor, a former lady in waiting to his first wife Jacqueline, whom he had married soon after the first match was annulled. The couple had been childless for over a decade but, as Henry's closest living relative and a son of Henry IV, any son of Gloucester's would automatically be second-in-line to the throne until such time as the king fathered children of his own. Wishing to conceive a child, Eleanor consulted a 'wise woman' known as Margery Jourdemayne, the 'witch of Eye', who advised her with certain potions, practices and rituals, as was common at the time. However, it appears that Eleanor went further, enquiring about the young king's health and likelihood of a long life. Her personal physician and clerk, Thomas Southwell and Roger Bolingbroke, were implicated in heresy and witchcraft, for imagining Henry's death by casting him an unfavourable horoscope. Both were executed and Jourdemayne was burned at the stake. Eleanor was forcibly divorced from Gloucester and made to carry out a public penance barefoot through the streets of London, carrying a candle to four churches on four different days.

The scandal arising from Eleanor's case impressed upon the regency council just how fragile the Lancastrian hold was upon the throne. With John, Duke of Bedford having died without legitimate issue, and the Gloucester marriage failing to produce any, as well as the early childless decease of their elder brother, Henry had no direct male cousins. If anything did happen to him, as Eleanor's associates had been aware, there would be a struggle for power between the various descendants of Edward III, including the Duke of York and the Beauforts. Henry was 19 at the time of these events, a suitable age for marriage – perhaps even old by the standards of royal expectation. The danger the council had just averted prompted them to turn their thoughts to finding a bride for the king.

*Chapter Two*

# Margaret 1430–1444

## I

Margaret of Anjou was born on 23 March 1430 at Pont-à-Mousson, in the French Duchy of Lorraine. The town sits on the Moselle river, a tributary of the Rhine, winding its way from the Vosges mountains through modern day Luxembourg, Germany and France, past castles, monasteries and fields. Originally a small village, the place was named after the Roman bridge that spanned the river, a crossing which has been in use ever since. The mountain overlooking the river provided an excellent defensive location for the local Counts, offering views that stretched for miles in each direction across the rolling hills and fields of the region, mid-way between Metz and Nancy.

It was in the chateau-fort built at the top of the mountain that Margaret's parents settled, and where their children were born. Little remains today of the home they would have recalled but the large chunks of masonry that survive in the back gardens of houses, and the upright posts that once held gates, serve as a reminder of the settlement that stood there for centuries, sometimes known as the Chateau Keure.[1] A sixteenth-century drawing shows the castle's large central keep dominated by a square, bulbous-topped Grosse Tour, or Large Tower, beside a second Tower of the Great Hall, along with the houses of the Seigneur, the Comte of Mousson. The state apartments on the inside were spacious and decorated, topped with special tiles from the factory at nearby Atton, hung to withstand the winds on the mountain top. The castle's chapel and the chaplain's house were also close by, creating a sealed unit of domesticity, defence and devotion. The second ring of ten-metre-high walls enclosed roads, rows of houses and more churches, including one dedicated to the Knights Templar and the hospital of St Anthony.[2]

By the fifteenth century, the chateau was in the possession of the Lorraine family, given to Margaret's mother by her grandfather, Duke Charles, a knight who took part in the Last Crusade of 1396. He married Margaret of the Palatinate, from the house of Wittelsbach, who bore him at least four children in thirty-one years together. However, their two sons died young leaving their eldest daughter Isabella as heir, so she was given a careful education, and became known for her ability to make decisions in difficult circumstances, as well as for her beauty, intelligence and wit. Charles arranged a political match for Isabella with the Angevin René of Anjou to ensure a French alliance, to protect his lands and Duchy against the ambitions of the Burgundians. It was also a good match in terms of land and titles, uniting two families that held a wealth of power between them.

Isabelle's bridegroom, René, was the son of Louis II of Naples, Duke of Anjou, and Yolande of Aragon, queen of the four kingdoms of Aragon, Catalonia, Valencia and Sicily. Their marriage had taken place on 2 December 1400 at Montpellier, and the 17-year-old Yolande had made quite an impact on her first reception at court the following year. Michel Pintoin, the monk of St Denis, and chronicler of Henry VI's court, who observed her at first hand, described how she 'captivated everyone with her rare beauty, by the loveliness of her face, by the air of dignity that radiated from her entire being'. She was, he concluded, a 'veritable treasure of graces'.[3] Louis had married his cousin, Yolande, in the hopes of gaining the realm of Aragon through her claim, which descended from her father, the Francophile John I. Yolande was a cultured and influential woman, who would lend crucial support to the campaign of Joan of Arc against the English and commission the Rohan book of hours with its beautiful and complex illuminations. The Bishop of Beauvais considered her 'the prettiest woman in the kingdom' while her grandson, Louis XI, attributed her with the same gender-transcending image later used by Elizabeth I, the existence of 'a man's heart in a woman's body'. She was also deeply devout, causing an oratory to be erected on the spot here a rabbit's burrow led her to discover an underground shrine to the Virgin.[4]

Louis was a cultured and martial figure, having fought to maintain his claim to the Kingdom of Naples, which he held for a decade. He also liberated Rome, suppressed a revolt in Provence in order to establish his Angevin inheritance and, in more peaceful times, founded the university at Aix, still operating today as the University of Aix-Marseille. At a time when the papacy was in turmoil, Louis supported the Anti-Pope, Benedict XIII, a relation from the Aragonese nobility, helping him to escape from the five-year siege of his papal palace and offering him shelter. Their first child, Louis, was born in September 1403, followed by Marie in 1404. A gap of over four years followed, when other pregnancies may have been lost, before Yolande bore her second son, René, at Angers Castle on 16 January 1409. He was considered 'remarkable amongst the children of his years, for an agreeable figure, a sweet, intellectual and precocious disposition and great aptitude to learn'.[5]

Typically for his time, René was raised by his mother and her ladies until the age of 7. There were at least four other children in the nursery at Angers Castle, with Louis, Marie and René being followed by Yolande, Duchess of Brabant and Brittany and Charles, Duke of Maine. The ninth-century chateau had been expanded considerably by their father Louis, who added royal apartments and a chapel to the imposing edifice overlooking the Loire. Framed by eighteen squat round towers at the river's edge, the chateau sits inside a semi-circular wall amid formal gardens. The young boy would have been familiar with the dark grey stone alternated with bands of a lighter colour; he would have driven across the drawbridge spanning the moat, through the double towers of the gatehouse, and prayed before the splinter of the true cross held in the chapel reliquary. The royal apartments, placed between the Tour du Moulin and the Tour du Diable, housed illuminated manuscripts, tapestries and other works of art that marked the family's statues as leading patrons during the transition from the late medieval style into the early renaissance. In the late 1370s, his grandfather had commissioned the famous Apocalypse Tapestry, hiring artist Jean Bondel to sketch the design, which was woven in Paris over the course of three years by Nicholas Bataille. Depicting ninety scenes in six sections from the Book of Revelation in red, blue and ivory, the tapestry would have been a feature of René's childhood, either hung in the great hall or displayed on stands. He would have been well-versed in its depictions of the four horsemen and the emaciated figure of death.

When René was 6 years old, a new chapter was marked in the ongoing conflict between the French and English. That October, the armies of Charles VI were defeated by those led by the Lancastrian Henry V at Agincourt, with crippling losses and casualties. Louis of Anjou was in Paris at the time but escaped his duty to fight as he was unwell, and fleeing to his family at Angers in the wake of the English victory. Louis's suffering in October 1415 was reputed to be a bladder infection, but his health took turn for the worse eighteen months later. He died at the chateau on 29 April 1417, at the age of 39 and was buried in Angers Cathedral. The imposing gothic façade was visible from the castle, just a five-minute walk away, and the 8-year-old René is likely to have taken his place in the procession to see his father's remains interred, or else visited his tomb there afterwards. After this, René was raised jointly by Charles of Lorraine and his great-uncle, Cardinal Louis I, Duke of Bar, at whose court he met some of the most significant artists of his day and was inducted into the Order of Fidelity in 1416. He chose the figure and motto of 'Ardent Desire' for his coat of arms.

After decades of hostilities, Agincourt was a humiliating defeat that paved the way for an increased English military and political presence in France. René and his siblings would have grown up hearing the name of Henry V, about his sieges of Rouen in 1418–19, Montereau and Melun in 1420, and the atrocities committed in the process. While his countrymen lauded their king's martial ability and stamina in poems such as soldier John Page's *Siege of Rouen*, news of the English soldier's brutality would have spread to Angers, 200 miles south of the city. Page's account is not unsympathetic to the plight of Rouen's citizens, who died in droves from starvation and illness. Yet the condition and treatment of its women, old people and children, driven out in order to save food, merely to starve in the ditch outside, helped to spread considerable anti-English sentiment. This led to further divisions between the unstable Charles VI, who was prepared to enter an alliance with Henry, and Charles's eldest son, the dauphin. René and his family were safe, at a distance; these years would not only have impressed upon him a complex message about the might and brutality of their enemies, but also about their potential, and thirty years after Agincourt, he would choose to marry his daughter to the son of the man whose name had been whispered and cursed during his childhood.

In May 1420, Charles VI and Henry V signed the Treaty of Troyes. It was a decision that would not only divide the French royal family, as Charles disinherited his son in favour of the English king, but it set the seal on the wedding of Henry V and Princess Catherine of Valois, which would result in the birth of the future Henry VI. The key players may have anticipated that such a repudiation would not readily be accepted by the independent and rebellious dauphin, but they were not in a position to foresee how the treaty and disinheritance would find an echo in England, forty years later, forcing a division between Henry VI and Margaret over their son's right to rule. René's sympathies lay with the dauphin, seeing France's future and national identity vested in Charles of Valois, but he also offered him his support for personal reasons. As his father's fifth son, and the third to survive childhood, it had initially seemed unlikely that Charles would inherit the throne. In 1413, he had been betrothed at the age of ten to René's sister Marie, but two of his surviving elder brothers were still ahead of him in line to the throne. However, following the deaths of Louis in 1415 and John in 1417, Charles was suddenly promoted to the position of king-in-waiting, in opposition to Henry V as heir to the kingdom, and Marie was set to become Queen of France.

Five months after the signing of the treaty, on 14 October 1420, René of Anjou and Isabelle of Lorraine were married in Nancy, at the home of Isabelle's mother.[6] He was three months short of his twelfth birthday while she was 9 or 10. Victorian biographer Mary Hookham describes her as tall, with beautiful features and a 'gentle piety', while painting young René in very nineteenth-century terms, as 'distinguished by an open physiognomy'.[7] Their wedding contract specified that Isabelle was the Hereditary Duchess of Lorraine while Rene would inherit Bar and Pont à Mousson, but their heir would be entitled to both their claims, uniting their lands. This allowed Isabelle to retain her rights rather than signing them over to her husband, but even though she held Lorraine in her own name, she would be expected to rule jointly with her husband and follow his guidance, so her freedom came within clear perimeters. On 10 November, formal proclamations were made in every large town in Lorraine to the effect that full rights of succession and government had been given to Isabelle and René, then under the guardianship of Yolande, Charles of Lorraine and Louis, Cardinal of Bar. The match was seen as a positive move for France, creating an alliance that would be strong enough to resist the enemies that had been weakening the country.

Two deaths that took place in the late summer and autumn of 1422 redefined the European stage. René was still too young to play an active political role in the transfer of power but his situation was considerably improved, as were the prospects of his future daughter. On the last day of August, Henry V died of dysentery, leaving a 10-month-old son as King of England and removing the dauphin's rival heir to the throne. This smoothed the path for his succession as Charles VII when his father died on 21 October 1422. The news was probably broken to him in Anjou because, the previous summer, Charles had made a tactical withdrawal when confronted by Henry's larger army at the siege of Chartres and sought protection from Yolande and Louis in Lorraine. Their Angers court was, for a while, home to the anti-English and Burgundian faction, the safe house of the future king, and would provide Charles with a wife and lover. The new king's marriage to Marie took place on 18 December 1422 at Bourges, capital of the former province of Berri, home of her great-uncle. A 20-year-old maid in Louis and Isabelle's household named Agnes Sorel accompanied Marie to her new life, to serve her as Queen of France. Matching the late medieval ideal of beauty, as her pale-skinned, high-browed portraits attest, it was Agnes not Marie who stole Charles's heart, and she went on to bear him three children before her death from mercury poisoning. Marie would produce fourteen legitimate heirs, including the next king of France, Louis XI, who was born in Bourges on 3 July 1423. Whatever the politics of the royal bedroom, René of Anjou was now the king's brother-in-law. He was also soon to become a father.

On 5 February 1424, according to the *Chronicle of Lorraine*, Isabelle made her ceremonial entrance into Pont à Mousson, where her presence was celebrated with jousts and tournaments. She was in the early stages of her first pregnancy and remained at the castle on the mountain in order to give birth, bearing a son named John on 2 August. Her second child, Louis, arrived in 1427 and, the following year, she bore twins Yolande and Nicholas, although Nicholas died before his third birthday.

In the year between the birth of his twins and the arrival of his daughter Margaret, René's life overlapped with one of the most famous women in the history of medieval France. Jeanne d'Arc, or Joan of Arc, was born in Domremy in the Duchy of Bar, fifty miles from Pont à Mousson and just twenty miles from Toul, making her one of René's subjects.[8] At the age of 12 she had seen visions of Saints Catherine and Margaret, before being told by St Michael that her country was being divided and torn by enemies (English and Burgundian) while the real king, Charles VI, was a fugitive, as yet uncrowned. If René's marriage uniting Anjou and Lorraine had engendered hope for France, the emergence of Joan was heralded as the fulfilment of an old prophecy that the country would be saved by a maid from Lorraine. In 1429, Joan was brought before Charles of Lorraine at Nancy, at a time when he was overseeing the dispute between René and his cousin Antoine, Count of Vaudemont, over the inheritance of the Duchy of Lorraine. Reputedly dismissed by the duke, she received a far more sympathetic audience from the 20-year-old René, whom she chose to ride with her on campaign to liberate the city of Orléans that April. Their connection gave rise to scandalous rumours about the nature of their relationship, but there is no foundation to these, being part of the wide discourse of defamation that found an easy target in Joan's gender and sexuality. René was given the commission to oversee examinations into the orthodoxy of Joan's religious views, while his mother Yolande headed the panel of matrons that investigated her to find indications of her chastity.[9] Outside Orléans, Joan dictated, or guided, the letter René wrote to John, Duke of Bedford, to cease the destruction of France and return the keys to the city. René's forces repelled the English from the city, which was considered a sign of her divine approval, leading Charles to agree to her request to march on to Reims.[10]

Now supported by the Duke of Alençon and other leading French generals, Joan's army went on to take Jargeau on 12 June, Meung-sur-Loire on 15 June and Beaugency on 17 June, before defeating a much larger English force at Patay the following day. It may be that René was no longer with her at this point, taking the opportunity to return briefly to Angers, or else his wife Isabelle travelled to see him on campaign, because it was around this time that she fell pregnant with their second daughter Margaret. Working back from Margaret's birthdate on 23 March 1430, a typical forty-week pregnancy would place the date of her conception around 16 June 1429, the day between the sieges of Meung and Beaugency. However, a slightly longer pregnancy would allow for more flexibility, as the army then headed north-east, in the opposite direction to Angers, reaching Gien before the end of June and accepting the surrender of Auxerre on 3 July. René was certainly present when they entered Reims on 16 July, where Charles VII was crowned the following day. It would seem likely, given their direction of travel, that Margaret of Anjou was conceived in early June, perhaps if her mother was present at Nancy or travelling with her husband in the weeks preceding the campaign.

It has been suggested that Margaret was born a year earlier, in March 1429, a date which the nineteenth-century historian Mary Hookham and Margaret's biographer of 1976, Jock Haswell, accept, as do some more recent authors. Edgcumbe Staley adds that René was far from home at the time of her birth, 'escorting La Pucelle to Chinon'.[11] This would neatly circumvent the difficulties of placing her conception between René's military engagements, meaning that Margaret was born just weeks before the lifting of the siege of Orléans. However, this only circumvents a difficulty if, in fact, a difficulty exists. Isabelle is likely to have been with her husband for part of her journey, accompanying him until the first or second week of June 1429, before departing for the safety of Angers. The presence of Joan of Arc may even have encouraged her to remain at her husband's side, a safe distance behind siege lines but close enough to share his bed. The birthdate of 23 March 1429 may have been a misreading of the Catholic calendar year, which at this time formally dated the new year from Lady Day, or 25 March. A convincing case for the late birthdate has been made by C. N. L. Brooke and V. Ortenberg in the Journal of Historical Research, and most modern historians accept her arrival as taking place in 1430.[12]

On 23 March, Isabelle went into labour at Pont à Mousson and delivered her second daughter, whom she named after her mother, Margaret. The baby was baptised in St Stephen's Cathedral in Toul, around twenty miles to the south-west of the mountain castle, by the Bishop of Toul, Henry II de la Ville-sur-Illon. Her godparents were her maternal grandmother Margaret and her father's elder brother Louis, King of Naples.[13] Being cradled in her grandmother's arms, Margaret was carried through the gothic entrance, along the thirteenth-century transept, choir and nave, where light poured down through windows topped with roses. Margaret was nursed by the woman who had cared for René in his infancy, Theophaine le Magine, a native of her grandmother Yolande's court at Saumur. Two months later, Joan of Arc was captured by the Burgundians at the siege of Compiègne, and handed over to the English. She was burned at the stake in Rouen on 30 May 1431. Margaret of Anjou was only 2 years old at the time but there is no doubt that she would have heard first-hand tales of the legendary Joan, of her determination and martial skills, her piety and importance in the history of France. The church at Pont à Mousson later housed a statue of Joan, but given the involvement of her family, an earlier memorial may have been placed to her there during Margaret's life time.

## II

The first years of Margaret's life were defined by her parents' struggles to claim their inheritance. Their methods and efforts, especially those of her formidable mother and grandmother, would impress upon her the need to be active in the face of challenges, to be strong and unyielding in dealings with the enemy, and the complicated nature of factional politics that could redefine loyalties and test individuals to the limit. She learned that death was final, but it also offered a moment of transition, opening doors for the survivors, and that imprisonment and exile could be overcome by the tireless work of allies. A woman's loyalties were defined by her family, by blood or by marriage, and it often fell to a wife to assume the reins of power during her husband's absence, to govern his estates and look after his interests. Essentially, she saw that a woman sometimes had to play the male part. It was a lesson she never forgot.

Upon the death of his great-uncle Louis I, Duke of Bar, in 1430, René inherited the Barrois Duchy, followed by that of Lorraine, when his father-in-law passed away the following year. Although he had been named as heir for the decade since his marriage to Isabelle, René's right to Lorraine was challenged by his cousin by marriage, Count Antoine de Vaudemont, who cited Salic Law, and the loss of the title through marriage, as reasons why the Duchy should pass to him. The cousins clashed at the Battle of Bulgnéville in July 1431, when Vaudemont allied with the Burgundians, surprising René with an unexpected artillery attack which decimated his forces within an hour, leaving heavy casualties. René was half-blinded by an arrow wound on the left forehead, which left him scarred for life.[14] He surrendered to the Burgundians, who handed him over to the count, whose terms included the return of certain castles and a ransom of 20,000 crowns. This, in addition to the further debt to the man who had captured him, and costs to the Burgundians in charge of the castles he had lost, exhausted René's slender finances.[15] Isabella was left to negotiate his release and head the family at Nancy. With the support of her mother; she raised an army to keep Vaudemont at bay and appealed to the Emperor, who ruled in her favour in 1434. She may also have taken her two daughters, Yolande and Margaret, south to the court of Charles VII, in Vienne, in an attempt to rouse his sympathy and support.[16] She certainly gained the trust and assistance of Emperor Sigismund, who became an advocate of René's cause. The Lorraine inheritance was settled by the betrothal of René's elder daughter Yolande to Frederick, son of Vaudemonte, but the count was angered by the emperor's intervention, broke off negotiations and ordered René to return to captivity along with his two eldest sons, John and Louis, aged 10 and 7. Margaret had to say goodbye to her brothers, not knowing whether she would see them again.

As it transpired, John would be released in time, but Louis would die while still incarcerated.

On 26 August 1434, Isabelle lost an important source of support with the death of her mother Margaret, her little daughter's godmother. That autumn there was also conflict over the inheritance of the kingdom of Naples, which had been held by René's elder brother Louis III, but that November he died from malaria, leaving no legitimate children. His claim had been previously disputed by Joanna of Naples, to whom the title now reverted. Isabella went to Naples to argue in favour of René's inheritance, and the timely death of Joanna the following February allowed her to assume the regency. The tension in the region, however, meant that she would remain there, protecting her husband's interests until 1538. During her absence, Isabelle sent Margaret to live with her paternal grandmother Yolande of Aragon at Saumur. Her elder sister Yolande was being raised in the Vaudemont household of her future husband, as was customary in the case of aristocratic betrothals.

Overlooking the confluence of the Thouet and the Loire in the Maine-et-Loire, the tenth-century chateau of Saumur was built to repel incursions south by the Normans. Restyled by the English Henry II in the twelfth century, its fairy-tale white turreted walls and pepper-pot domes are familiar from the *Très Riches Heures du Duc de Berri*, depicted as the castle appeared in the second decade of the fifteenth century. Yolande had acted as regent for her son as the head of the house of Anjou since her husband's death and had served as a substitute mother-figure for Charles VII, when his own parents acted against his interests by favouring the English. An important influence upon the king, she had promoted and funded Joan of Arc's campaign to restore his rights and achieve his coronation. Her household was established in the castle but later in life, she adopted the habit of a nun and resided in a house in the Faubourg des Pontes, seeking a more simple and devout existence.[17]

It is unclear exactly when Margaret arrived in Saumur, but it was probably around 1435, when she was 5 years old; she would remain there until Yolande's death in December 1442, when Margaret was 12. Yolande's was a cultured household, where her granddaughter read Boccaccio and other works of romance and chivalry. She would also have been present on diplomatic occasions, as fragments surviving from René's accounts from 1442 include the direction to his treasurer to 'dress Mme Marguerite for the arrival of the Emperor's ambassadors in Saumur and Angers'.[18] Yolande also made efforts to provide for the girl's future, negotiating a marriage for her with the Austrian Hapsburg Frederick III, King of the Romans, and future Holy Roman Emperor. When René was finally released from captivity in November 1436, he headed for Isabelle in Naples, calling in at Saumur on the way, and being reunited with his daughter for the first time in years. He and Margaret were also together for the marriage of his eldest son, her brother, John of Calabria, which took place at Angers in April 1437. Margaret and Yolande acted as the hosts for a visit of the king and queen, Charles and Margaret's aunt Marie, who stayed at Saumur in 1440, giving the girl a taste of the Angevin court.

Yolande's death left a power vacuum in Anjou. Giving up their costly and ultimately doomed venture in Naples, René and Isabelle returned to Angers, where Margaret joined them. Keen to repair his property after their absence and the ravages of war, René of Anjou developed his court into a cultured, artistic and chivalric environment. His surviving accounts detail the clothing, jewellery, library, furniture and entertainments purchased at the time, including the expenses for his garden with its collection of specialist plants and his large zoo and aviary, in which he kept lions, elephants, camels, leopards, tigers, wolves, stags, boars and exotic birds from around the world. He hosted musical and nautical spectacles, mystery and passion plays for thousands of spectators, gave a warm welcome to pilgrims, employed leading figures as his secretaries and doctors and retained the famous dwarf Triboulet as an entertainer, whose image was immortalised in 1461 by a medal struck by Francesco Laurana.[19]

In addition to the artists of the Avignon school, René employed the Burgundian Barthélemy d'Eyck, whose stepfather supplied the family with cloth, as artist and valet de chambre. Probably related to Jan Van Eyck, whose reputation is better known today, Barthélemy was considered a leading artist of his day during his lifetime and was active from 1440, meaning that Margaret is likely to have been familiar with his oeuvre. It is likely that he encountered René during the duke's imprisonment at Dijon or during his later time at Naples, but it is certain that René commissioned illuminated manuscripts from him, leading Eyck to be known as the Master of René of Anjou, and contributing to the calendar details of the *Très Riches Heures de Duc de Berri*, created by René's great-uncle. There has also been some confusion between his work and that of René himself.

At the time of Margaret's residence at Angers, her father commissioned additions to an earlier manuscript, known as the *Hours of Rene of Anjou*, which was embellished in 1442–3 by the Rohan Master, which included portraits of Rene, his father Louis, Isabelle and Margaret. Some of the miniatures appear to be the work of d'Eyck, but the entire manuscript is a composite of several influences, including those made before it came into the hands of Margaret's father. René's contribution included three personalised prayers, offices of the dead and Latin poems attributed to Walter Mapes, a twelfth-century Welsh cleric who studied at the University of Paris and visited Champagne.[20] René's hours also contain the labours of the months tied to the astrological signs, just as the Duke of Berri's do, but with slight differences, giving a picture of the rural year as Margaret's family experienced it. The early year from January to March depicts a man warming himself before the fire, cutting down a tree and working in an orchard. The spring months of April and May show a nobleman looking like the portraits of René dressed in red robes against a blue sky and vivid grass, out for a walk, carrying a tree branch over his shoulder, followed by a similar figure riding on horseback with a bird of prey on his left hand. Interestingly, the 'twins' depicting the astrological sign of Gemini that feature alongside the hawker, or falconer, are not the usual blood-related siblings but a naked couple in an embrace, about to copulate in what appears to be a field, or sparsely planted wood, indicating that this time of year was also associated with lovers. June, July, August and September show images connected with the stages of harvest, scything, harvesting grain, threshing the corn and pressing grapes underfoot. The final quarter of the year is reserved for sawing wood, feeding acorns to pigs and slaughtering animals in preparation for the winter. It is a reminder that even the most important families in France, fighting over their dynastic claims, were still dependent upon the cycle of the year.

The Hours also provide a more intimate window into Margaret's world. Its illustrations depict exquisite interiors with lead-paned windows, stone archways and pillars, the walls painted bright colours or hung with fleur-de-lys curtains, the floors covered in complicated patterned tiles or two-tone designs, in black and white, or dark and light shades of blue. People pray in stone alcoves screened by hangings or recline on beds under canopies. In one scene, a group is seated at a feast, along the sides of a trestle table covered in a white cloth; another sees a crowned king ensconced in a carved throne, topped with winged dragons, over which hangs a harp. The external views show rolling green landscapes around mountains and winding rivers, with woods and stony outcrops. The family's piety is constantly re-enforced by the content and illustrations, but also their mortality, by the memento mori depicting René as a corpse, his stomach split open to show the worms eating his organs inside.[21]

Renés's library contained more than 200 books, including a silver Bible, botanical, legal, medical, historical, astronomical, geometrical and similar works, in as diverse languages as Hebrew, Catalan, Occitan, Latin, Greek, Turkish and Arabic as well as German and French.[22] At Angers, the writer Antoine de le Salle was appointed tutor to Margaret's brother, John, Duke of Calabria, and fulfilled the role of overseer of tournaments. Salle created the didactic text *La Salade* in the 1430s and 40s, a book of guidance for the education of Princes and contributed to the series of famous jousts held by René in the 1440s. During this time, René was compiling his own *Le Livre de Tournais*, the Book of the Tournament, but also wrote *The Book of the Love-Smitten Heart*, a sophisticated courtly allegory of the lover's quest with the narration framed in three ways, by letter, romance quest and dream vision. The text was completed in 1477, but had its genus in the 1450s, exposing the kind of story that was favoured by the Angevin court.[23] Margaret's years of young womanhood, from her arrival at Angers until her marriage, were spent in a refined atmosphere of literature, art, music and culture alongside the national and personal dynastic tensions of the era.

In January 1443, René was at his castle of Tarascon to receive an embassy from the Duke of Burgundy, proposing a match between Margaret and his nephew Charles, Count of Nevers. A dowry of 50,000 livres was agreed and a contract was signed at Tarascon on 4 February 1443, by which Margaret's children were to inherit Sicily, Provence and Bar, taking precedence over the children of her elder sister Yolande. This provoked Antoine Vaudemont and his son Ferri, or Frederick, to bring the matter before Charles VII, with the result that Margaret's marriage was postponed. Had she become the wife of the Burgundian count, the course of European history would have been significantly different but, as it happened, she was soon to receive a far more significant proposal which would ally her to another of Anjou's formidable enemies. The King of England was seeking a wife, and he hoped to find her in France.

*Chapter Three*

# Marriage 1445

## I

The marriage of an English king to a princess of France was hardly a new occurrence. In fact, by 1445, it had practically become an English tradition. Stretching back over more than three centuries, the previous eleven kings all had a French wife, with only one exception. The twelfth-century King Stephen had chosen Matilda of Boulogne, while the first Angevin monarch, Henry II, wed Eleanor of Aquitaine. His sons followed tradition with Richard I wedding Berengaria of Navarre and John taking Isabella of Angouleme as his second wife. In the mid-thirteenth century, Henry III's consort Eleanor was a native of Provence while Edward I had made a second marriage to Margaret, daughter of Philip III of France. The unfortunate union of Edward II and Isabella of France, Margaret's niece, still lingered in the popular imagination, with the infamous 'she-wolf' siding with her lover against her husband and agreeing to his deposition, and perhaps even his death. It may have been reaction against his mother, or new connections to the Low Countries, that led her son, Edward III, to choose a wife from Hainault. Since then though, Richard II had wed Isabelle of Valois, Henry IV chose Joan of Navarre and Henry V had returned to the house of Valois, to marry Isabelle's younger sister Catherine. It was almost an expectation of an English king that he should select a wife from some region of France, and especially in recent years, this had been an important part of the fluctuating fortunes of the Hundred Years' War.

Yet, historically, not all these marriages had been received the same way. Circumstances in 1444, when René of Anjou met William de la Pole, Duke of Suffolk, at King Charles's court at Montils, had changed considerably since the reception of Catherine of Valois as the wife of Henry V. Then, in the wake of Agincourt and the Treaty of Troyes, with Henry's military victories, the English were in the stronger position, allying themselves with the crown of France against the dauphin's faction which opposed their presence. Twenty years later, the dauphin was an established king and the English had lost lands and authority. The death of the steadying figure of Henry VI's uncle, John of Bedford, had followed soon after the 1435 Treaty of Arras, which saw the

French ally with Burgundians instead. A disastrous campaign in the early 1440s by John Beaufort, Duke of Somerset, had proved expensive and unproductive, perhaps even corrupt; modern speculation has his death in 1444 as a possible suicide, resulting from his failures.

The union of Henry VI and Margaret was a good strategic move for the French. Charles VII and René were poised to launch a joint attack against the Burgundians, an enterprise which could only benefit from having English support, or at the very least a peace. England and Burgundy had signed a treaty of perpetual peace in 1443, creating fears of a joint attack upon France that Charles wished to pre-empt. Pope Eugenius was also keen for France to heal its wounds, after the damaging schism when the house of Anjou sided with the anti-popes, and he hoped for Valois support following his own recent defeat at the hands of the Turks. Plausibly, Margaret's candidacy arose at the French court in response to an English suggestion that the English seek a bride for their young king. The natural choice for Henry's ambassadors would have been a daughter of Charles VII, echoing the choices made by Henry V and Richard II, and paying tribute to Henry's mother. There were, in fact, four Valois princesses available at the time, and although they were still young, they were not too young: Yolande, approaching 10, and Joan, who was just 9, were the most likely candidates, although the 5-year-old Joanna and the infant Magdalena were also in the nursery. However, Charles was not prepared to offer Yolande, or one of her sisters, but he was keen to back his niece Margaret as a candidate for the match. Although Margaret's credentials have been questioned, as she brought no dowry beyond nominal titles, there were a number of good reasons for this. If Henry had married a French princess, this may have created the same problem of dual inheritance as vested in Henry VI by the Treaty of Troyes. Also, a daughter of Charles VII would be closely related to Henry VI, both sharing the same grandfather, from whom it was thought the strain of madness was thought to have been inherited, doubling the likelihood of an heir inheriting the condition. Margaret was close enough to the French throne, a Princess from the powerful Angevin line, to be sufficiently royal. It would also create a further debt of loyalty between René and Charles, and hopefully ensure future long-term English support.

Half the English court had been pressing for a peace deal with France, perhaps through a marriage, since at least 1439. John de la Pole, Earl of Suffolk, soon to become duke, and the king's half-great-uncle, Henry, Cardinal Beaufort, were in favour of the match while the opposing faction, headed by the king's uncle Humphrey, Duke of Gloucester, attempted to thwart their efforts and promote the continuance of war. Henry VI, now in his early twenties, was keen to marry and had a natural preference for peace over war; he hoped that by marrying into the house of Anjou, he would also gain a friend in the Valois court. The Victorian historian Agnes Strickland, and her contemporaries, relate a romantic story about Henry dispatching an Anjou man, Champchevrier, then a prisoner of Sir John Fastolf, to accompany an artist to obtain a portrait of Margaret 'in plain kirtle, her face unpainted and her hair in coils'. He wanted to know 'her height, her form, the colour of her skin, her hair, her eyes, and what size of hand she hath', if this did take place, the image no longer survives. In 1912, Edgcumbe Staley named Hans of Antwerp as Henry's favourite artist, whom he had earlier sent to paint the three daughters of the Count of Armagnac,[1] but this cannot be the well-known goldsmith and artist, painted by Holbein, as this Hans was not born until 1497. Perhaps some earlier Dutch artist by the name of Hans also served Henry VI, and was also dispatched to Anjou after his sojourn in Armagnac. Victorian authors referred simply to 'one of the finest artists in France'.[2]

The choice of Margaret, instead of one of King Charles's daughters, was considered something of a disappointment among Gloucester's faction, a situation that was not aided by the bride's lack of dowry and prospects, as her elder brothers precluded her from inheriting from her father. When Parliament decided to send Suffolk into France to negotiate on Henry's behalf, he was dubious about accepting their mission, fearing, rightly, that he would be seen as its author, so insisting that he was accompanied by a delegation of four other leading officials. Henry chose his Lord Privy Seal and Dean of Salisbury, Adam Moleyns, his secretary Richard Andrew and his trusted servants Sir John Wenlock and Sir Robert Roos and supplied letters of declaration that they should experience no blame should the embassy not prove a success. Despite his support, it was Suffolk who was charged with the potentially explosive charge of bargaining with the French, with permission to cede Maine and Anjou in return for the English being allowed to keep the lands in Normandy and Aquitaine that had belonged to Henry V. This deal was not widely known in England in 1444 and the Duke judged, quite rightly, that it would prove unpopular. He was also empowered to offer that Henry would meet the costs of the wedding and waive the proposed £20,000 dowry. The English were aware that the Burgundian Count of Nevers was seeking Margaret's hand, which added further impetus to Suffolk's negotiations, in order to avoid being excluded by another Franco-Burgundian alliance.

Suffolk and his party landed at Harfleur on 15 March 1444 and travelled to the English stronghold of Rouen, before heading south to Le Mans in Angevin territory. They met at Vendôme on 8 April, from where Suffolk and his party were taken by boat along the Loire to the magnificent chateau of Blois, as a guest of Charles, Duke of Orléans. Suffolk would have been familiar with the duke, whose capture at the Battle of Agincourt had led to a twenty-five-year imprisonment, only ending with his release in 1440. From there, they continued to Tours, where René and Charles VII were waiting at the chateau of Montils-les-Tours, (later known as Plessis-les-Tours) the eleventh-century fortress that had been acquired by Charles that year. Margaret was brought by her mother from her Angers home to the Abbey of Beaumont-les-Tours, where Suffolk visited them to pay his respects on 4 May. Following eighteen days of further negotiation they signed the Truce of Tours, by which the terms of the marriage were set out.

Margaret and Henry were formally betrothed on 22 May in the mixed Romanesque and gothic St Martin's Cathedral at Tours. The ceremony was conducted by Piero da Monte, Bishop of Brescia, a papal legate, who provided the dispensation required for their mutual descent from John II of France. Beside the 14-year-old princess stood the duke, acting as proxy for Henry VI, repeating his vows and making his promise to the young girl. More than a decade older than Margaret's father, Suffolk was an experienced statesman of 48, and Margaret appears to have trusted him from the start. He was her first connection with England, her proxy husband, even her mentor, whom she perceived as the champion of her cause without being aware of his initial reluctance. That moment, in Tours Cathedral, was the start of a long friendship that would endure until Suffolk's death. It was the legal contract by which she was handed over from one man to another but, with Henry VI's youth and pacifist character, the safe pair of English hands was that of the duke. Suffolk was the figure of strength and authority that Margaret looked towards, to fulfil the role of father and guide through the coming years. Their mutual interest was political but there was also a personal element, of affection and respect. Rumours that they became lovers did not arise until the sixteenth century; it is far more likely that codes of chivalry dictated a more innocent nature to their friendship from 1444.

The festivities began with Charles and René leading a colourful procession of the French nobility through the streets of Tour. In addition to the two kings and their queens, this included the Dukes of Brittany and Alençon, the dauphin Louis and his wife Margaret of Scotland. At the banquet that followed, Margaret was treated with all the honours due to a Queen of England and René organised a tournament featuring knights dressed up as figures from the Arthurian stories and a wooden castle named Joyeuse Gard, after the one owned by the character Lancelot. As part of the occasion, Margaret was presented with a bound volume of the stories, which was probably an edition of the Chrétien de Troyes version. The truce was confirmed on 28 May and the English left the following day.

It is difficult to make a fair assessment of the English reception to Margaret's marriage, given the weight of hindsight and the narratives of her enemies, which gained the credibility of law and dynasty under Henry's successors, the Yorkists. Nor was there one single uniform response, with reactions varying across issues of gender, class, location and self-interest, as well as the likelihood that much of the country may have barely reacted at all, or merely registered the fact of the marriage, rather than the identity of the bride. It did not take long for Margaret's perceived failings to identify her as a scapegoat to her enemies and history would colour her as warlike, aggressive and unfeminine in her reactions to the fragmentation of her adoptive country. But those conclusions were processes that took years in the construction, as the result of a complex factors of gender, identity, historiography and faction. Nor could she have predicted, or been held responsible for, the brevity of the Anglo–French peace and the losses of territory that England suffered in the later 1440s and early 1450s. In 1444, Margaret as an individual was untried, untested; she had yet to marry, produce a child, lead a faction, forge alliances: the tide of history might easily had ebbed a different way. The dissenting voices raised against her betrothal belonged to a courtly clique against whose aspirations the match jarred, but this was not necessarily representative of the country, or Parliament, or the court in general, nor did it have to be permanent. In 1444, the nature of her queenship and relationships was still to be determined. The course of her life would be determined by the tensions between her influence as an individual and her nationality, her status as a symbol of Frenchness as viewed by an increasingly xenophobic nation.

The Truce of Tours was considered a poor deal for England by the Duke of Gloucester and his supporters, who would have preferred Henry to marry a daughter of the Count of Armagnac. However, those English residents of Normandy saw it rather differently, welcoming the first cessation of hostilities in twenty-five years, with 'immense and incredible joy … dancing and feasting with yesterday's enemies', according to the French chronicler Thomas Basin.[3] The fifteenth-century historian John Capgrave, a great supporter of Henry, believed 'this marriage will be pleasing to God and the realm, because that peace and abundant crops came to us through it'.[4] However, the later writer, Edward Hall, offered a retrospective view, stating that the marriage seemed to many 'both unfortunate and unprofitable to the realm of England' because 'the king with her had not one penny' and the English made an enemy of the Count of Armagnac. He went further to contradict Capgrave, saying that the match displeased God, and was the start of Henry's subsequent misfortunes.

Yet at the time, without Hall's insight, Henry was very keen for the marriage to go ahead and showed his gratitude to Suffolk by elevating him to the title of marquis and awarding him the wardship of another young Margaret, this time the infant daughter of the deceased Duke of Somerset. Born in May 1443, and without any surviving brothers, Margaret Beaufort was undoubtedly the most significant heiress in England and would soon be betrothed to Suffolk's son. Somerset's death brought Suffolk to greater prominence at court, along with Margaret's uncle Edmund Beaufort, Marquis of Dorset, who now succeeded to the family title and estates. Quickly establishing himself as a favourite with the king, the 37-year-old Beaufort cut an imposing figure and used his influence to promote those in his circle such as Adam Moleyns, who gained the see of Chichester in 1445.

Five months elapsed during which Margaret made her wedding preparations. Suffolk was issued with his instructions on 28 October 1444 and promptly embarked for France on 7 November, with a large entourage ready to accompany the queen of England to her new home. It was a court in miniature, with 'chief nobles, barons, ladies, damsels, knights, squires and other officers, besides servants, sailors and running footmen', all requiring 'diet, offerings and almsgivings, necessaries, salaries and wages'.[5] Each baron received 4s 6d a day and had three squires and two valets, who were paid 1s 6d and 6d respectively. A baroness had the same wage, as did her retinue of one valet, one squire, one chamberer and two damsels. The initial cost of the expedition had been estimated at just under £3,000[6] but it ended up taking much longer, running to a total of 182 days and, therefore, costing much more, adding fuel to existing criticism.

Included among the party were the high-ranking women who had been chosen for the queen's entourage. Without exception, they were married and mature in age, many of them being mothers: Jacquetta, Duchess of Bedford, from a prominent Burgundian family, was the youngest at 28 or 29, and she was Margaret's aunt by her marriage to Henry; the 40-year-old Alice, Marchioness of Suffolk, granddaughter of the poet Geoffrey Chaucer, who would become Margaret's lifelong friend; Beatrice Talbot, Countess of Shrewsbury, the mother of children Margaret's age; Isabel Dacre, Lady Grey; Alice Neville, Countess of Salisbury, then in her mid-thirties, who would end up on the opposite side from Margaret in the years ahead as would Ismayne, or Emma, Lady Scales. Mary Ann Hookham[7] also places Elizabeth Grey (née Woodville) among the women, a future queen of England, as that name is listed in the Egerton MS, but this is a case of mistaken identity, as Elizabeth was only 7 or 8 at the time, and certainly not known by her married surname at this point. It is more likely to have been Woodville's future mother-in-law, Elizabeth Ferrers, Baroness of Groby, who had married Edward Grey.

A few details about Margaret's movements survive from mid-November, recorded by John Breknoke and John Everdon, clerks of the comptroller's wages, which indicate how quickly the English party met up with their queen. On the thirteenth of the month she was recorded as being at 'Cambec,' (probably Caudebec-en-Caux) from where she was conveyed to Rouen in the boat of a John Oliver, who received 6s 8d for his trouble. Caudebec-en-Caux sits about twenty-two miles west of Rouen as the crow flies, but it would have been a long slow journey for Margaret through the three oxbow bends of that stretch of the Seine. The English would have landed at Le Havre or Honfleur, thirty miles further west; they were not mentioned on 13 November, but had definitely arrived by 28 November, when Margaret travelled to Honnflete/ Hounfleet, (Honfleur?) and returned to Rouen accompanied by 'Beatrice Lady Talbot, and other ladies and damsels appointed to attend her.'[8] As René of Anjou was currently laying siege to Metz with King Charles, it would have been Duchess Isabelle who met with Suffolk, travelling up from Angers to conduct the English to the city of Nancy, where the wedding was scheduled to take place. By 12 December Margaret was at Vernon, forty miles to the south-east of Rouen[9] after which she appears to have returned east to Harfleur.

The whole process was slowed by her father's siege at Metz, which was not lifted until 3 March, and a lack of funds. Francis Lancelott in *The Queens of England and their Times*, states that Margaret left her father's court with 'no money and but little apparel' and had to wait until Henry was able to petition parliament for aid in February 1445. Once that was granted, and René had returned victorious, the ceremony could go ahead. The state of Henry's finances remained dire though, and although he sought the desperate solution of raising loans against the crown jewels, he later realised he would require them at his wedding, so was forced to redeem them and pawn some of his own personal plate and jewellery.[10] Margaret had been raised in a court already drained by ransom payments and the costs of war, but it is unlikely she had a full understanding of just how poor her future husband had become. Her eyes would soon be opened though, as she would be forced to pawn some of her silver wedding gifts to the Marchioness of Suffolk, in order to pay her boatmen in the coming weeks.[11]

The wedding took place early in March, again with Suffolk standing proxy for Henry. It was officiated over by Louis de Haraucourt, Bishop of Toul, a godson of Louis, Duke of Bar, René's great-uncle. Margaret's motif of the daisy, or marguerite, featured prominently in the decoration and clothing: she wore white satin with the flower embroidered in gold and silver.[12] At the same time, Margaret's elder sister Yolande was married to Frederick, son of Antoine Vaudemont, to settle the Lorraine claim. A week of festivities ensued, with feasting, tourneys and jousts, presided over by King Charles's mistress, Agnes Sorel, formerly a member of René's household, who appeared in a suit of silver armour studded with gems. The jousting was held in Nancy's Place de la Carrière, still a wide, tree-lined avenue today, where René defeated Charles VII and Frederick was named as champion, being presented with his prize by Margaret.[13]

Margaret's parents accompanied her as far as Bar-le-Duc and her brother John continued with her to St Denis, in Paris. The Duke of Orléans escorted her on the next stretch of her journey, through Paris, arriving at Pontoise on 18 March, where the border between English and French possessions lay, and the French lords turned back, as she was welcomed by Richard, Duke of York. The following day Margaret paused in Mantes to distribute 22s 4d in alms, along with shoes and grey clothes for fourteen poor women on Maundy Thursday and on 20 March she spent three days at Vernon, attending Mass at the castle on Palm Sunday and leaving a gift of cloth and 6s 8d.[14] From there she and York took a barge to Rouen, the capital of English-held Normandy, arriving on 24 March, but Margaret was indisposed at the time of her arrival, either seasick or unwell, or unhappy, as her place in the grand entry festivities was taken by the Countess of Shrewsbury. While staying in the city that had witnessed the burning of Joan of Arc thirteen years earlier, Margaret gave 13s 4d to the Monastery of the Blessed Mary of Rhotomarensis, an additional 6s 8d when attending mass in Rouen Castle and the same amount again on Easter Day.[15]

Hookham relates that Margaret visited the Abbey of 'Bocamshard' on 31 March, while Lancelott has 'Bokamsbard'. As with other entries, the spellings of place names are phonetic, as they fell on fifteenth-century English ears, so this was almost certainly the Benedictine St Georges de Boscherville Abbey, set in a bend of the Seine close to Rouen, with a twelfth-century church and chapter house. The Abbey lies on the way to Pont-Audemer (Hookham) or Pountamder (Lancelott), which Margaret had reached by 1 April, before reaching Honfleur again, the following day. She left an offering at the Church of the Blessed Mary of 3s 4d, before being conveyed by a boatman named Collin Freon and three sailors to the *Cok John*, a ship from Cherbourg which awaited her in the harbour. Her attendants travelled in the *Mary of Hampton*, but a total of fifty-six ships were required to shift her entire household across the Channel.[16] Waiting for favourable weather conditions, the fleet eventually set sail on 9 April.

## II

Margaret's ship limped into Portchester, then a village close to Portsmouth, in Hampshire. The voyage had taken her from Honfleur to the closest, most direct English harbour, past the Isle of Wight, through the gap defined by Bembridge and Selsey, into the Solent, but it had not been a smooth crossing. Suffering from seasickness and an outbreak of 'the pokkes' (the pox) Margaret was unlikely to have been able to appreciate her first sight of her new home, of the country over which she was to rule, with its long beaches, white cliffs and rolling green hills. The following day, the party sailed along the coast to Southampton where Suffolk carried Margaret ashore. She recovered from her ordeal in the Hospital of St Julian, or God's House, just metres from the waterfront, probably in the prior's lodgings or one of the individual rooms reserved for the clerics, rather than in the two main halls. The resident brethren and sisters were more accustomed to tending to poor and needy travellers and pilgrims, than a queen. The grey stone chapel with its square tower still stands in Winkle Street, incorporated into the south-east corner of the town walls. Over the next few days, Margaret slowly recovered and her physician Master Francisco was paid £3 9s 2d for 'various aromatic confections particularly and specially purchased by him and privately made into medicine for the preservation of the health of the queen, as well by sea as by land.'[17]

Meanwhile, Henry was anxious to meet his bride. News of her illness had already caused the marriage to be delayed, but a romantic story related by Raffaelo De Negra to the Duchess of Milan in 1458, suggests that Henry hastened down to Southampton to see her in person:

> When the queen landed in England the king dressed himself as a squire, the Duke of Suffolk doing the same, and took her a letter which he said the King of England had written. When the queen read the letter the king took stock of her, saying that a woman may be seen over well when she reads a letter, and the queen never found out that it was the king because she was so engrossed in reading the letter, and she never looked at the king in his squire's dress, who remained on his knees all the time. After the king had gone the Duke of Suffolk said: Most serene queen, what do you think of the squire who brought the letter? The queen replied: I did not notice him, as I was occupied in reading the letter he brought. The duke remarked: Most serene queen, the person dressed as a squire was the most serene King of England, and the queen was vexed at not having known it, because she had kept him on his knees. The queen afterwards went from thence. The king really wrote to her and they made great triumphs.[18]

The use of disguise and the adoption of a lower status identity in order to conceal a king's true status evokes memories of chivalric romances and courtly love conventions that later fuelled the matrimonial games of Henry VIII. De Negra's account is the only source for this meeting, and it does not sound much like the image of Henry VI that has survived into the twenty-first century. Portrayals of the Lancastrian king tends towards the pious, austere, even asexual and mentally unstable, but this discrepancy may be the fault of historiography, the fault of hindsight and symptomatic of the scant descriptions that survive of Henry. If the image of Henry hurrying to meet his queen, dressed as a humble squire and kneeling at her feet, is an unfamiliar one, it is partly because our general impression of Henry is not a rounded one. He had already written to René to say how much he was looking forward to meeting Margaret, and he was within riding distance at Southwick, along the coast in West Sussex.[19] Henry was 23; he was not yet the man who fell ill, or who was captured and controlled by his enemies. Nothing suggests he was not a normal, healthy young man, perhaps more gentle and pious than some of his contemporaries, but fully able to anticipate a wife, family and long reign. He had been waiting for the conclusion of the match for over a year, and the news that Margaret had arrived, would have peaked his curiosity as much as her illness created concern. Rather than being unusual for its 'romance', this supposed meeting is quite in keeping with Henry's quiet, unshowy and sensitive character. He did not claim the stage, or declare his identity, he slipped in unobtrusively in a humble way, in order to observe his bride. He also used the occasion to assess whether or not she was well enough for the wedding to go ahead, considering that she may have tried to rise to the occasion and fulfil her duty before she had fully recovered. Seen in this light, the event appears more sensitive and considerate than the act of romance it evokes.

Henry had been making eager preparations to welcome his bride to England. There had been no queen's apartments in use in any of the royal palaces for years; Catherine of Valois had died in 1437, but she had retired from the public view long before that. Henry's improvements were necessary to establish suitable living quarters for his wife, including repairing lodgings and chambers at Westminster, building a new hall, serving space and kitchen rooms at Eltham, and cosmetic repairs at Sheen, adding to the gatehouse and walling the garden. Preparations also went ahead for Margaret's coronation, with scaffolding being erected in Westminster's Abbey and instructions given out to the London guilds to prepare their pageants for her entry into the city.

Presumably, Henry and Margaret officially met soon after Suffolk revealed the king's identity. This event has been dated to 14 April and took place, according to chroniclers Holinshed, Stowe, Lingard and others, at Portchester Castle, located at the north end of Portsmouth Harbour. Two days later, Henry wrote to his Lord Chancellor, John Stafford, Archbishop of Canterbury, explaining that he would not be returning to Windsor in time for the Garter celebrations on St George's day on 23 April, 'because the queen is not yet free of the results of the sea-sickness by occasion of which the pox being broken out upon her'.[20] The man Margaret met, at some point during the third week of April, was tall and dark-haired, to judge by the various portraits of Henry and the details established by the examination of his skeleton in 1910. That report established him as standing between 5ft 9 and 10in and to be a 'fairly strong man'.[21] As a child, Henry had been described by French witnesses as 'a very beautiful boy', 'of beautiful appearance', dignified, well-mannered and 'every inch a king'.[22] Images in the contemporary Talbot-Shrewsbury Book of Hours show him with dark hair, a gentle expression and a forked beard. Margaret would have been relieved to discover that her husband could speak fluent French.

Far less is known about the new queen's appearance. The same book of hours depicts her with the long blonde hair that was a conventional accoutrement of queenly appearance, but she was described by De Negra as being somewhat 'dark', although it is not clear whether this related to her hair or complexion. Portraits of both her parents suggest they were dark haired yet this is no guarantee of inheritance, or artistic accuracy. Edward Hall, who never saw her, relates that 'this woman excelled all other, as well in beauty and favour, as in wit and policy, and was of stomach and courage, more like to a man than a woman', but although his final point relates to the queen in later life, some of her mettle may have shown already as a young woman, upon being taken from her family, crossing the sea, enduring illness, entering a strange country and becoming the wife of a stranger.[23] She needed to remain composed and retain her dignity through the difficulties of travel and sickness, let alone the public receptions she was given at various stages of her journey. What would have mattered to each party involved in such a negotiated match was the pedigree, position and power of their future spouse. What they could bring to the marriage table was of most significance, followed by that individual's conduct, their appropriate projection of authority within its context, as well as the appearance of physical health and strength for the purpose of procreation. Character was significant, but as a function of their ability to act as a conduit for successful rule. Quirks could be tolerated so long as they did not weaken an individual's majesty; good looks and attraction were a personal bonus, but not essential. There is no reason to believe that Margaret and Henry were not each satisfied with their future spouse.

On 23 April Margaret and Henry were married at Titchfield Abbey by William Ayscough, Bishop of Salisbury. A dispensation had been issued to allow the wedding within the prohibited season of Lent. While the opening speech of Parliament back in February had concerned the importance of peace, the sermon focused on the dynastic imperative of Henry producing an heir, with a reading of the 128th Psalm, describing wives as fruitful vines upon the wall of a house and children as olive branches around the table. Five miles from Portchester, the abbey had been home to the white-robed order of austere Norbertines, or Premonstratensian canons since the early thirteenth century.

Although little of the original building survives under the post-reformation century additions, the expensive, multi-coloured tiles and carvings indicate that it was a luxurious, high-status building, fit for a wedding. Henry could have made the decision to marry Margaret in Westminster Abbey, or St Paul's, playing to a large crowd in his capital city, but arranging the ceremony in the privacy of Titchfield meant that Margaret would enter London as its queen, and head straight for her coronation. The focus would be on her, not on the king, with her status and position already established.

Henry had ordered Margaret's wedding ring to be specially made from one given to him by his uncle, Henry Beaufort, at the time of his Parisian coronation in 1431. Back in January, he had ordered the Treasurer of his Chamber and Keeper of his Jewels, John Merston, to deliver up a '*Ring of Gold*, Garnished with a fair Rubie, somtyme given unto Us by our Bel Oncle the *Cardinal of Englande*, with the which we were Sacred in the Day of our Coronation at Parys', to be sent to a *Matthew Philip*, 'to Breke, and thereof to make an other Ryng for the Quenes Wedding Ring'.[24] Now the gold ruby ring, especially adapted for the queen's use, was placed upon Margaret's finger. Other items Henry requested from his treasury for Margaret's use included gold tablets, set with gems and pictures of the Virgin Mary and saints, gold cups, gold brooches, with rubies sapphires and pearls, another one made in the form of a woman, and one other in the shape of a gold fleur de lys.[25]

Among Margaret's wedding presents was the magnificent manuscript of the Talbot-Shrewsbury Hours, depicting a blonde-haired queen at her wedding, similar to the image reputed to have been drawn of Margaret by her father in his own book of hours, being presented with the book bound in red leather with gold and blue clasps. The image shows Margaret and Henry, hand in hand, as Talbot kneels before them, identifiable by the white dog at his side, his dynastic symbol. She is crowned, with her long fair hair loose, dressed in flowing lilac robes which reveal the white and gold of her dress beneath. An illustration later in the manuscript of the queen of the Amazons is almost identical in colour and detail to that of the young queen. Accepting the book, Margaret's gaze is down, upon the giver of the gift, but Henry's eyes are upon her, his expression gentle, even deferential, sitting in blue robes lined with ermine. They are seated under the grey stone arches of a perpendicular building, perhaps the abbey, with the ceiling painted blue with old stars and before a backdrop of the combined English-French royal arms. To Margaret's left are her waiting women, dressed in the fashionable horned hennin headdress of the day, while members of Henry's court appear behind him.

The manuscript was commissioned by Lord Talbot specially for the occasion and made in Rouen, written in a French gothic cursive script, and contained a table of the descendants of Louis XI, the deeds of Alexander the Great, epic poems, 'chansons', or songs of heroic deeds, prose romances, writing by Christine de Pisan, Giles of Rome, Guy of Warwick and others. The one specific English-focused entry was the Statutes of the Order of the Garter. A tapestry had also been commissioned for Margaret, a hunting scene featuring ladies wearing the marguerite, or daisy, and the letter M sewn into the horses' bridles. The new queen was also given the unusual gift of a lion, which cost 65s 4d to transport to Robert Mansfield, the keeper of the menagerie at the Tower of London. Exactly who gave her the gift, and where the lion came from, is unclear, although Hookham claims it was 'from one of her attendants' and the unlikely beast raises more questions than can be answered with any satisfaction. Most of all, it is tempting to speculate what the gift was intended to symbolise; whether it was merely a status symbol, a gift worthy of a queen, or if there was some heraldic intent?

Henry and Margaret spent their wedding night at the abbey, remaining together there until 27 April. Although Henry was a deeply devout king, there is no reason to suspect the marriage was not consummated successfully, on that occasion, or soon afterwards. It is not possible to assert, as Paul Murray Kendall does, that Margaret was 'already a woman; passionate, proud and strong-willed' or, as he continues, that she was humiliated by her discovery that she was 'married to a monk', or that Henry was overawed by her strength and beauty and became her 'humble vassal'.[26] Henry was reputedly advised by Ayscough not to 'have his sport' with the queen, or 'come nigh her' unless for the procreation of children, but this does not exclude intercourse at all, and the king was keen to father an heir. The report is also more likely to have sprung from hatred of the Bishop than the reality of the marriage, as it had been Ayscough himself who had married the pair. Another image in the Talbot-Shrewsbury Hours depicts Nectanebus and Olympius in bed, providing detailed information about the intimate environment in which the new couple would have sealed their union. The bed is placed under a fixed canopy, the underside of which is covered in red material with gold stars. Floor to ceiling curtains in green and gold hang on three sides, while they are tied up out of the way on the fourth, allowing sight of the bed itself. The couple lie between white sheets, over which a red floral coverlet is draped, reaching down to the floor. No details survive about the wedding night, or the subsequent reaction of the court, which may well be the result of Henry's choice to make it a quiet, private occasion. Another image from the same manuscript shows a new mother, lying in a similar bed, beside a long wooden cot containing seven babies. It was clear where the English expected Margaret's duty to lie.

At Titchfield, Henry discovered the extent of his new wife's poverty. It may be that her wardrobe was found to be inadequate, or equally that Henry wanted to dress Margaret according to her new station, for he dispatched to London to bring back a dressmaker named Margaret Chamberlayne, to prepare clothes for the queen, at a salary of twenty shillings. This may account for her slow progress back to the capital, as word was sent ahead to prepare the city for the queen's reception. Henry returned to Westminster, while Margaret was entrusted to Henry's uncle Cardinal Beaufort, one of the leading supporters of the truce with France. Margaret's first impressions of England would have been gleaned from the beautiful green countryside of the South Downs and Surrey hills as they passed south of London, through the home counties. She was a guest at Beaufort's home of Bishop's Waltham, a moated, newly renovated palace mid-way between Portsmouth and Winchester on the Downs, and also at Archbishop Stafford's home at Croydon, before reaching the red brick Eltham Palace in the middle of May. Henry was back in Westminster on 25 May, where he met with the Privy Council. Three days later, on 28 May, Margaret and Beaufort rode along the Thames to the awaiting reception at Blackheath, just outside the village of Greenwich.

The Mayor, Sheriffs and Aldermen of the city had assembled to await Margaret's arrival, their crimson and scarlet robes, along with the red hoods, embroidered sleeves and blue cloaks of the Guildsmen making for a colourful sight as the queen approached through the early summer fields. This is also the last point at which Margaret could have met her husband's uncle, Humphrey, Duke of Gloucester, who was present with 500 men in livery and welcomed her, despite his opposition to the match. She may well have met him before, having accepted his offer to stay at his Palace of Bella Court to break up her journey before her entry into London.[27] Later renamed Placentia, Pleasaunce and then, Greenwich Palace, this was Margaret's first glimpse of the newly built red-brick house on the bank of the Thames where she was to spend significant time and refurbish to reflect her own tastes. It was a conciliatory gesture from Gloucester, intended to reassure her that his objections to the marriage had been diplomatic, not personal, and to establish a connection in the hope that Margaret's sympathies would not be given wholly to his enemies. In this aspect, Gloucester would fail; Margaret's loyalties had already been won by the Dukes of Suffolk and Shrewsbury and their wives, but she was shrewd enough to play the diplomatic game and accept his hospitality with a good grace.

From Blackheath, Gloucester conducted Margaret the five miles to Southwark, passing through the main street with its many inns and market place, right past the spires of Southwark Priory, now renamed as its cathedral. From there, the procession headed towards London Bridge, with its tall buildings crammed along the entire length and the Thames rushing beneath its nineteen arches. At the gatehouse, which allowed access to the bridge from the Southwark side, Margaret was confronted by a pageant representing the figures of Peace and Plenty, with the suggestive motto from the Book of Genesis attached: 'Ingredimini et replete Terram', or 'Enter and replenish the earth.'[28] The celebration verses, reputedly written by the poet Lydgate, described Margaret as England's 'pleasure and joy', as welcome as any princess ever was, as the bringer of joy, wealth and abundance. As she progressed along the bridge, with its many shops, latrines and chapel, through its narrow span of eight metres, Margaret encountered a pageant of Noah's Ark, bearing the legend 'Jam non ultra irascar super terram', or 'Henceforth there shall be no more curse upon the earth.'[29] The comforting sun would begin to shine upon the earth again and the flood of vengeance between England and France would cease. The verses presented her as the bringer of peace, like the dove after the Ark, the symbol of unity between the two nations:

> *So trusteth your people, with assurance*
> *Through your grace and high benignity.*
> *Twixt the realms two; England and France,*
> *Peace shall approach, rest and unity,*
> *Mars set aside with all his cruelty*
> *Which too long hath troubled the realms tweyne*
> *Biding your comfort in this adversity*
> *Most Christian Princess, our Lady Sovereign.*[30]

Coming off the bridge, Margaret passed through Bridge Ward, along Bishopsgate and New Fish Street, in the shadow of narrow houses and the churches of St Magnus, St Margaret and St Leonards. The streets would have been lined with people, probably kept back behind railings, or hanging out of windows overhead, to witness the arrival of their new queen. The procession headed up the gradual hill of Gracechurch Street, past the conduit there, past St Benet's, All Hallows and St Peter's to the conduit at Leadenhall, one of the highest points in the city. Here, Margaret paused to observe a speech made by Madame Grace and many other 'sumptuous and costly'[31] pageants, including the cardinal virtues, appearing from artificial woods, scattering flowers and garlands.[32] Turning left, the procession headed into Cornhill, the wide road that bisected the city along its east–west axis, where more verses and performances greeted Margaret at the inn that bore her name, emphasising parallels between their new queen and the martyr St Margaret and extolling her as the symbol of peace:

> *Conveyer of grace, Virgin mooste benigne.*
> *Oo blessed martir holy margarete*
> *Maugre the myght of spirites maligne*

> *To god above hire praier pure and swete*
> *Maketh now for Rest pees and quiete*
> *Shewed here pleynly in this storie*
> *Oure queene Margarete to signifie…*
> *God in hevene comaundynge abstinence*
> *Noo wicked Angel schall do more grevaunce*
> *Erthe see and Trees shall ben in existence*
> *Obeisaunt to mannes wille and pleasaunce*
> *Desired pees betwixt Englande and ffraunce*
> *This tyme of grace by mene of Margarete*
> *We trust to god to liven in quiet.*[33]

She was saluted again at the Great Conduit on Cheapside, outside the Mercers' Hall, where a pageant of 'five wise and five foolish virgins' waited, then continued past Chepe cross and along Goldsmith's row, the workshops that were to dazzle visiting Italians to the city a half century later with their shining displays of plate. From there she saw the great spire of Old St Paul's Cathedral, rising above the city streets. At its gate she saw a performance of the judgement and resurrection, accompanied by more verses by Lydgate.

Margaret spent Friday night in the Tower of London. Henry had created forty-six Knights of the Bath in an overnight ceremony, who processed with Margaret through the streets the following day, for the service at St Paul's. John Stafford, Archbishop of Canterbury, preached a sermon about the benefits of justice and peace brought by the marriage. The *Brut* chronicle describes Margaret wore white and rode in a 'horse-bier' hung with matching white cloth of gold and draped with white damask. She wore a gold crown on her loose hair and, around her neck, the 'Ilkyngton Collar', a gold collar set with rubies, sapphires and pearls, which was reputed to have been a favourite piece owned by Henry V during his time as Prince of Wales.[34] Henry had written to request the collar on 18 April:

> To oure trusty and welbeloved Squier John Merston Keper of oure Jewell Greting. For asmuch as we, by oure other Letters, under our Prive Seel, have yeve in Commawndement to the Tresorer and Chamberleins of oure Eschequier, to Deliver unto you a Puson of Golde called Iklyngton Coler, Garnisshed with iv Rubees, iv greet Saphurs, xxxij greet Perles, and liij other Perles, and also a Pectoral of Golde Garnished with Rubees, Perles, and Diamondes, and also with a greet Owche Garnishede with Diamondes, Rubees, and Perles, somtyme Bought of a Marchant of Coleyn for the Price of Two Thousand Marc, We Wol and Charge you that, for such things as oure moost entierly right Welbeloved Wyf the Queene moost necessaryly bere for and at the tyme of the Solempnitee of hir Coronation, ye Deliver unto hir the said Pusan and Pectoral of oure Gyft.[35]

From the collar hung a pendant known as the Jewel of St George, made for Margaret at Henry's request, by the companies of Goldsmiths and Silversmiths, at a cost of £4,000.[36] Behind her were seventeen chariots carrying her ladies.[37] She rode out of London, probably through Ludgate and along the Strand, past Charing Cross, to what was then the village of Westminster. Situated on the bend of the river, the community surrounded the palace and abbey, the imposing seat of royalty in London, where Margaret spent the Saturday night.

Margaret was crowned in Westminster Abbey on Sunday, 30 May 1445 by the Archbishop of Canterbury. Henry had requested 8 yds of scarlet from the Keeper of his wardrobe, John Norreys, to be delivered to John, Lord Dudley. Feasts were held afterwards and a tournament lasting three days took place in the Westminster tiltyard. Margaret had become England's queen amid much ceremony and lavish spending. She was characterised as the dove, the symbol of peace, the conduit by which England and France would lay their quarrels aside. And yet, just three days later, Suffolk admitted in the House of Commons that the fragile peace may very well collapse. If it did, Margaret's situation as a costly French Queen of England could become very difficult indeed.

*Chapter Four*

# The Young Wife 1445–1453

## I

Margaret's coronation marked the high point of her reign. With the distractions of celebrations and festivities, brightly coloured clothes, jewels and feasting, the summer of 1445 represented a highpoint of national unity and international peace that was the best England had experienced in years. War was temporarily halted with France, the English had a new queen, King Henry was happy, even the Duke of Gloucester was lavish in his greeting and tensions between the aristocracy took second place to the collective welcome. Parliament conferred upon Margaret a generous income of £4,666 13s 6d a year, with an additional £2,000 in revenues from lands,[1] and her household was established, enjoying newly renovated queen's apartments. On the surface, Margaret was given every reason to feel welcome but, in her youth and naivety, she may not have initially seen the complexities of her situation. It was a fragile peace that reigned that year, with the problems of personalities and government still too entrenched to disappear despite the king's best efforts. However, young as she was, Margaret would have soon become aware that Henry's efforts were not always enough, that his mild, pious disposition left him open to influence.

Over the coming weeks, Henry and Margaret slowly got to know each other, against the backdrop of Westminster and Eltham in early June, before they set off on a brief trip through Kent, visiting Canterbury on 12–14. As her first official visit to an English city as its queen, she was welcomed outside the city by the bailiffs and conducted down to the cathedral, where she visited the shrine of St Thomas Becket. After returning to London, their time was divided between Windsor and Westminster, with a brief foray into Oxfordshire and Woodstock in September. Their first Christmas together was spent back at Westminster Palace.

It has been the consensus of historians and biographers through subsequent centuries that Margaret was a more forceful character than her husband. Their personalities have tended to be presented in polarised terms, with Henry too pious, inept and inactive, and Margaret the scheming woman –

overpowering and militant. Some have gone further, following Shakespeare's famous description of Margaret as a 'she-wolf of France', with a tongue 'more poisonous than an adder's tooth, a vizard-[mask]-like face unchanging, like an Amazonin trull [sic]'. While king and queen could occasionally conform to certain behavioural extremes, particularly under duress, the reality was that of two individuals capable of a range of behaviours, with Margaret equally contemplative and shrewd and Henry sometimes outgoing and attempting an active kingship. It is in the interpretation of their behaviour according to lines of gender, loyalty and nationality that such caricatures have arisen. Margaret's strength of character was seen as a compliment to Henry's rule by the Duke of Orléans, who wrote that she was 'formed by Heaven to supply her royal husband the qualities which he required in order to become a great king', yet later English chronicler Edward Hall reflected the sixteenth-century view that Margaret was a gifted woman, but that her abilities were in conflict with her gender.[2] During her lifetime Margaret was described as a 'great and strong laboured woman' who 'spares no pains to pursue her objectives towards and end and conclusion favourable to her power', but she was also called 'wise and charitable' by those who served her.[3] History has judged her harshly because the majority of surviving sources about her life were overwhelmingly male-authored pro-Yorkist, and for their purposes, Margaret was too masculine a woman and Henry too effeminate a man.

Henry's mildness is well known from the accounts of his confessor, John Blacman, who was the probable author of the tract *A Compilation of the Meekness and Good Life of King Henry VI* in the years following Henry's death. This remained the prevailing view into the sixteenth century, when Hall described Margaret's new husband as possessing a 'meek spirit' and 'simple wit' preferring 'peace before war, rest before business, honesty before profit and quietness before labour'. There was none 'more chaste, more meek, more holy, nor a better creature'. In him, 'reigned shamefastedness, modesty, integrity and patience to be marvelled at, taking and suffering all losses, chances, displeasures and such worldly torments in good part and with a patient manner ... he gaped not for honour, nor thirsted for riches, but studied only for the health of his soul'.[4] This comes close to hagiography, with the king painted as a devout, holy figure, tallying with later perceptions of him as a martyr and early Tudor efforts to secure his canonisation. Hall allowed that Henry was not exclusively passive, but his masculinity was that of a divine figure, rather than the martial, chivalric example set by his father and grandfather.

Retrospectively, the characterisation of king and queen was also a question of shifting blame for Lancastrian failings, with Margaret being defined in opposition to Henry's character, the negativity to his positivity, the action to his passivity, the strength to his gentleness. Not only Henry VII, but also Richard III, made efforts to record miracles reputed to Henry's intervention and to achieve his canonisation. If the subsequent generation saw Henry as a potential saint, Margaret's character had to be blackened to make the narrative of her evil influence all the more believable. Hall acknowledged that 'the Queen his wife was a woman of a great wit' or cunning, but to the Tudor mind it was an unnatural wit that led her to display masculine traits; in fact, the very qualities they praised in earlier medieval kingship. Margaret was,

> yet of no greater wit than a hot stomach, desirous of glory and covetous of honour, and of reason, policy council and other talents and gifts of nature, belonging to a man, full and flowing. Of wit and wiliness she lacked nothing, nor of diligence study and business, she was not unexpert.[5]

To the Duke of Orléans, Margaret's strength could only make Henry stronger, adding weaponry to his arsenal, but to Hall's mind, Margaret was usurping the male role when she tried to be strong and industrious; her strengths were unfeminine but her faults were occasioned by her gender. In addition, she was accorded the worst contemporary cliché of female mutability: 'but yet she had one point of a very woman for often time she was vehement and full bent in a matter, she was suddenly like a weather-cock, mutable and turning'.[6] Margaret's forceful character raised doubts about whose control she really came under: her husband's, Suffolk's or France's.

Besides the difference in expectations of gender, nationality played a role in Margaret's queenship and the perceptions of her new subjects. She arrived in England with an alternative concept of female leadership than the passive, dynastic ideal that the English were hoping she would fulfil. What Hall perceived to be her desire for glory and honour, was the fighting spirit that had led her grandmother Yolande to back Joan of Arc, and her mother Isabelle to campaign to free her husband from prison and to fight for his title in Naples. Had Margaret been married to a warlike man, of the character of Henry V, her qualities would have appeared complementary, but secondary, to his. In French eyes, perhaps even in European eyes, her dedication, action and drive were admirable qualities to be desired in a wife. Her reputation suffered from her efforts to play the active part. Yet a parallel situation in France, when René underwent his long imprisonment and was unable to act, did not lead to the censure of his wife when she took up the reins. England did not possess the French tradition of the rule of strong women in the smaller kingdoms and duchies in times of national conflict. The rift in the Valois family had allowed for greater power to devolve to key families which was shared with their women to an extent that just did not happen across the Channel. Margaret did not identify or appreciate this difference, nor was she willing to abandon the interests of her family and homeland. She was shrewd enough to realise that real power was not invested in Henry himself; he was the nominal face of kingship while the aristocrats behind the scenes influenced him. He was tolerated by the powerful nobles so long as it did not interfere with their plans, and she had already allied herself with those who worked to bring the match about. In France, the factions at court worked well for Charles VII because he had the personal strength and authority to keep them in check. This divided the nobility against each other meaning he could exercise greater control, but Henry VI was a very different personality.

Nor would France allow Margaret to forget the purpose of her marriage. According to Edward Hall, René wrote to Margaret and Henry that they should 'take upon them the rule and governance of the realm and not to be kept under, like young wards and desolate orphans' and that when she did, Margaret 'bore the whole swing as the strong ox does when he is yoked in the plough with a poor silly ass'. Hall adds that when Margaret 'perceived that her husband did not rule as he would', but was under the influence of his uncle, Humphrey of Gloucester, and did not hold 'much authority and governance of the realm', she 'determined with herself, to take upon on the rule and regiment, both of the king and his kingdom, and to deprive and evict out of all rule and authority the Duke'.[7] By the nineteenth century, more sympathetic interpretations of Margaret emerged, authored by Strickland and Hookham, Abbott and Tout, but even they acknowledged the imbalance of power in the marriage, with Lancelott stating that she 'gained the ascendancy over the easy mind of her husband'.[8]

However, hindsight makes it easy to overstate the situation in 1445. Margaret was only 15 at the time of her marriage, still very young and lacking in experience or any real understanding of the nature of politics and the complexities of the English court and its characters. It would be unrealistic to expect that she had any degree of control over the many older, experienced statesmen who had served Henry IV and V, and spent more than two decades wielding real power during the minority and young adulthood of an easy-going king. More than likely, they saw her as an opportunity, an alternative regal figure who could advance them and their cause over their opponents. Her preference was quickly established, and is very understandable, given the role Suffolk's party played in her relocation. Effectively, a transition took place whereby Margaret was handed over by her family to the close-knit group surrounding her husband, whose closest surviving relatives were elderly uncles. Henry's parents were both dead and he had no siblings, so Margaret cleaved to the new 'family' offered her by the Suffolk-Shrewsbury-Beaufort faction. She had already invested in them by the time she arrived in England and they met her more than half way in an alliance that was mutually beneficial to them all. One difficulty arising from the strength of Margaret's partisanship was that it jeopardised her ability to act as a mediator. Medieval queens were traditionally seen as a path to royal mercy, receiving petitions from their subjects and smoothing over tensions at court. Dozens of letters survive from her during this period, written on behalf of individuals who needed help or patronage, or were suited to a new position, or required the backing of the law. Yet later, by allying herself so closely to one party, Margaret was perceived as being unable to fulfil this role fairly. Her Lancastrian bias, as the gulf widened between the king and the Yorkists, prompted comparisons with a former French queen, Isabella, who had conspired with her lover Roger Mortimer to overthrow Edward II in the 1320s.

Margaret had more influence in the traditionally female sphere of love and courtship, influence and patronage. On a personal level, there is little to indicate that she and Henry were unhappy with each other or that she was unable to influence him; in December he wrote to Charles of his 'most dear and well-beloved companion, the queen', who had 'requested us to do this many times'.[9] In the early years of her reign, Margaret's letters encouraged marriages and interceded for the appointments of certain individuals to clerical positions and other preferments, including testimonials for her servants and sought to right certain wrongs. Among others, she appealed to the Abbess of Shaftesbury regarding the promotion of her Chaplain, Michael Tregory of Corfe Castle, to the Abbess of Barking, for her secretary Robert Osbern, asking her to be a 'good and favourable lady' and show him and his wife 'tender benevolence', to the Mayor of Southampton on behalf of 'the right able and sufficient' Robert Bedale and asked the Duke of Somerset to advance her gentlewoman, Margaret Stanlowe, with all the 'ease, favour and tenderness that ye goodly may by right of truth'.[10] Margaret also made efforts on behalf of those seeking a wife, such as her servant Thomas Shelford, who desired 'full hertly to do … worship by way of marriage' to a daughter of a Mr Hall of Larkfield', and she urged the widow Jane Carew to consider the suit of her sewer, Thomas Burneby, 'for the great zeal, love and affection that he hath unto your person'.[11] As queen, she tried to help those who were suffering illness, poverty or injustice, writing to the Master of St Giles in the Field, to admit a 17-year-old leper, Robert Uphome into the hospital there, and asking for alms for a W. Frutes and Agnes Knoghton, a young couple, newly married.[12] She also championed the causes of Nicholas Carent, to obtain goods from the deanery of Wells Cathedral; her tenants at Enfield whose horses had been taken by the corporation of London; John Reignold, who had wrongfully been put out of a certain livelihood and a draper named Rauf Josselyn, who had been wrongly removed from the manor of Aspendon.[13] In 1448, Margaret founded Queen's College, Cambridge, for the continuing benefit of the poor scholars, established by Henry at Eton. The college's charter was issued on 30 March, and the first stone was laid by her chamberlain, Sir John Wenlock, on 15 April. Margaret persuaded Henry, Suffolk, Somerset and York to contribute, but it was the last time she would manage to get them working together.

## II

The storm clouds began to gather early. When negotiating the marriage, Suffolk had been empowered to offer to return Maine to the French and, once the celebrations were out of the way, the question arose of when this would take place. This concession was not widely known, but it was already deeply unpopular, given that the territories had been won through the shedding of English blood. The arrival of a joint French–Anjou embassy hot on the heels of the wedding on 3 July, brought the issue to the fore. Led by Louis of Bourbon, they were welcomed into London on Wednesday 14 July and were received in state by Henry at Westminster the following day. Dressed in regal finery, Henry was warm and welcoming, addressing them in French, doffing his hat and clapping them on the shoulder. One of the ambassadors left a description of Henry:

> they found the king upon a high stool, with a bed stretched over it, of blue tapestry, diapered, of the livery of the late king [Henry V] … and his motto 'Jamais' of gold and a back-piece of tapestry representing some ladies who present to a lord the arms of France; and the whole was of gold, very rich … and he himself was clothed in a rich robe down to the ground, of red cloth of gold.

As soon as he saw they had arrived, Henry 'came down and stood exactly in front of his chair, and there waited for the said ambassadors, and took by the hand all those of the king's party right humbly, taking off his hat a little to the said count and archbishop'.[14] He gave 'a very good appearance of being well pleased and very joyful, especially when the king, his uncle, was mentioned, and the love which he bore towards him, it appeared that he rejoiced at the heart'. The French party spent about three weeks in England, during which time Henry agreed to meet Charles VII in person, in France, and to surrender Maine by 1 October.

The date came and went but Maine remained in the hands of the English. On 12 November, Henry appointed Suffolk, Moleyns and others to negotiate with the French for an extension of the treaty of Tours. Charles decided to appeal to Margaret directly, hoping she would use her influence with the king to honour his promise. Margaret was more than willing to do so. On 17 December 1445, at Sheen, she acknowledged letters sent from her uncle Charles VII and confirmed her desire for peace:

> But in as much as perceive the good love and the entire will that you have towards my lord and myself, the great desire which you have to see us, and also the fruitful disposition and liberal inclination and good concord between both of you, we herein praise our Creator and thank you thereof with a good heart, and as kindly as ever we may, for no greater pleasure can we have in this world, than to see an arrangement for a final peace between him and you, as well for the nearness of lineage in which you stand the one to the other, as also for the relief and repose of the Christian people, which has been so long disturbed by war. And herein to the pleasure of our lord, we will, upon our part, stretch forth the hand, and will employ ourselves herein effectively to our power in such wise that reason would that you, and all others, ought herein to be grateful.[15]

It was a tactful, diplomatic letter for a 15-year-old, in which Margaret reassured her uncle that she would do what she was able, according to the pleasure of her husband, to bring about peace. She continued, with more specific reference to Maine:

> And as to the deliverance which you desire to have of the Comté of Maine and other matters contained in your said letters, we understand that my said lord has written to you at considerable length about this, and yet herein we will do for your pleasure the best that we can do, as we have always done.[16]

This loyalty was reaffirmed on 20 May 1446, at Windsor, when Margaret's secretary, Michael de Paris, wrote to Charles on her behalf, asking if he had any more requests and signalling her intent to arrange a meeting between her uncle and husband, at which she would try to be present. By the arrival of summer, Henry had agreed to travel to France and take Margaret with him, meeting Charles at Le Mans. On 1 June he appointed commissioners to negotiate him a loan to fund the trip, with Moleyns and Dudley being sent to conclude arrangements on 20 July, but the visit never happened, for reasons that are unclear are unclear. The return of Maine was deeply unpopular, amid fears that England was falling under French control and Henry may have been unwilling to oppose the very popular Duke of Gloucester, who as his surviving uncle, was still heir to the throne. In addition, the royal finances were considerably depleted, after the expenditure on Margaret's arrival, wedding and household. When the royal couple travelled to Bristol, they stayed in the Hospital of St

John the Baptist, perhaps from inclination, but also perhaps to avoid having to spend money renovating the neglected Bristol Castle, which was said to be on the verge of collapse by 1540.

Painfully aware of the promises he had made, Henry decided to employ subterfuge, writing in secret to Charles on 22 December 1446, to confirm the surrender of Maine and Le Mans, as his 'most dear and wellbeloved companion the queen' had been requesting him to do.[17] Charles was to have Maine by 30 April 1446, but still this intention was not made public and no strategies were put in place for the current English residents. Once again, the date came and went, without Maine being returned. Charles, and Margaret, must have grown impatient with the broken promises. By February 1447 Moleyns and John Dudley were back in France, negotiating at Charles's court, in advance of the expiration of the extended Truce of Troyes, due to take place on 1 April. On 22 February they achieved a second Treaty of Tours, allowing them until 1 January 1448, with Henry still insisting that he would be going to meet Charles in person.

Early in 1447, the tensions between Suffolk and Gloucester came to a head. Following the conviction of Humphrey's wife, Eleanor Cobham, for witchcraft, in 1441, Henry became convinced that his uncle was plotting to overthrow him or bring about his death, in order to claim the throne. Gloucester had retaliated by attacking the influence Suffolk wielded over the king, now coupled with his closeness to Margaret, possibly even hinting at an inappropriate closeness between them. Suffolk now took steps to pre-empt what he believed to be an impending attack from Gloucester, but the extent of his influence, and Margaret's, is unclear. Parliament was summoned to meet at Bury St Edmunds, in the heart of Suffolk, where its Duke could be certain of support, calling out his retainers and asking the local knights to attend armed.[18] Gloucester was popular in London and although Parliament was not exclusively held there, the shift in location was sinister given the state of tension between the two men. Yet Gloucester could not ignore a summons of attendance, and Henry did nothing to intervene. The session opened on 10 February, but Gloucester did not arrive for another eight days, when he approached with a retinue of eighty horsemen and was intercepted outside the town by two members of Henry's household. He was instructed that the king did not wish to see him, but that he should go to his lodgings at St Salvatores, near the North Gate of the city. There, he was visited by Suffolk, Humphrey Stafford, Duke of Buckingham, Richard Neville, Earl of Salisbury and others, who read out a string of charges against him and informed him that he was under arrest. Gloucester stood accused of having 'not so much advanced and preferred the commonwealth and public utility as his own private things and peculiar estate'.[19] He was forbidden to leave the building and an armed guard was placed around it. Five days later, on 23 February, 1447, Gloucester was found dead in his bed.

Contemporary accounts did not consider the event to be suspicious. William of Worcester related that 'there died Humphrey, the Good Duke of Gloucester, the lover of virtue and state', Gregory's chronicle and the monk Richard Fox, both simply reported the fact of his death, while Abbot Whethamsted of St Albans commented that 'after being placed in strict confinement, he sank from sorrow'. Hardyng's chronicle, which was certainly favourable to Gloucester, pointed out that he was not a well man; at the age of 56 or 57, he 'died incontinent, for heaviness and loss of regiment [self-control] and oft afore he was in that sickness at point of death'.[20] If this is true, it seems likely that his demise was a heart-attack or stroke brought about by the shock of his arrest. This did not prevent rumours circulating that the duke had been smothered in his sleep, prompting the display of his body in the cathedral the following day. Fifty years after the event, chronicler Robert Fabyan refused to commit himself on the topic of Gloucester's death, writing that 'of whose murder diverse reports are made, which I pass over', but he did add that no wound was found upon his body. Fabyan represented Gloucester as the last bastion before the loss of France; 'it was thought that during his life, he would withstand the delivery of Anjou and Maine, before promised'.[21] By the time of Hall's account, though the murder was presented as fact and the crime was being laid at the doors of Suffolk and Margaret: 'It was furthered and set forward by such, as of long time had borne malice to the duke ... which venomous serpents and malicious tigers, persuaded, incensed and exhorted the queen, to look well upon the expenses and revenues of the realm and therefore to call an account'.[22]

For a while it seemed that the main voice of criticism against Suffolk had been silenced. Another key figure at court also died early the same year, but this time from the pro-France faction. Henry, Cardinal Beaufort, was in his early seventies at the time of his death on 11 April 1447, having been a supporter of Margaret since before her arrival and leaving her the bequest of the 'bed cloth of Damascus' and an arras from the bedroom set aside for her use at his Waltham Priory home. Gloucester's cause was taken up by his loyal adherent, Richard, Duke of York, who had been angered at having been replaced in Normandy by the Duke of Somerset in 1445. Fully expecting to return to service in France, York found himself increasingly side-lined and, in September 1447, was appointed Lieutenant of Ireland, which was seen by his supporters as an exile. This may have been the reason why he was reluctant to actually take up the position, and leave England, until 1449.

In 1448, Henry and Margaret undertook at least two pilgrimages that appear to have been connected with conception and childbirth. That June, they had just marked the third anniversary of their marriage as they travelled to the shrine of Our Lady of Walsingham, a favourite intercessor on matters of women's health.

Traditionally, pilgrims removed their shoes in the slipper chapel and crawled or travelled the final mile on their knees to venerate the famous 'black Madonna' statue to whom women hoping to bear a child would leave a gift. On the way back south, they also stopped at Bury St Edmunds and Woolpit, other key locations along the East Anglian Marian route, no doubt with the same intention. That September, they travelled north to the shrine of St Cuthbert at Durham. One of the most important pre-Reformation saints, the seventh century Cuthbert's relics had been translated to the newly completed shine behind the cathedral altar in 1104. Adorned with expensive gifts, it had a base of green marble, gilded and set with four seats for pilgrims to receive his blessing, and a gilt cover, depicting Mary and the baby Jesus, and Christ on a rainbow. The deeply devout king needed no excuse to visit the tomb, but the sheer distance from his usual home territory suggests the same purpose as the Norfolk visit.

Margaret must have felt her childlessness keenly, aware as she was that this was considered to be her primary function. Until she bore a son, the question of inheritance would remain unresolved, as the death of Gloucester meant that the Duke of York had now become Henry's closest living relative. One voice of malcontent, raised against the queen by a Canterbury man, stated that:

> oure quene was none able to be Quene of Inglond, but an he were a peer of, or a lord of this realm, he would be one of them that should help to put her down, for because that she beareth no child, and because that we have no prince in this land.[23]

Blacman's comment that Henry 'used' his wife 'with all honesty and gravity' has often been taken to suggest the pair had something of an infrequent, or joyless, sexual relationship, but his words do confirm that they were intimate, so the question of Margaret's childlessness through these early years of marriage, cannot be satisfactorily explained, beyond the fact that fertility in a couple can be a complex and difficult balance.

The model of queenship to which Margaret conformed in the late 1440s was typical of former English consorts like Philippa of Hainault, Anne of Bohemia and Joan of Navarre. It was essentially quiet, dignified by demure compliment to their husbands' kingly activities, focused on the household, patronage and piety. Like them, Margaret was influential behind the scenes, within the confines of the bedroom or in private discussion, conforming to gendered ideals about the subordinate place a woman should occupy, even in the case of a queen. She was deemed to be a model to all wives, an earthly incarnation of those qualities venerated in the Virgin Mary, with queenly adoration correlating to the most popular cult of the day. Not published until 1474, Caxton's *A Game of Chesse* typified this view of the quiet queen but drew on influential texts from the fourteenth and early fifteenth century by Christine de Pisan and Jacobus de Cessolis. Advice written by Geoffrey de Tour Landry advised women to let their husbands be their 'spokesperson and master' but when they were alone, a wife might 'talk to him pleasantly, and advise him to mend his ways if he has done wrong'. This applied to queens too, as Landry cited in his example:

> a good woman ought to do this, like Hester the queen of Syria. Her husband the king was fierce and quick tempered, but when he was angry she would say nothing until he had calmed down. When his anger was over, she might rule him as she pleased. This was very clever of her, and so should all women do.

Margaret's situation was rather different: Henry was the opposite of the King of Syria, as pacific and gentle as Hester's husband was fierce and angry, but she still had to find her own way to rule him, and walk the delicate path of being supportive and exercising her own influence. There is nothing to suggest that she was not successful in this during the first years of their marriage.

Despite Henry's prayers, the question of Maine remained unresolved. A diplomatic solution was required, not a spiritual one. By January 1448, Charles was running out of patience with Henry and the large presence of French troops on the border, ready to seize the province, was causing alarm among the English at Rouen. Despite the renewal of the Treaty of Tours and the assurances of Henry, who also returned nearby Le Fresnay to the French, a stalemate had been reached. In July 1449 Charles declared that the truce was over, making Henry obliged to arm and equip his garrisons and soldiers from already depleted coffers. Then came the news that Rouen had fallen and the English were driven back almost to the Norman coast. The Duke of Somerset, who had replaced York as Normandy's lieutenant, was forced to surrender a number of Norman properties as the price of his freedom, and offer John Talbot, Earl of Shrewsbury, as a hostage. The reaction in England was of fury and disbelief; by early November, Somerset was being accused of treason and cowardice, but the malcontents were aiming higher. As he had predicted in 1444, Suffolk was considered the architect of the French marriage and came under attack for his role, despite the assurances he had secured from Henry against this very eventuality. When parliament met on 6 November, the order was given for Suffolk's arrest and imprisonment in the Tower, ahead of his impending impeachment. Bishop Adam Molyens surrendered the Privy Seal but when he arrived down in Portsmouth to pay the wages of sailors and soldiers, he was set upon by a mob and murdered. Upon their reassembly in January 1450, Parliament began to formulate charges against Suffolk of having sold English territories to France and attempting to place his son on the throne, through the marriage he made for the boy with the Beaufort heiress, which Henry had fully supported six years before.

Both Suffolk and Somerset had advanced with the support of King Henry, as rewards for loyal service, and even with formal guarantees of royal support. At this point, it may have been considered incumbent upon the king to remind Parliament of this and support his councillors, but no such assurances came from Henry. It was Margaret who urged her husband to take the advice of the lords and protect his friends from the increasingly angry mob.[24] Henry may have felt he needed to make concessions for the recent failures of foreign policy and appease his enemies. Suffolk was an obvious scapegoat, having become so deeply unpopular that the king may have considered it prudent to remove him before the danger extended to the throne. Nor was Margaret free from attack, as the symbol of the now-despised French deal. The chronicle of Mathieu d'Escouchy states that rumours were spread about Margaret's legitimacy, with her enemies claiming she was the result of a liaison her mother enjoyed while her father was in prison. D'Escouchy claims she remained publicly dignified in response but gave vent to her tears in private.[25] She must also have been angered at the treatment of the man who had protected her in France, stood proxy for Henry at her wedding and carried her ashore, and feared for his future. It must have been difficult for her not to see this as an extended attack upon herself, with her closeness to Suffolk providing further excuse for his unpopularity. It was a rapid turnaround from the welcome she had received less than five years before, an indication of how much the political mood had changed: she would also have been acutely aware that Suffolk himself had predicted such a shift.

## III

John de la Pole, Duke of Suffolk, was impeached on 7 February, 1450 and the list of accusations was read to the king in Parliament five days later. They included the standard practise of self-advancement at the expense of the crown, but also the very specific charges of the loss of Rouen and the surrender of Maine and Anjou. On these last two counts, the finger should have been pointing firmly at Henry, so perhaps he was only too grateful that it was directed elsewhere. He did attempt to gain control over the bill to ensure that the decision lay in his hands, but was overruled by the lords, who pushed the impeachment through. On 17 March, Suffolk was sentenced to be banished for five years. The London mob were calling for his blood, so it may have been Henry's influence that commuted the death sentence to banishment but, in reality, this only led to a slight stay of execution. His last meeting with Margaret would not have been an easy one, given the role he had played in her life for the last five years, as protector, guide and almost a quasi-paternal figure since he had received her from her father and carried her ashore at Portsmouth. It is impossible to imagine Margaret's feelings, beyond the regret and loss of a good friend; perhaps she understood the necessity of sending Suffolk away, perhaps she blamed Henry for not protecting him more. Maybe she took consolation from the thought that he would be able to return in five years, perhaps even sooner if the political climate changed. She had no idea that she would never see him again.

Swearing that he was innocent of all charges, Suffolk took to the safety of his own boat at Ipswich, sending letters ahead to Calais in hopes of a welcome there. He had formerly been Captain of the town and had every reason to believe they would receive him, and he could live out his exile in some comfort. However, his ship was intercepted in The Channel on 2 May, by the warship *Nicholas of the Tower*, belonging to the Duke of Exeter. Suffolk was greeted with the ominous words: 'Welcome, traitor', and ordered aboard, where the sailors put him through a mock trial and executed him with a rusty sword. His naked body was washed up on the beach at Dover, reputedly with his head on a pole beside it, where it remained for days, while the terrified local sheriff awaited instructions from London as to how to proceed. The news of his death spread through Kent, filling the locals with fear that they would suffer reprisals. Many believed believed that a furious Henry would raze the county and return it to woodland, and this served as a trigger to action, resulting in the greatest challenge the king had yet experienced.

Across the country, disorder and tension were reaching dangerous levels. Personal feuds brewed unchecked among the nobility, especially the Nevilles and Percys in the north, Courtenays and Bonvilles in the west. Taxes were heavy, ex-soldiers went unpaid, judges and sheriffs were open to bribery. Henry's coffers were empty; he and Margaret sat down to dinner one day, only to be told there was none, as the palace suppliers were refusing to cooperate due to unpaid bills. Amid his desperation, Henry began to sell letters instructing judges which parties to favour, and tried to raise funds by selling titles or borrowing from the lords. While the Suffolk crisis unfolded, the French laid siege to Le Mans, and then Maine, which the English were forced to surrender in March 1450. Afraid of reprisals, Henry issued a proclamation stating that he had done his duty by honouring the terms of his marriage agreement. This did nothing for his popularity, or that of Margaret, and the loss was now public knowledge. Henry was right to be afraid.

In May, an uprising took place in Kent under the leadership of a shadowy figure named Jack Cade. Calling himself the Captain of Kent, Cade distributed a manifesto called the Complaint of the Poor Commons of Kent, listing fifteen counts of complaint and grievances, with the support of representatives from all walks of society. More worryingly, Cade also adopted the name John Mortimer, the surname of the heir of Richard II, who had been displaced by Henry's grandfather, Henry IV, when he usurped the throne in 1399. This was a direct attempt to undermine the king and it was accompanied by rumours that Richard, Duke of York, as the direct descendent of the Mortimers, would be a better ruler than Henry. A Kent man named Stephen Christmas was executed for saying that the duke should replace Henry, for 'havynge more favyr unto the Duke of York thenne unto the kyng'. York wrote letters to reassure Henry of his loyalty and hurried back from Ireland, but he was clearly the popular alternative to the Lancastrian rule, and the damage had been done. Henry and Margaret fled to the safety of Kenilworth Castle in Warwickshire to await news. The rebels marched to Blackheath and, on 24 June, defeated a royal army at Sevenoaks, killing the commander Sir Humphrey Stafford. Five days later, William Ayscough, Bishop of Salisbury, who had married Henry and Margaret, was dragged out of the church at Edington where he was celebrating Mass and murdered. Two other unpopular figures, Margaret's chancellor William Booth and Walter Hart, or Lyhart, Bishop of Norwich, were threatened with a similar end but managed to escape. By 1 July, the rebels were in London, where Cade oversaw the execution of Lord Saye, Henry's treasurer, and his son-in-law, William Cromer, Sheriff of Kent, under the Standard at Cheapside. Their main target was the deeply unpopular Duke of Somerset, who was confined to the Tower of London for his own safety. Eventually, the Archbishop of Canterbury, John Kemp, persuaded Cade to call off his men, with the promise of pardons. At first Henry agreed to this, but then revoked rebuked the pardons, because they had not been approved by Parliament. With a price on his head, Cade fled into Sussex, where he was captured and wounded, dying on his way to trial in London in mid-July. His body was put through a mock trial, beheaded at Newgate and then dragged through the streets to be quartered, each section being sent to a different part of Kent as a deterrent.

The uprising left Henry and Margaret shaken to the core. Yet Henry recognised the need to return to London quickly, reaching St Albans by 24 July and arriving in the capital four days later. A service of thanksgiving for his safe return was held in St Paul's Cathedral. But Henry did not simply see this as a question of rebellion, as on 1 August, he appointed a court to investigate Cade's criticisms. Overseen by the bishops and lords, it held sessions in the key seats of disorder; Rochester, Dartford, Maidstone and Canterbury, with the result that a number of landowners were indicted for thefts, assaults and lawless entries while pursuing the rebels. Henry also travelled in person to Canterbury, Lewes and Salisbury when the sessions were sitting in order to present the face of majesty and oversee justice.

This may have contained the men of Kent but did little to console Henry's former supporters, including Alexander Iden, the man who had captured Cade, who was now indicted for seizing money from one of the leader's supporters. Although Cade's death and the inquiry were intended to deter other rebels, this was not the end of the matter. Just days after his capture, two Sussex men, John and William Merfield, stated in Salehurst market place that King Henry was a 'natural fool' and would often play with a staff with a bird on top, and that 'anoder kyng must be ordayned to rule the land.'[26] Through the late summer and autumn, they gathered men from the Sussex towns of Chichester, Hastings and Eastbourne, calling on those who had previously risen in Kent to join them. While Cade's attack had targeted those unpopular advisors close to the king, the aim of the Merfield uprising was to remove Henry and replace him with someone more competent. They wished to remove all lords and clergy, appoint a council of twelve commoners to run the country and that all lands and property should be held in common. This time, there was no large-scale uprising; the Merfield brothers and a handful of the ringleaders were arrested and swiftly dealt with.

Yet other voices of discontent persisted, with smaller uprisings breaking out as Kent stirred to arms again in September 1450 and January and April 1451.[27] The Duke of York's name was constantly evoked, with his former Chamberlain, Sir William Oldhall, attempting a coup in his favour in the summer of 1451, York's retainers rising in September and his supporter Thomas Yonge being imprisoned in November for raising in Parliament York's right to be named as the king's official successor. Further acts of brutality aimed at government officials were recorded across the country during this period, including the murder of the Duke of Suffolk's former steward and chaplain, the arrest of his secretary, the mutilation of a sheriff and clerk, attacks upon the property of bishops and servants in the employ of unpopular figures close to the throne.[28] John Paston petitioned Henry to complain that he had been forcibly ejected from his own property at Gresham in Norfolk, as part of a family feud, but also warned the king of growing dissent: 'if this great insurrection, riots and wrongs … done against your crown, dignity and peace … be duly punished, it shall give great boldness to them and all other misdoers to make congregations and conventicles riotously … to the subversion and final destruction of your liege people and laws.'[29] In addition, the soldiers from Normandy were returning home, wounded, unpaid and angry, arriving in carts in London in early August 1450, having made a hasty departure.[30] The mood was ugly.

Since the death of the Duke of Suffolk, Margaret had drawn closer to Edmund Beaufort, second Duke of Somerset, brother of the John Beaufort, who had died after his disastrous French campaign of 1444. Edmund's unpopularity among the mob kept him in the Tower until April 1451, but upon his release, he was awarded the Captaincy of Calais and Margaret gave him a 100 mark annual salary for his good service and friendship. This award was nothing out of the usual, but it allied her to another unpopular figure, considered the architect of the more recent failures in France. Typically, as with Suffolk, rumours arose about an improper relationship between Somerset and the queen, which was considered credible due to the popular belief that he had previously enjoyed a liaison with Henry's mother, Catherine of Valois. Yet there were no visible cracks in the royal marriage for the gossips to exploit. Margaret was frequently with Henry, rarely spending time apart except for occasions when politics demanded, perhaps to create a deliberate show of unity. This had the additional benefit of cutting domestic costs, as her expensive household was scaled down in an attempt to save money. They spent Christmas 1451 together at Eltham and, the following year, embarked upon a tour of the south-west and Welsh borders. The attacks upon Suffolk, Ayscough, Saye and others united the close-knit group around the throne, who were in a reactionary, defensive position, conscious that the mood of the country was volatile and that the question of French losses and surrenders had been more unpopular than anticipated.

Their main opponent, taking Gloucester's position and even adopting some of the recent complaints of the rebels, was Henry's immediate heir, Richard, Duke of York. After returning from Ireland in response to Jack Cade's uprising, York made little secret of his enmity towards Somerset, having immediately preceded him in the role in which he saw Somerset to have failed. As a former governor of Rouen, York blamed his adversary for its loss, and the collapse of the English regime in Normandy, with some justification. Early in January 1452, York decided to act to pre-empt more rumours that he was plotting against Henry. On the ninth, he issued a statement of loyalty, claiming that the king's mistrust of him was the result of lies spread by his 'enemies, adversaries and evil-willers'.[30] However, he then took the dangerous step of raising troops from his loyal Welsh borders and marching to London with the intention of demanding the removal of Somerset, whom he felt responsible for the slurs against his name. In contrast to some accusations of weakness and inactivity, Henry took decisive action and marched north to meet York, travelling through Barnet, St Albans, Dunstable, Stony Stratford and Northampton. It was only then that he learned that York had passed him and was already approaching the capital. Ignoring a delegation sent by the king to convince him to stop, York arrived at Blackheath at the start of March with around 8,000 men. He found the gates of the city locked against him, as Henry had commanded.

Henry turned around, marching swiftly south and entered London ahead of his enemy on on 27 February. The following day, he passed through Southwark and Blackheath, to learn that the rebels had camped upon Dartford Heath. Uncertain of York's intentions, Henry went to confront him. The duke had raised a considerable force, estimated at between 10,000 and 20,000 men, with seven ships lying in the Thames with their guns trained on the meeting. However, Henry's army was almost three times the size, reflective of his status and greater support; a clear indication of the strength of his kingship at this point. With York's mission starting to look foolish at best, treasonable at worst, Henry sent a delegation of amenable lords to persuade his cousin to submit. Even York's close family, his brother-in-law, the Earl of Salisbury and the Earl's son, Richard Neville, Earl of Warwick, saw that negotiation was the only way. York allowed himself to be swayed, with promises that concessions would be made to his hostility towards Somerset. Yet once he had conducted York into the royal tent, Henry was able to order the duke's disarmament and his removal to London, where he was kept under house arrest at Baynard's Castle for two weeks. After that, he was marched to St Paul's and forced to swear an oath of loyalty. Smaller pockets of rebellion that named York as their figurehead were swiftly crushed that spring in Ludlow and Kent. Henry had outsmarted York, but it did little to dispel the rivalry between the duke and Somerset, or solve the immediate problem of the succession. However, he had survived two serious crises and a challenge to his leadership: By the summer of 1452, Henry had reasserted his kingship and been a visible presence through the dispensation of justice. The issues of the royal finances and English territories in France still remained, but considerable steps had been taken along the road to rebuilding a strong rule and reasserting Henry's personal rule.

That summer, Henry headed off on a summer progress through the west country with a large entourage including the Duke of Somerset, while York remained at home in Ludlow. Margaret stayed behind at Greenwich, parted from Henry for the first substantial period of their marriage to date. It was a response to the recent civil unrest: to be a visible presence, to inspire loyalty in distant parts and, occasionally, to see the execution of justice. It could also have been potentially dangerous. The king left Eltham on 23 June, travelling west, through Kingston, Chertsey, Guildford, Farnham, Alton and Alresford, reaching Southampton on 4 July. From there he headed to Beaulieu, Christchurch, Ringwood and Kingston Lacy in Dorset, which was in the possession of the Beaufort family. During his visit, Henry may have met the 9-year-old Margaret, who was soon to marry his half-brother Edmund Tudor and become the mother of the future Henry VII. From there, he continued his journey to Poole, Milton Abbas, Sherborne and Crewkerne in Somerset.

Henry was at Forde Abbey on 14 July, and possibly visited the home at Shute of William Bonville, a staunch supporter of the Duke of York, but a firm enemy of York's other ally, the Duke of Devon. Henry's patronage of Bonville was an attempt to display strong Lancastrian leadership in hostile territory, but also to show approval for one party involved in the feud. From there, he went to Ottery St Mary 'and there was received with great solemnities and lodged in the college two nights'. On the afternoon of 17 July, he approached the city of Exeter, arriving after dinner, with a warm welcome from the Mayor and 300 citizens who rode out to greet him. The visit was recorded by a John Hoker, who wrote that 'he came to this citie upon Moneday, at the afternoon, being then the feast day of St Kenelme ... being accompanied by a great trayne of noble Gentlemen and others.'[32] While friars incensed him with frankincense, Henry kissed the cross and was presented with the keys of the city. He entered through the South Gate, which was covered with painted scenes, and the Mayor led him up South Street, which had been hung with tapestries and silk, through the High Street and Broad Street to the Cathedral Close, where the king dismounted and walked to the high altar of the cathedral to make an offering.

After Exeter, Henry headed to Honiton, then to Donyatt near Ilminster where, on 20 July, the Duke of Somerset presided over the Sessions in the Bishop's Hall. Two men were condemned to death and then reprieved by the king, in a staged show of royal clemency. From there, he went to Bridgewater and Glastonbury, where he stayed two nights, and on to Wells, Bristol, Bath, Malmesbury and Cirencester by the start of August. Next, Henry passed through Gloucester and Monmouth, before turning north at Hereford and approaching the Yorkist stronghold of Ludlow, where the castle was the seat of the York family. However, although Henry intended to make an impression upon those Yorkist retainers who had risen against him, he was not prepared to lodge himself under the roof of his enemy, choosing instead to spend the nights of 12 and 13 August with the local Carmelite Friars. The king's coming would have been anticipated well in advance and it would have been no coincidence that for three days leading up to his arrival, judicial sessions were held at Ludlow to make examples of the duke's supporters. The Yorkist *Six Towns Chronicle* stated that the accused were forced to appear before the king naked, their necks in a noose, in terrible weather, to ask forgiveness.[33] This cannot be verified, and with the chronicler stating it was the idea of the Duke of Somerset, the Yorkist bias is clear, but there was clearly some reassertion of Lancastrian majesty in Ludlow that summer as part of Henry's plan to regain authority.

Leaving Ludlow, Henry passed through Bridgenorth, Birmingham, Kenilworth, Coventry, Banbury, Woodstock, High Wycombe and Sheen, arriving at Eltham on 6 September. After such a long absence from Margaret, the pair were reunited in Kent and spent the next month together, dividing their time between Eltham, Greenwich and Sheen. That October, Henry set off again through the Eastern counties: Cambridgeshire, Essex, Hertfordshire, Lincolnshire, Northamptonshire, with a similar intention. He attended more trials, visiting Hitchin, Huntingdon, Peterborough, Newark, Stamford, Cambridge, Saffron Walden and Barking before returning to Eltham on 11 November. Henry's extensive travels, through the second half of 1452, had been deliberately targeted at Yorkist heartlands, with the intention of modelling kingship, dispensing justice and suppressing dissent. As the end of the year approached, he hoped that a long-lasting peace had been restored to the country, by which the feuds and challenges might be controlled, if not quietened. And it may have done, were it not for the exceptional circumstances that arose in 1453. As long as Henry remained a visible king, coupled with the recent demonstrations of justice, the status quo might have been preserved. But then Henry fell ill. It was a disaster that neither Henry or Margaret could have seen coming.

The royal couple spent Christmas together 1452 at the manor of Bella Court at Greenwich, granted to Margaret from the estate of the Duke of Gloucester, or 'seized' by her, according to her enemies. It had become her favourite residence, renamed Pleasaunce or Placentia, as early as 1447, and had undergone an extensive building program to transform its interiors and decor using her symbol of the daisy in pink brick, white stone, carved into the woodwork and glazed into windows. She threw out the reed matting which covered the floor and replaced it with terracotta tiles monogrammed with her initials, decorated the pillars and archways, built a vestry to house the crown jewels and erected a pier to allow greater access from the river. The costs of the new courts and pavilions, pavements, windows and wainscoting were recorded by Margaret's Clerk of the Works, Robert Ketewell, and included the Flanders tiles used to floor her bedroom, the dais built at the far end, and a new door with 200 tin nails and double hinges. She had a state bed costing 8s 6d delivered from London and paid 5s for a bathing vat – an early bath. Beds were also ordered for Henry's half-brothers, Edmund and Jasper Tudor, which were made by a Greenwich carpenter, Richard Henham, at 4s each, and set up 'in the lodging within the little garden'.[34]

On New Year's Day 1453, Margaret made an offering of a gold, jewelled tablet, bearing the name of the Virgin Mary, one of the traditional figures to whom women prayed for assistance in matters of conception, pregnancy and birth. With the festivities and celebrations planned for that season, it appears to have been a happy time. £25 9s was paid to a Richard Bulstrode for 'stuff and wages' for a disguising made before the king and queen.[35] On 5 January, the king and queen were at the Tower for the investiture of Edmund and Jasper Tudor, then in their early twenties, as Earl of Richmond and Earl of Pembroke respectively. On 8 February, Henry set out again, to travel through Essex, Suffolk and Norfolk, visiting Norwich on 18 February, ending up at Berkhamsted Castle and then Reading, where a new session of Parliament opened on 6 March. During this session, the Tudor brothers were declared legitimate, on account of Margaret's failure to have conceived a child in almost eight years of marriage. However, what the lords, and perhaps what even Henry himself did not know, was that shortly after the end of the festivities, around the middle of January, Margaret had indeed fallen pregnant. Finally, after so many years of waiting, she was to bear an heir to the English throne

*Chapter Five*

# Madness 1453–1455

## I

Until this point, Margaret's queenship had been conventional, even formulaic. She was frequently at Henry's side, fulfilling her role as the young, foreign consort, a symbol of royalty, piety and patronage. Her sphere was largely domestic, in which she functioned as a supporting partner, overseeing her household, enjoying ceremonies, feast days and occasions of worship, ostensibly a female counterpart to her king. But events 1453 changed her role, as motherhood and her husband's unexpected crisis forced her into a position that was unfamiliar, perhaps even unwelcome, but in which she demonstrated great bravery in attempting to steer the Lancastrian ship through its period of troubles. She may have been ill-equipped to try to step into the shoes of government, but she had the advice of her husband's leading councillors, and she understood that Henry's recent efforts to stabilise the crown needed to be re-enforced. That this period of turmoil happened to coincide with her pregnancy and delivery, followed by her post-partum recovery, is indicative of the inner reserves of strength upon which Margaret was obliged to call.

That April, Margaret undertook a visit to Norfolk without Henry, but with one of the Tudor brothers as her escort. According to a letter written by local woman Margaret Paston to her husband, recording the two days of her visit. Keen to be an advocate of marital bliss, the Queen sent for Margaret's cousin, an Elizabeth Clere, 'and when she come into the quene's presence, the quene made right muche of her, and desired her to have a husband'. Whatever answer Elizabeth made, the visitor was 'right well pleased … and reported of her in the best wise, and said, by her troth, she saw no gentlewoman since she came into Norfolk that she liked better than she doth her.'[1] With her pregnancy confirmed, this incident could indicate that Margaret was keen to spread her happiness. She may have taken the opportunity to visit the shrine of Our Lady at Walsingham, lying to the north of the city, at the culmination of the East Anglian pilgrimage route. Particularly associated with female health and fertility, Margaret is likely to have knelt before the dazzling shrine, bright with gold and jewels, and left an offering of her own. She also appears to have visited the Lady Chapel at Canterbury Cathedral around this time, probably with a similar objective. Henry was delighted to learn of her condition, awarding Richard Tunstall a life annuity of £40 for bringing him the news to his 'singular consolation ... grete joy and comfort.'[2]

On the way back south from Norfolk, Margaret made the unusual choice to stay with Cecily Neville, Duchess of York, at Hitchin, in Hertfordshire. Given the duke's recent challenge to Henry, this act may have been the effort of the two women to build bridges, or else was initiated by Margaret as her own means of asserting royal authority, in counterpart to Henry's efforts on progress. Hitchin manor, an L-shaped building attached to a priory, contained within its grounds a holy well dedicated to St Winifred, which may have given the queen another reason to visit. Perhaps Cecily, who had recently delivered her twelfth and penultimate child, made a gesture of conciliation towards a young woman who was pregnant for the first time. The Duchess appears to have taken the opportunity to advocate her husband's cause, as her letter to Margaret that summer reveals. First, she spoke warmly of Margaret's pregnancy as the result of intercession by the Virgin Mary, who had helped the queen to 'fulfil your right honourable body, of the most precious, most joyful and most comfortable earthly treasure that might come into this land'. Then she moved on to express the 'immeasurable sorrow and heaviness' which did 'diminish and abridge' her days and her 'worldly joy and comfort', as the result of York's estrangement from the crown. She hoped that Margaret would be a 'tender and gracious' means by which Henry would show his grace and favour to her family.[3] And indeed, York had lost much goodwill and support among the nobility for his rash actions at Dartford. Former friends had abandoned him, or were in prison, and the lieutenancy of Ireland was taken from him in March 1453, forcing him to retire into private life.

Through 1452 and early 1453, Henry had functioned as a strong and active king, both in terms of his presence and authority, in restoring justice to England. Next, he moved to act in France, where English possessions had recently been lost. Shortly before Easter, a grant was levied upon the nobility to help pay for the campaigns of Sir John Talbot, Earl of Shrewsbury, by which it appears Henry was making serious efforts to regain control of his former French territories. Having proved indispensable to Henry during Cade's rebellion and York's disloyalty, Talbot was now in his sixties, although some accounts place him closer to 80. In October 1542, the Earl had been dispatched across the Channel and round the tip of Brittany, with his son Viscount Lisle, and an army of around 3,000 men. They had retaken Bordeaux soon after their arrival, and extended their occupancy through much of Western Gascony by the end of the year. At the arrival of 1453, the English situation in France was successful enough to give Henry hope that, if he could not equal his father's conquests, he might at least regain some control of the Plantagenet inheritance. Henry had taken active control of his kingship in a way that was unprecedented in his entire reign. He was finally shaping into a strong king, and it is probably no coincidence that it was during this personal resurgence that he had fathered the all-important heir.

Mindful of his success the previous summer, Henry prorogued Parliament at Reading on 2 July, in order to undertake another progress through the country. Before he did so, disputes arising among the nobility which required his attention. On 21 July, Henry presided over a court at Sheen to settle the case of a lordship in Wales, which was claimed by both Richard Neville, Earl of Warwick, who had the historical ownership of the lands and was holding them by force, and Edmund Beaufort, Duke of Somerset, to whom Henry had recently granted their keeping. In the meantime, Henry ordered the Neville forces to be disbanded and the lands to be temporarily held by Lord Dudley, until a formal hearing could rule on the matter. The inclusion of Somerset in the Council proceedings did not incline Warwick to surrender, but served to alienate him from the crown, and this, coupled with his ongoing feud with the Percy family, drove him firmly into the Yorkist camp. He was still at Sheen on 21 July, but ten days later, had reached the manor of Kingston Lacy in Dorset, before arriving at the former hunting lodge of Clarendon, in Oxfordshire, at the start of August. It was here that Margaret's world would be turned upside down.

Clarendon sat on what was then the main road just outside Winchester, connecting the city with Salisbury. It appears Henry was heading north-east, perhaps beginning the return stretch of his journey back towards London. The lodge was maintained by a tenant, in good repair for Henry's intermittent use, although it was coming towards the end of its period of royal occupation. Sections of the ruined east wall and great hall survive, along with the interiors of gravelled walls, giving a sense of what the place was like, but the greater attraction was the deer park, the largest of its kind. It is unclear who was travelling in the king's reduced household, but the assertion of Gregory's chronicle that Somerset accompanied Henry seems likely; however, it may be that Margaret remained at Greenwich, as she was due to enter confinement in the middle of September. Having waited so long for a child, she may have been unwilling to jeopardise the pregnancy in its final months, with all the discomforts and rigours of daily travel. It was probably at Clarendon that news caught up with Henry of the Battle of Castillon, which had been fought in Gascony on 17 July. A complete disaster, it had resulted in the defeat and death of John Talbot and the loss of all English territories in the area. What happened next is one of the greatest medical mysteries of late medieval England.

While at Clarendon, Henry slipped into a catatonic state. No source records the exact moment of this, or the events immediately preceding it. The sources disagree as to whether this situation arose as the result of a shock, an accident, a head injury or a breakdown, such as the modern world would recognise, and it is uncertain whether this was a slow decline over a series of days, or an abrupt transformation, as if the king was discovered in this condition one morning. Benet's chronicle states that Henry 'became very ill' on the feast of St Peter's Chains, which was 1 August, yet it appears that Henry was able to receive a visit from Sir William Stourton on 7 August. According to the *Chronicon Angliae*, he 'suffered a sudden and unexpected fright, becoming so ill that ... he lacked both natural sense and intelligence sufficient to govern the realm' and that 'no doctor or medicine could cure him',[4] while Bede's chronicle has that he 'suddenly became indisposed ... his wit and reason withdrawn. He was 'deprived of his senses and memory, unable to speak or use his limbs, incapable even of moving from the place where he sat'.[5] Bale's chronicle described how Henry was 'indispost sodenly' and was 'smyten with a ffransy' as the result of his 'wit and reason [being] withdrawn.'[6]

Henry certainly had a hereditary predisposition to 'madness', as the grandson of Charles VI. Reigning over France from 1380–1422, the father of Catherine of Valois experienced a more vigorous, violent manifestation of instability between periods of comparative sanity, or calm, although he was rarely able to make decisions or to rule even at this time. In 1392, under conditions of extreme stress, Charles had developed a fever, unable to pronounce his words and became over-excited, attacking and killing suspected assassins among his own men before falling into a stupor. At other times he was unable to recognise his wife and children, did not bathe or change his clothing for months, roamed the corridors of his chateaux howling like a wolf and believed himself to be made of glass. Reactions among the French to Charles's condition had largely been driven by fear, that his behaviour represented the disapproval of God, or some form of sorcery, especially as his first outbreak coincided with a period of prolonged drought. He was prescribed rest and relaxation at one of his country residences where the air was thought to be cleanest. When this did not result in his long-term recovery, two Augustinian friars attempted to exorcise his demons using magic incantations, then administered the king a drink made from crushed pearls. The royal council put its foot down, though, when they proposed trepanning, or drilling holes into Charles's head to release the unhealthy vapours gathered there. Abbot Whethamsted, compiling a chronicle contemporary to Henry believed that the king's health was undermined by his genetic inheritance, as he was 'his mother's stupid offspring, not his father's, a son greatly degenerated from the father, who did not cultivate the art of war ... a mild-spoken, pious king, but half-witted in affairs of state.'[7]

Even more significantly, Margaret was well-placed to appreciate that the illness of Charles had catapulted France into a state of civic turmoil, torn between rival factions. The situation had weakened the country to the extent that the English had been able to exploit its weakness and win significant victories under Henry V. Now the same situation appeared to be unravelling in England. Charles's queen, Isabeau, had been closely associated with her chief advisor and brother-in-law, Louis Duke of Orléans. Rumours that they were conducting an affair, coupled with rivalry between Louis and the Duke of Burgundy, culminated in the brutal murder of the queen's favourite in 1407. The pairing of Margaret and Somerset had already given rise to some rumours, and the new vulnerability at the apex of the English power structure was ripe for exploitation by Henry's enemies. Margaret must have hoped that her husband's illness was a temporary condition, rather than the debilitating, unpredictable episodes of Charles. It was perhaps the different characters of the two kings that led them to manifest their illness in different ways, with Charles volatile and violent, while Henry became withdrawn, passive and trance-like.

Instability was a question that baffled contemporary medicine, with its over-reliance upon astrology, the Galenic humours and religion. Madness could be any deviation from behavioural norms, in an emotional, physical or spiritual sense, so could encompass sadness, fits, memory loss, abusive or repetitious actions. Some forms of spiritual behavioural 'madness' were acceptable, even prized in certain contexts, such as prophecies and states of religious trance. This connotation aligns Henry with the most devout members of society, and stresses what was perceived as his predilection for saintliness in contrast with his less successful leadership. Unnatural behaviour was frequently explained as the manifestations of demonic possession, but had this diagnosis been taken seriously in England, it would have posed a threat to Henry's kingship, even to the Lancastrian dynasty. Medical 'madness' might be the result of the imbalance of the humours, bodily abuses, or the indulgence of vices, although Henry was known for his asceticism, so this was not considered likely either. The Bethlehem hospital for the insane, later 'Bedlam', had been founded in London in 1330, from the old priory for sick paupers, but even the most expert doctors there were baffled as to how to treat cases like that of the king.

Henry has been recorded by history as being 'mad', a term which reflects the instability he suffered during two phases of his life, first in 1453–4 and in a less debilitating recurrence in 1455. However, how these periods relate to his general mental health is still open to debate debate; whether they were isolated incidents or the eruptions of a long-term underlying condition. The critical question is whether he was considered 'mad' before this, by his household, allies and family, and if the episode made him unstable or unsuitable to rule after 1455. Hostile chronicles like Whethampsted, and enemies to the Lancastrian cause referred to Henry as weak and simple, silly and feeble, but these character attacks were often intended to highlight Henry's unsuitability for kingship, rather than realistically depict his mental health. Do such accounts exploit his mental fragility to represent his 'madness' as a long-term phenomenon, or are they representing a reality, that Henry was unbalanced throughout his life? Before the breakdown of August 1453 there is no indication of Henry experiencing mental illness or significant poor health. He was not the strong ruler that his father had been, and he may have been easily led by unpopular favourites, but the signs in 1452 suggest that he was taking kingship into his hands and restoring justice. Was this new-found strength a contributing factor to his collapse, or an unhappy coincidence? If Henry was indeed weak, and unsuited to rule, this sustained effort may have proved too much, with the disastrous news from France being the final straw. Or, alternatively, he was shaping up to be a good king when unanticipated illness laid him low.

Henry was brought back to London under the pretence that everything was normal. However, he was hidden away at Windsor, a situation that could only provide a short-time solution, while his physicians and councillors debated their options. Acting under Somerset's direction, the Council continued to act in the king's name, meeting in the hope that he would soon recover his wits. It was amid this period of secrecy and uncertainty that Margaret entered her confinement, probably in mid- to late September, into specially prepared rooms at Westminster Palace. On 13 October, the feast day of Edward the Confessor, she delivered a son whom she named Edward, breaking the three-generational line of Henries. A healthy male Lancastrian heir changed the aristocratic dynamic significantly. Prince Edward pushed York's claim one remove away from the throne, as he was now his father's inheritor, conceived and born in wedlock, and potentially a sign of other children the king might produce. The baby was christened in the Abbey, by William Waynfleet, Bishop of Winchester, with the font arrayed in russet cloth of gold and a mantle embroidered with pearls and precious stones costing almost £555.[8]

Leaving her confinement, Margaret was reunited with her husband, only to discover that he did not recognise her and could not interact with her in any way. Nor could he recognise his infant son, as recounted by the Duke of Norfolk: 'at the Prince's coming to Wyndesore, the Duke of Buckingham toke hym in his armes and presented hym to the Kyng in godely wyse, besechyng the Kyng to blisse him and the Kyng gave no maner answere'. The duke tried again, but then the queen arrived and 'toke the Prince in her armes, and presented hym in like fourme as the Duke had done, desiryng that he shuld blisse it, but alle their labour was in vayne'. But Henry still made no answer, only once looked at the prince and then cast his eyes downwards again, saying nothing.[9] Predictably, such behaviour gave rise to rumours about the child's paternity, which were also founded in disbelief that Henry possessed sufficient virility to father a child, coupled with his known ascetic character. Yet, as Blacman recorded, the indications are that Henry and Margaret had a sexual relationship in keeping with the king's character and contemporary expectations, never using his wife 'unseemly' or 'dealing unchastely with other women', even during her absence.[10] In such, Henry may have been the exception not the rule among his contemporaries, where double standards of sexual behaviour were prevalent, even encouraged for the sake of masculine good health. It is unlikely that Margaret would have been foolish enough to jeopardise the line of succession, but as the *English*, or *Davies Chronicle*, related, 'the queen was defamed and denounced, that he who was called prince was not her son but a bastard conceived in adultery'.[11]

The reputed fathers of Edward were Margaret's long-term friend, even a possible father-figure, Edmund, Duke of Somerset, who was approaching 50 and James Butler, Earl of Ormond and Wiltshire, then in his early thirties. It did not help that Somerset was named as the boy's godfather, along with John Kemp and Anne Stafford, Duchess of Buckingham, or that by this point, he was the most powerful figure in the country. Rumours of illegitimacy were commonplace during these decades, as the rival houses of York and Lancaster struggled for master. In the 1460s they would be used by the Yorkists against their own family members, as Edward IV's brother claimed him to be a bastard, and Richard III later using the same line against the princes in the Tower in 1483. It was an easy, yet devastating weapon if it was taken seriously. Sexual impropriety was the easiest way to politically discredit a queen and while such rumours could not be proven, they could equally not be disproved, and could resurface at points of vulnerability. It was also a predictable response to the political step Margaret was about to take, which propelled her outside the restrictive gender definitions of her role. Once he had recovered, though, Henry never questioned Edward's paternity and recognised him as his son.

The suggestion that Margaret was unfaithful have been embraced by John Ashdown-Hill, an historian noted for his Yorkist sympathies, who argued that Edward was conceived during the period of Henry's incapacity. Yet the dates are clearly against this. Assuming a straight-forward nine-month pregnancy, conception occurred in the second week of January, while Henry and Margaret were together at Greenwich, in the aftermath of the happy Christmas season of 1452. Had Edward been a week or two early, this still dates the event to the end of January, long before Henry fell ill in August. Steps were taken in 1454 to eradicate any rumour-mongering, with apprentice lawyer John Helton suffering a traitor's death for 'producing bills asserting that Prince Edward was not the Queen's son'.[12]

## II

The situation for Margaret in the winter of 1453 was a delicate one, dependent upon the duration of the king's illness, which could not be predicted. With her husband incapacitated, and with a new-born child, she could envision the dangers that lay ahead for Henry's rule and the inheritance of her son. Even though York had been quietened, he was still waiting in the wings, and would not hesitate to press his advantage. When a council was summoned on 23 October, the initial intention had been to exclude him but, behind Somerset's back, he was issued with an invitation to attend. Thomas Tyrell was instructed to inform York that the purpose of the meeting was to 'sette rest and union betwixt the lords of this lande ... for asmuch as there hath bee and yit as it is supposed variance betwixt him (York) and sum othre of the lords.'[13]

York arrived in London on 12 November, followed by Norfolk, who immediately launched accusations of treason against Somerset, who was arrested and committed to the Tower. York then complained that Henry, Margaret and Somerset had attempted to ostracise him over the previous two years by warning his potential allies to stay away from him or risk royal displeasure. To Henry and Margaret, this may have appeared a sound political policy given the trouble that York had stirred and their desire to prevent further disruption. Yet on 21 November York was granted a public declaration, under the great seal, that all men were free to serve him. This directly threatened Margaret's chief purpose to ensure the continuance of the Lancastrian dynasty by producing a male heir.

In the wake of York's call for support, it must have seemed to Margaret, that she had a greater mission: to keep Henry's kingship afloat during his absence, and prevent York from encroaching upon her husband's position. In order to achieve this, she needed the imprisoned Somerset released in order to provide the foundation upon which she would uphold Henry's reign. In the absence of the two men she most relied upon her husband and the duke, Margaret saw the mantle of responsibility pass to her. Just as her mother and grandmothers would have done, she prepared herself to step into the void. Isabeau of Bavaria had acted as regent for Charles VII during his madness and former French Queens, Blanche and Joan, had ruled while their husbands, Louis VIII and Philip IV, were away on crusades. Margaret intended to overturn English expectations of her age, gender and tradition, and take on the mantle of governance until Henry's recovery. Previously she had played a quiet, supportive role to his comparative 'activity'. Now that the king's incapacity reduced him to a passive role, Margaret attempted to become the essential active, political figure, to supply his deficiencies and counterbalance him. As highlighted by Joan of Arc's fate at the hands of the Lancastrians in France, the fifteenth century did not readily embrace women who attempted to assume what were perceived to be masculine roles and made themselves 'unfeminine', or a 'perversion' of the norm. It would be a slur from which her reputation would never recover, not even among historians of the twenty-first century.

In January 1454, the 23-year-old French-born queen, who had given birth for the first time just three months before, took a remarkably brave step. Until that point, despite her close personal connection to Somerset, she had remained ostensibly politically neutral.[14] Perhaps she felt that neutrality made her a viable figure to stand above the dynastic disputes; perhaps she would have ruled equally fairly in favour of Somerset and York, Neville and Percy, through their ongoing feuds. Forced by necessity, in a bid to save her husband and his kingdom, but also believing it to be her natural right as his anointed queen, Margaret presented herself to the royal Council as Protector of England. The extraordinary moment was recorded on 19 January in a letter now in the Paston collection, written by a John Stodeley to the Duke of Norfolk:

> The queen has made a bill of five articles, desiring them to be granted, the first of which is that she desires the whole rule of this land, the second is that she may appoint the chancellor, treasurer, privy seal and all other officers of this land, with sheriffs and all other officers that the king should make; the third is that she may give all the bishoprics of this land, and all other benefices belonging to the king's gift; the fourth is that she may have sufficient livelihood assigned to her for the king, the prince and herself. As for the fifth article, I cannot yet find out what it is.[15]

Margaret's five articles, or four, as they survive, were never going to be accepted by Henry's Council. Had she taken such a step in one of the smaller French kingdoms, she may have been trusted and supported, but her nationality was the first, immediate barrier. Although she had been crowned as Queen of England, a certain level of distrust would always surround her birth, especially given the difficult Anglo–French relations of recent years. If she was not to be considered, at the most extreme, a spy, or actively working to turn the country over to the Valois, she was at least ill-equipped to understand the nature of English politics and the nuances of allegiance in her new realm. It was a legitimate concern that her background meant that she was not aware of the subtleties of England's recent history, political allegiances, and the complex aristocratic feuds, in the way that veterans like York were. Thus, her nationality, education and inexperience counted against her in spite of her bravery, sense of responsibility and dedication. She must have anticipated this, but perhaps counted upon her influential friends in the council to sway the disbelievers. Some though, could not be convinced and supporters were returning to York, such as the Duke of Warwick who had previously been neutral, and the Duke of Norfolk, who had been estranged from York over the Blackheath debacle. A growing presence of the Yorkist faction in the Council contributed to the rejection of Margaret at regent. They would also have objected to her having sole power to appoint figures to key positions of Henry's household, which could result in greater representation of York's enemies. However, the subtleties Margaret lacked could have been supplied by seasoned councillors like Somerset, Fortescue, Archbishop John Kemp and others, with the queen as their figurehead. Thus, it was not so much Margaret that York and his allies rejected, as the coalition her rule implied, which would effectively end all Yorkist ambitions.

Yet it is possible that Margaret was playing a shrewder game. Aware of the composition of the Council, and with the advice of her close friends, she may have been deliberately casting her net wide in an attempt to obtain her lesser demand of suitable support. The royal finances had been in trouble for years, with credit being denied them since 1451, so she may have hoped that with the inevitable rejection of her political request she would at least receive funding with which to bide her time. This is, in fact, what happened. She was given an income and retreated to Greenwich with Henry and Edward to await further developments. Her focus was firmly on her husband and new-born son and she had to trust in Somerset and others to maintain balance on the Council. If her intention had been to make a powerful declaration on behalf of her son's inheritance, then her rights had been noted her rights had been noted and she had been successful. On 15 March, at Windsor Castle Edward was created Prince of Wales, Duke of Cornwall and Earl of Chester, and York was one of the signatories approving the act. The boy was to receive an allowance of £1,000 annually until he was 8 years old, transferring all other revenues from his lands and estates to the king, in whose household he was intended to reside until his majority at 14.[16]

When Parliament finally convened, after six months of denial regarding the king's health, Archbishop Kemp raised the question 'to whomm the kinges power sholde be committed for the holding of ... at this tyme'. With Somerset still in the Tower, the decision was taken that, during Henry's incapacity, power should rest in the hands of his immediate adult successor, the Duke of York, who was named as the King's Lieutenant. Until this time though, everything had been done in the king's name. Yet there may have been dissention, or unwillingness to participate in these events during the king's absence, as the turnout rate among the lords was very low, prompting the introduction of fines for non-attendance. It was the death of Archbishop of Canterbury and Chancellor John Kemp, on 22 March, which effectively brought matters to a head. There could be no progression without a Chancellor, who had control of the royal seals, but the role could not be appointed without royal approval. The day after the death of John Kemp, the House of Lords sent a deputation to Henry in order to ascertain whether he was capable of advising them, or if his illness continued. The record of their visit, in the Rotuli Parliamentorum, gives a good indication of the level at which Henry was functioning at this point:

> Lords Spiritual and Temporal were in the king's high presence in the place where he dined. Articles were put to the king expressing great concern for his health and the great diligence of the lords in his parliament, but from him they could get no answer or sign. After dinner they came to the king again and urged him for an answer, by all ways and means they could think of, but they received none. From that place, the king was led, between two men, into the chamber where he slept, and the lords pressed him once more, but they received no answer, word or sign.[17]

As a result, York was appointed Protector on 27 March, 1454. Less than a week later, the central role of Chancellor went to the Earl of Salisbury, York's brother-in-law. The appointment was ratified by an Act of Parliament on 3 April, for 'so long as it pleased the king' or until 'Prince Edward should reach years of discretion' and, if he chose, could 'assume the dignity and title himself'.[18] After all, Henry's reign had set the precedent for rule by the royal Council, during his minority, and a similar system of care might be resurrected until Edward came of age. That summer saw a comparatively quiet period, with Margaret, Henry and Edward remaining in seclusion while York conducted business in the north.

That autumn, significant reductions in the royal household were introduced as a means of countering the spending that had led to the royal pair being refused credit. It was considered necessary,

> to advise, ordain and establish a sad [serious] and a substantial rule in the King's household by the which should grow to his highness not only great honour and worship in this, his realm, and comfort to his people, but also it should be to his singular renown, fame and laud in other lands and countries.[19]

Ordinances published in November at the instigation of York, allow an insight into the organisation of Henry's world, from the individuals who served him to the jobs they fulfilled. Far from being a sinister act of control, this represented an effort to return the king's household to the regime followed by his father. The Ordinances listed those who were entitled to bring a retinue to court, who might be housed and fed at the king's expense, including bishops, earls, viscounts, barons, secretaries and those fulfilling specific roles like Lord Cromwell, the Lord Chamberlain, Henry's carvers Edward Hungerford and Philip Wentworth, chaplains John Arundel and John Kirkby, physicians John Fauceby and William Hatcliff, surgeons Robert Waren and Thomas Bekbank, four squires of the body and four gentlemen usher, and a compliment of henchmen, squire, yeomen and grooms. His minstrels were Thomas Ratcliff, William Wicks, John Cliff and Robert More Wayte; four people kept the jewel house, twelve were employed in the counting house, thirteen in the bakehouse, eight in the pantry, eight in the cellar, four in the buttery, three as 'ale-takers', six in the pitcher house, four in the spicery, four making confections, four in the chandlery, two in the waffery and many more in the kitchen and its other offices. As queen, Margaret kept the figure of 120 that comprised her establishment, with thirty-nine individuals serving Prince Edward. The royal stables were significantly reduced, with forty-six horses reassigned, leaving only twenty-five, and the staff cut from thirty-nine to nine, but this was probably a temporary measure, reflective of the fact that Henry was not travelling or using such resources. It made sense for the horses to be employed elsewhere instead of just waiting indefinitely in the stables, although this did not stop some from interpreting the cuts as malign.

Then, as unexpectedly as he had fallen ill, Henry recovered. He was soon speaking 'as well as he ever did' and was able to recognise visitors. It must have been the most immense relief to Margaret when, on Christmas Day 1454, he was finally able to acknowledge his son, then fourteen months old. She carried Prince Edward to Henry, and their stilted conversation allowed hope for a full recovery and the resumption of rule and family life. The encounter was described in a letter written by Edmund Clere, to his cousin John Paston, at Greenwich on January 10:

> On Monday afternoon the Queen came to him, and brought my Lord Prince with her, and then he [Henry] asked what the Prince's name was, and the Queen told him, Edward; and then he held up his hand, and thanked God thereof. And he said he never knew him till that time… and he asked, who were godfathers? And the Queen told him and he was well apaid. [content].[20]

There is no indication that Henry understood what had happened to him; he gave no explanation or comment upon his condition, nor what had roused him from it. Rapidly though, he had to become acquainted with the changes of the last eighteen months, and Margaret would have been instrumental in explaining to him the latest developments. Whether she did this in an impartial tone, or with caution for fear of upsetting his mind again, or if she complained of the imprisonment of her favourite, the Council's rejection of her, or the presumptions of the Duke of York, it is impossible now to know. Yet Henry emerged with some degree of understanding that the York–Somerset rift had widened and that regal authority was required to restore balance. He gave thanks for his recovery on 9 January, by hearing mass, saying matins, commanding his almoner to undertake a pilgrimage to Canterbury on his behalf and his secretary to make an offering in Westminster at the shrine of St Edward.

The fortunes of the York and Lancastrian dynasties turned upon the health of the king's mind, and the Council had become polarised between the two, to the discomfort of those who wished to remain neutral, or simply loyal to the throne. Localised problems were now factored into national politics. The long-running Percy–Neville feud, which had largely been confined to the north, had also reached a head, with York backing the Nevilles, to whom he was related by marriage, and the Percies aligning with Somerset. Now these lords appeared in the Council after periods of absence or neutrality, in order to support their powerful backers. Increasingly, people were starting to take sides. By the time the Council met on 5 February, Henry, and perhaps Margaret, had been able to exercise sufficient influence to ensure that Somerset was officially granted his freedom from the Tower on bail. A month later, though, when he had still not been released, Henry was forced to issue a public statement professing his belief in the duke's loyalty and Somerset was freed with a 'declaration of his innocence in all criminal charges against him, leaving all other matters to arbitration'.[21] This was bad news for York, who anticipated reprisals for Somerset's arrest, but with Henry's re-emergence, the reins of government had been taken back into Lancastrian hands. And when Henry was in control, it meant that Margaret's influence, in favour of Somerset, found its voice again. In spite of York's allegations of corruption in France, Somerset was reappointed Captain of Calais. The Earl of Salisbury was removed as Chancellor in favour of Thomas Bourchier, who also took the Archbishopric of Canterbury and other pro-Yorkist supporters like the Earl of Worcester found themselves replaced. The king was sufficiently recovered to be able to anticipate that tensions would brew between the two factions and bound York and Somerset over to keep the peace until 20 June, under bonds of 20,000 marks each, to allow for the process of arbitration to take place over their disagreements. It was a sound, sensible decision, designed to dispel the situation, and it involved sufficient financial penalty that should have guaranteed its success.

Fragile though it was, Henry's leadership had been reasserted, and many of the changes made in his illness were reversed. With the Protectorship at an end, and bound over to keep the peace, York and his immediate circle retreated to the north. In their absence, Somerset called a meeting of selected councillors on

15–18 April. Whatever was discussed, and the main topic was probably York, the resulting decisions required legal sanction, for which Somerset summoned the Great Council to meet at Leicester. The stated intention was to make provision for the king's safety, but this was interpreted by York and his allies as a 'mistrust to some persons'. They feared that their attendance at the meeting would be taken as an opportunity to facilitate their arrests and began to gather men around them.

Historian R. L. Storey has stated that if Henry's illness was bad for England, his recovery was a disaster. Although this denies Henry's right to rule, its recognition of his unsuitability to rule, and the ensuing consequences is difficult to dispute. During Henry's absence a sort of status quo had been established, with York as a strong, active figure of authority, working on behalf of the national interest while the Lancastrian royal family were the figureheads of royalty, living quietly at Greenwich. This situation could have continued indefinitely, although trouble would have arisen if York followed through his intention to put Somerset on trial. The country could accept an unwell king because it received a more competent replacement: in effect, Henry's illness could be considered a neat solution to his weak kingship. However, this overlooks the very real development Henry had shown in recent years towards building a strong personal presence and to create stability in the wake of Cade's rebellion. It is true that conflict was made almost inevitable by Henry's return to government, demoting York and freeing Somerset, unleashing the dissatisfaction of both. Another way of looking at the question though, is that the responsibility for the imminent drama lay with York who had been a constant agitator, in opposition to Somerset who had the king's favour. Yet York felt that he was being overlooked and Henry was being misled. Nor was he just an over-mighty subject; if he chose, he could argue that had a better right to rule, since his line of descent had been usurped by Henry's grandfather. Ultimately, though, Henry was the king, and it was his responsibility to control the feuds between his nobles and curtail their personal vendettas. He failed to do so but, to be fair, it would have taken an exceptionally able and strong ruler to keep Richard, Duke of York, in check.

The potential dangers of Henry's illness, and recovery, had been spotted by another French commentator as early as 1453. Charles, Duke of Orléans, who had welcomed the young Margaret at his Château of Blois in 1445 and accompanied her on part of her journey to England. Orléans had spent twenty-five years in captivity in England and recognised the potential for treachery arising from Henry's vulnerability, writing in a ballad:

*Have not the English always betrayed their kings?*
*Certainly, everyone knows of it.*
*And, once again, their king is in a precarious position.*
*Each Englishman pushes himself forward by speaking ill of him.*
*They show sufficiently by their evil words that they would readily injure him.*
*There is a great dispute among them about who would be king.*[22]

On 19 May the new Chancellor, Thomas Bourchier, received instructions to compose letters under the great seal informing York, Warwick, Salisbury and Norfolk that they would be considered traitors, and treated as such, if they did not disband their troops. The following day, York replied that 'neither by our coming, nor by the manner thereof, do we intent to proceed to any matter except what, with God's mercy, shall be to his pleasure, and to the honour, prosperity and welfare of our Sovereign Lord'.[23] When Somerset and Henry headed to Leicester, York, Warwick and Salisbury marched down from the north with an army. On the morning of 22 May, when the king's party reached the little Hertfordshire town of St Albans, Henry and Somerset had the first indications that the tension might erupt into violence.

Windsor Castle, where Catherine of Valois gave birth to the future Henry VI on 6 December 1421. It would remain a favourite palace for the young king throughout his childhood. *Karen Roe*

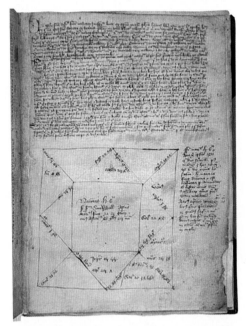

A horoscope drawn up for the date of Henry VI's birth. It was customary to examine the astrological influences under which a monarch was born, and this chart was composed retrospectively, during Henry's childhood. However, predicting negative events such as illness, danger or even death, could lead an astrologer into trouble. *British Library Egerton MS 889 f5*

The Arms of René of Anjou, Margaret's father, depicted in his Book of Hours by Barthélemy d'Eyck. The second son of Louis II, Duke of Anjou, King of Sicily and Naples, E inherited considerable territories and influence, although little wealth. *British Library Egerton MS 1070*

View of Saumur Castle, the residence of Margaret's paternal grandmother Yolande of Aragon, with whom she stayed during her childhood. *Paul Fairbrass.*

The fairy-tale Saumur Castle, with its white towers, is depicted in the illustrations for the Très Riches Heures du Duc de Berri. Dominating the skyline in for the month of September, it overlooks a scene of peasants gathering in the harvest, showing the castle as it was in around the year 1410. *Laurent Goujon.*

The marriage of Henry and Margaret, which took place on 23 April 1445, depicted in another illustration in the *Talbot Hours*. The book was commissioned and presented to her by John Talbot, Earl of Shrewsbury, as a gift to Margaret before her marriage, and contained fifteen texts including romances, chansons, works on chivalry and the order of the garter.

Illustration depicting Henry and Margaret, kneeling at prayer, in the company of their patron saints, St Edward and St Margaret.
*BL Harley MS 318*

Titchfield Abbey in Hampshire, where the wedding ceremony of Henry and Margaret was conducted.
*Ozzy Delaney.*

The joint arms of England and Anjou, symbolic of the union between Margaret and Henry. For many reasons it proved an unpopular match in England, although the couple themselves appear to have lived harmoniously together. *BL Royal 15 E VI MS*

St. Peter's Street, St Albans, Hertfordshire. By 1455, tensions between the rival factions at court had become so great that conflict became inevitable. Henry's army, led by the Duke of Somerset, met that of Richard, Duke of York, in the town of St Albans. The fiercest fighting was concentrated in St Peter's Street, culminating in the death of Somerset.
*Ruth Hartnup*

St Mary's Guildhall, Coventry. In reaction to the Yorkist loyalties of London and the south, Margaret and Henry established a northern power base, centered at Coventry. A tapestry depicting their visit to the city still hangs in the Guildhall. *Elliott Brown.*

Kenilworth Castle, in Warwickshire, another location where Henry and Margaret lived with their growing Lancastrian court. *David Merrett.*

The great hall of Kenilworth Castle, which must have been well-known to Henry and Margaret, dining and meeting loyal friends here during their exile from London. *Laura la Rose.*

Statue of Margaret and Prince Edward in the Jardin du Luxembourg, Paris. *Amy Licence.*

A depiction of Henry, crowned and seated on the throne, dating from 1488-9 when his posthumous cult was being established. Angels flank him and offer their blessings. *BL Hargrave MS 274*

In 1461, following victories at Mortimer's Cross and Towton, Edward, Earl of March entered London and was declared Edward IV. Henry and Margaret fled into Scotland. Edward's depiction in the same manuscript as Henry, in 1488-9, is a more secular image, with no angels, reflecting his different relationship with the new Tudor king, Henry VII.

*BL Hargrave MS 274*

A romanticised Victorian illustration of the legend in which Margaret met with a robber whilst fleeing from the Yorkist armies. *Patrick Gray.*

Margaret, depicted in stained glass in a window on the west of the aisle, at St Mary's Church, Saffron Walden, Essex. *Martin Cooper.*

Lincluden Abbey, depicted in a postcard of 1905, where Margaret and Prince Edward were offered shelter by Mary of Guelders, dowager Queen of Scotland. *Ashley van Haeften.*

Harlech Castle, in Wales, a Lancastrian stronghold which continued to hold out against the Yorkist regime until 1468. Margaret fled here after the Battle of Northampton. *giborn_134*

Henry was captured in 1465 and sent to the Tower of London, where he was lodged in the Wakefield Tower, the circular tower in the centre of the wall running parallel to the river. *Dun Can*

The guest house, Cerne Abbey, where Margaret, Prince Edward and Anne Neville were lodged upon their return to England in April 1471. Here, news of the death of the Earl of Warwick forced them to reconsider their plans. *Peter Broster*

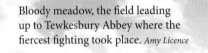

Bloody meadow, the field leading up to Tewkesbury Abbey where the fiercest fighting took place. *Amy Licence*

Tewkesbury Abbey, where the army of Edward IV met that of Prince Edward on 4 May, 1471, resulting in a definitive victory for the Yorkists. Margaret's son was killed during, or shortly after, the battle and Margaret, heartbroken, surrendered to her enemy. *Amy Licence*

Memorial slab to Edward, Prince of Wales, set into the floor between the choir stalls at Tewkesbury Abbey. *Amy Licence*

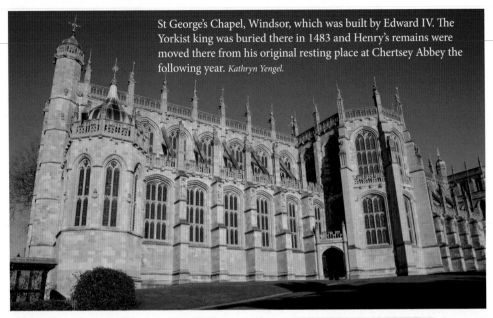

St George's Chapel, Windsor, which was built by Edward IV. The Yorkist king was buried there in 1483 and Henry's remains were moved there from his original resting place at Chertsey Abbey the following year. *Kathryn Yengel.*

Angers Cathedral, where Margaret was laid to rest next to her parents in 1482. Her remains were scattered by revolutionaries ransacking the cathedral in the late eighteenth century. *Dennis Jarvis*

Daisies, or Marguerites, symbolising Margaret, in the Talbot Book of Hours, British Library.

## Chapter Six

# War 1455–1458

## I

The town of St Albans lay at the end of a day's ride from London. Travellers approaching through the surrounding hills and fields would have had their first glimpse of the imposing Norman abbey, dominating the skyline with its huge nave and square tower. Inside, the remains of the saint reposed under a glittering tomb, where pilgrims flocked to leave gifts and murmur their prayers. By the middle of the fifteenth century, an extensive town had grown up around the abbey, with a square and streets lined by narrow-fronted, wattle-and-daub buildings, owned by residents who engaged mostly in hospitality or fulling, the preparation of wool. It was an unlikely location for the coming conflict, where the tensions that had been building over recent years, finally spilled over in an encounter that shocked those involved with the extent of its brutality.

After Margaret and Prince Edward had been safely established at Greenwich, Henry and Somerset travelled from Westminster via Watford, before reaching St Albans as a stop-over on the way to Dunstable. There, they heard the news that York was approaching the city with an armed force and paused, wondering whether this would be a repeat of the Dartford incident of 1452, or if York would commit the ultimate treason of raising arms against the king. The duke had acted in the national interests when he took on the position of Protector but, now that Henry had returned to his senses, York appeared to have made a transition, to acting to promote his own cause or, as he would say, in self-defence. In anticipation that Somerset would be made a target, Henry asked him to step aside, replacing him as Constable of England with the Duke of Buckingham, who advised them to negotiate with York, who was also his brother-in-law. Somerset's advice to stand and prepare themselves to fight where they were was rejected, in spite of his greater military experience. Henry may have considered he was protecting his friend, but the decision was possibly a hasty one, plunging the royal army into the town while York had already taken up his position. This has been described by one historian as a 'wayward' decision and the Duke of Buckingham as 'temporising',[1] but it is difficult to assess the situation without the influence of hindsight: Henry was not certain that combat would follow, and occupying the town was a mark of his authority. He made his stand at a place, or property, which the Paston Letters refer to as 'Boslawe', formerly known as 'Sandeforde'. With the royal party based in the central square and the rebel York in the Key (or Kay) field to the east, messages went back and forth, containing the predictable accusations against Somerset and professions of York's loyalty. Henry appears to have been prepared for the possibility of a fight as he did not make for his usual lodgings in the abbey, although Buckingham did not believe it would actually happen. The notion that fighting was anticipated, but perhaps not so soon, is indicated by the notable absences from the field: the Duke of Norfolk arrived in St Albans with 1,000 men the day after the battle, followed by the Earls of Oxford and Shrewsbury, Lord Cromwell and Sir Thomas Stanley. Perhaps York decided to seize the moment and act before these additional forces had the opportunity to reinforce the royal defences. York agreed to lay down his weapons on condition that Somerset should be excommunicated and that a more representative council should be appointed to work with the king. Even worse, he demanded that his enemy be delivered into his hands, but Henry would not abandon Somerset, so he rejected this condition. He did not foresee that it would lead to Somerset's death.

Henry replied with dramatic fighting talk, if indeed the words recorded in the anonymous paper held among the Paston letters are his actuals ones. Equally, he may have been influenced by Somerset, or Buckingham, or other advisors as he threatened York and his allies with the terrible deaths of traitors. Under such circumstances any king would have done the same, or more. York had crossed the line in 1452 and was breaking the oath he had sworn not to take up arms against the king. Interestingly, Henry also blamed the dissention in the kingdom for his illness:

> I, King Henry, charge and command that no manner person, of what degree, or state, or condition that ever he be, abide not, but void the field, and be not so hardy to make any resistance against me in my own realm; for I shall know what traitor shall dare be so bold to raise a people in my own land, where through I am in great disease and heaviness. And by the faith that I owe to St Edward and the crown of England, I shall destroy them, every mother's son, they shall be hanged, and drawn and quartered, that may be taken afterward, of them to have example to all such traitors to beware to make any such rising of people within my land and so traitorously to abide her king and governor. And for a conclusion, rather than they shall have any Lord here with me at this time, I shall this day, for her sake, and in this quarrel myself live or die.[2]

Later accusations suggest it was the Yorkists who fired the first arrow that began the battle. Fighting broke out in what is now St Peter's Street, the central market street, and was short and brutal, little more than a skirmish, lasting about half an hour. York had the larger force at around 2,000 men, but Henry had the greater number of nobility on his side, including the Dukes of Somerset and Buckingham, Earls of Dorset, Stafford, Wiltshire, Northumberland and his half-brother Pembroke, and Lords Berners, Clifford, Roos, Sudeley and others. Henry stood his ground by the church in St Peter's Street, with his banner proudly displayed and a 'sore fight' ensued. The *English Chronicle* gives the first of the two most graphic accounts of the day, relating how York and his men 'violently broke down houses and fences' on the east side, 'slaying all that resisted them'.[3] Unable to break through the barricades erected by the king's men, Warwick circumvented the streets and crept through the back gardens of houses to join the fray. Fleeing from the scene, Abbot Whethamsted witnessed a man 'with his brains dashed out, there another with a broken arm, a third with throat cut, and a fourth with a pierced chest' amid a 'whole street ... full of dead corpses'. He related how the timid monks sheltering inside the abbey listened anxiously 'to the clash of arms and the groans of the wounded', before going out into the streets afterwards, to see the 'maimed and mangled corpses ... transfixed with barbed darts'.[4] An anonymous contemporary French account, known as the *Dijon Relation*, put the fighting at a little over three hours, beginning at ten in the morning, and giving a sense of the hand-to-hand fighting in the narrow streets: 'because the place was small, few combatants could fight there and matters became so critical that four of the king's bodyguard were killed by arrows in his presence'.[5] Others place the start later, at around eleven.

The king's physical presence was significant: bodily, he was the personification of his kingship, standing under the banner bearing his arms, in the thick of the fighting. For all York's protestations that he was defending the king, in legal terms anyone engaging in combat with any army fighting under the royal standard was committing an act of treason. Equally, Henry could very easily have been killed. He came very close, being wounded by an arrow, either in the neck or shoulder, and although the injury appears to have been superficial, this was more by accident than design. Had Henry moved slightly at the opportune moment, the arrow could have hit him in the throat or head, proving fatal. The sudden, dramatic onset of fighting unfolding before his eyes, with his loyal friends dying violently on either side, cannot have failed to affect such a sensitive man as Henry is known to have been. Benet relates that the king, finding himself deserted, fled to a tanner's house nearby. The *Dijon Relation* says that York learned of the king's retreat and ordered him to be taken to the abbey for safety.

There was never any doubt about York's intended target. The *English Chronicle* states that the plan was to seek his 'mortal enemy, and enemy to all the realm', and 'seize him by strength and violence'.[6] He and Warwick cornered Somerset in the market place, forcing the duke to seek refuge in one of the buildings. According to legend, the witch of Eye, Margery Jourdemayne, had made a prophecy back in the 1430s that Somerset would die in a castle. Now, barricaded inside the Castle Inn at St Albans, the duke saw there was no other option but to come out fighting. He launched a brave attempt to fight his way to freedom, killing four men with his own hands before, according to the *Dijon Relation*, he was 'felled to the ground with an axe, and at once wounded in so many places that he died'.[7] A newsletter from Bruges, reporting the details at several removes, stated that Somerset had been taken away and summarily executed. However he met his fate, Somerset's death effectively ended the battle. Other loyal Lancastrians such as Henry Percy, Second Earl of Northumberland and Thomas, Lord Clifford, were also cut down. Contemporary estimates of the death toll vary between Benet's 100, John Crane's 120, 'six score', and the *Dijon Relation's* 200. York went to find Henry in the abbey, where other loyal Lancastrian lords escaped dressed in the habits of monks, knelt before the king and professed his loyalty again. Reputedly, York claimed he had not opposed Henry 'but had been against the traitors to his crown' and, according to the *Dijon Relation*, the king blessed him before he departed.

The news would have reached London the same day. Waiting at Greenwich, Margaret learned that her husband was safe and alive, but her friend and mentor Somerset had been cut down by the Yorkists, who were now in control. Her reactions must have been mixed but they were not recorded. Her biographer of 1861, Jacob Abbott, plausibly imagined her 'waiting in the utmost suspense and anxiety' and, less plausibly, being 'thrown into a state of utter despair, so much so that she remained for some hours in a state of stupor, as if all was now lost, and it was useless and hopeless to continue to struggle any longer'.[8] Abbott allows her to have recovered from this state 'at length' and to begin to 'consider what was to be done', which is far more consistent with Margaret's character. It is not clear where or when her reunion with Henry took place, but she may have hurried to Westminster once she heard that the combatants were heading south.

After the battle, York and his men accompanied Henry back to London. The dynamics of this situation were reported differently by the chroniclers, some suggesting that Henry was a willing participant, others hinting at a more sinister sense of him being a captive. Bale related that 'on the second day after they brought the king to the city of London in great honour, the Duke of York riding on his right side and the Earl of Salisbury on his left and the Earl of Warwick bearing his sword'. Gregory's chronicle described how, 'after it was over, the Duke of York brought Henry to London as king, not as a prisoner', while the *Dijon Relation* wrote that 'the king, Duke of York and all the other lords came to London, where they have been received with great joy and solemn procession'.[9] A Bruges newsletter, kept in the Milanese State Papers, was more focused on the role of the Duke of York: 'they say he has demanded pardon from the king for himself and his men, and will have it. He will take up the government again, and some think that the affairs of that kingdom will now take a turn for the better.'[10] The historian Polydore Vergil, writing in the reign of York's granddaughter, Elizabeth, wife of Henry VII, recorded that the duke 'armed himself with mildness, mercy and liberality, and was so far from laying violent hands on King Henry that he brought him honourably to London, as conqueror of the field'.[11]

Henry was led through the streets of the capital before being taken to lodge at the bishop of London's Palace. That Sunday, York organised a crown-wearing ceremony at St Paul's where, according to one source, Henry received the crown from the duke's own hands. A proclamation, made in the king's name forbade anyone from talking about St Albans and a week of 'royalty and sport' followed.[12] York also needed to ascertain the king's mental fitness to enact the necessary business resulting from St Albans, so a Doctor Gilbert Kemer was summoned from Salisbury to attend him at Windsor. The summons, issued on 5 June, simply stated that the king had 'need of his medical knowledge':

> *Trusty and Welbeloved, we greet you wel.*
> *And for as moche as we be occupied and laboured, as ye knowe wel, with Sicknesse and Infirmitees, of the whiche to be delivered and cured, by the Grace of our Lord, as nedeth the Helpe, Entendance, and Laboure of suche expert, notable, and proved Men in the Crafte of Medicines, as ye be, in whom, among alle other, our affection and desire right especially is sette,*
> *We desire, wille, and hertily pray you that ye be with us at oure Castell of Wyndesore the Twelfth Day of this Moneth, and Entende upon oure Persone for the Cause abovesaid, and that ye faille not as oure singuler Trust is in you, and as ye desire and tendre of oure Helth and Welfare.*
> *Yeven undre oure Prive Seel at Westm. the v day of Juyn.*
> *Dors.*
> *To Maistre Gilbert Kemer, Dean of Salesbury.*[13]

Henry's neck wound would have received attention at the scene of the battle, but Kemer's advice may have been required to see that it was healing well, in addition to his consideration of the king's state of mind. Henry was judged capable, as he appeared in person when Parliament was formally opened on 9 July. Three days later though, the king relinquished the care of his colleges at

Eton and Cambridge for the duration of his life. Payments were made to three physicians in total for their 'great labour and care to the king's person at this time'.[14]

The inevitable recriminations did not take long to surface. On 19 July, a quarrel broke out between Warwick and Lord Cromwell, about who should take responsibility for initiating the bloodshed. A Londoner named Henry Windsor, wrote to John Bocking and William Worcester concerning the uneasy atmosphere:

> The king our sovereign lord, and all his true lords, are healthy in their bodies but not at ease in their hearts. Two days before the writing of this letter there was a quarrel between Lords Warwick and Cromwell before the King. When Lord Cromwell sought to excuse himself of all responsibility for the battle of St Albans, Warwick swore he was not telling the truth since it was he who originated all the fighting there ... Also, men of Lords Warwick, York and Salisbury proceed in armour daily to Westminster, having filled their lords' barges with weapons.[15]

Five days later, on 24 July, Parliament issued pardons for York and his allies for their roles at St Albans. This is interesting because the Yorkists then had the upper hand, as is evidenced by the passing of these pardons, but the Lancastrians were not issued with similar statements, suggesting that York did not feel secure in his position. The pardons were designed to protect him, then and in the future. Henry declared that,

> none of our cousins, the Duke of York, and the Earls of Warwick and Salisbury, nor any of the persons who came with them in their fellowship [to St Albans] be impeached, sued, vexed, grieved, hurt or molested for anything supposed or claimed to have been done against our person, crown or dignity.

The lords were required to swear an oath in his presence, to affirm their loyalty to Henry and 'do all that may be to the welfare, honour and safeguard of your most noble person and royal estate and pre-eminence and prerogative ... and I shall at no time consent to anything to the hurt and prejudice of your most noble person, dignity, crown or estate.'[16] Vergil described a situation where Henry was a puppet controlled by the Yorkists who worked in subtle ways to undermine his power: 'so Henry might be king in name and not in deed'. But they 'removed from him, little by little, his old councillors, put them from office and authority, and substituted in their places new men of their own'.[17] This Parliament was the first to censure Margaret's involvement in politics, with York's allies stating that until recently, government had been managed 'by the Queen, the Duke of Somerset, and their friends had been of late a great oppression and injustice to the people'.[18] If Margaret had not previously felt animosity towards York, his role in the death of Somerset, his manipulation of her husband and, finally, his accusation that she had oppressed her people, were sufficient to turn her into his implacable enemy. The following year, Benet's chronicle recorded that Margaret 'greatly loathed' both York and Warwick.

Henry's involvement in the Battle of St Albans, and his acquiescence to the Yorkist agenda in its aftermath has been received differently by historians. When it comes to the question of responsibility, Henry's identity as a king was in conflict with that of his personal mental health. From the little that is known, he appears to have stood his ground bravely until the point that his life was threatened, upon which he bid a sensible retreat. He did not lead his troops, or bear arms, but he did don armour. Perhaps he engaged reluctantly, in disbelief, unable to accept how the situation evolved around him, even fearing for his life. Perhaps his presence in the midst of the fray was coincidental. To rephrase the dilemma of Ophelia's drowning in Hamlet, the attacking Yorkists brought the fight to Henry, in St Peter's Street, rather than him advancing to meet it. It is problematic to regard Henry's outward acquiescence as a sign of weakness. The belief that York had his best interests at heart may have been essential to the narrative constructed by the king in order to make sense of the situation. He had to believe in York's support, as he had little choice at that point. His inner circle had been decimated at St Albans, under the aegis of the interests of the realm, and it was the same mantra that York repeated throughout their dealings with the Council that season. Even if he had considered York's actions to have been treasonous, or even heavy-handed, Henry was not in a strong enough position to mount any sort of opposition. There is also the persuasive point that, at this time, York's message was genuine: he believed he had acted on behalf of the crown, and would continue to do so for a number of years. In 1455, York still supported Henry's kingship and their cooperation was more complex than the taut façade some historians have maintained.

Equally, placing responsibility for the battle with Henry, as some historians have done, raises more problems than it solves. It has been asserted that the conflict was the result of Henry's inability to keep his warring nobles in check, to squash York's ambitions and keep Suffolk and Somerset's influence in perspective, but one cannot demand of an individual, retrospectively, what they are unable to give. Through weakness of character, or naivety, or ineptness, Henry was not able to exercise control over men who were stronger, more experienced and, in actuality, more powerful than him. It is true that Henry was an adult who had been king for most of his life, or as long as he could remember. Temperamentally, he was not suited to kingship but, by an accident of birth, kingship had chosen him. There is no question that he was unaware of the problems this created, in an era when strong leadership was as essential in the council chamber and court corridors as it was on the battlefield. In recent years, Henry had taken advice and attempted to reassert himself; the crises of 1450–2 provoked him to a semblance of strong kingship, with great emotional cost. He was simply not sufficient to meet the challenges that followed, but the alternative was to abdicate his power, certainly resulting in his death and a long minority, which warring magnates would have been able to exploit further. Those historians who see Henry as failing to fulfil his duty miss the point that he was incapable of fulfilling that duty. He could not 'simply exercise greater personal accountability' because to do so was not a 'simple' matter. The ideal situation, for England, had been the period of the first Protectorate, with the royal family at a symbolic remove and a competent adult male in charge. Had Henry been able to 'simply' turn on effective kingship, no doubt he would have done so.

Taking Henry's former illness of eighteen months as an indicator of his fragile mental health, it is not surprising that the events he witnessed at St Albans, and their political ramifications, set back his recovery. By the end of August he had retired to Hertford Castle and, by autumn 1455, rumours were circulating in London about his incapacity. He was too ill to attend the second session of Parliament, so the Council resorted to the obvious precedent of the Protectorship. On 11 November, power was granted to York 'by assent of the council, to hold and dissolve Parliament at the Palace of Westminster, as the king cannot appear in person',[19] and Parliament was reconvened the following day. On that occasion, requests were made for York to be reinstated as Protector but, reputedly, he 'protested his unworthiness' and 'required time to formulate his conditions'. He refused to accept the position 'during royal pleasure' but only until he would be formally relieved of it by the king in Parliament. A week later, York accepted the petition of the Commons, to become protector and defender of the realm and church, and the king's principal councillor, taking for his wages 2,000 marks a year as a reward for personal labour in journeying and riding on the businesses of the realm.[20] The reason given was 'the sickness with which it had pleased the Almighty to inflict the king'. The governance of the realm was committed to the council, recorded in the patent roll and affixed with York's seal. Effectively, Henry was no longer even the puppet. All power had been placed in York's hands, making him king in everything but name, even though he continually declared that it had not been his intention to replace Henry, but rather to support his kingship.

The balance by which kingship was vested in Henry and exercised by York can be illustrated by a letter sent on the king's behalf by the Privy Council on

5 December, 1455. There had been unrest in Devon and the letter, addressing those lords local to the disturbance, requiring their support. Framed as being 'from the King' to his 'trusty and well-beloved cousins', and signed by him, it nevertheless included, and verified, the delegation of action to the duke:

> our part is to provide for the restful and peaceable rule of this our said land, and to chastise such as neither fear God nor us, to example of others, we have willed and desired our right trusty and right entirely well-beloved cousin, the Duke of York, protector and defender of this, our said land, to address him into the said country for the setting apart of the said misgovernance.[21]

The lords were urged to meet with York, and offer their assistance, on behalf of the king, 'as our singular trust is in you and you desire the welfare of us and of this our realm'. It was a suitable division of labour: York as the active instrument and Henry as the symbol of kingship. As such, it may have proved a successful method of running the country, but in personal terms, it denied the king's autonomy and York's ability: he was acting as king but not being treated as one.

Henry and Margaret spent part of the autumn of 1455 at Hertford Castle, situated on a bend of the River Lea. It may be that the king was consulted about this, as the place would have had happy associations for him with his mother, and periods of time they had spent there together in the 1420s. One chronicler gives York an almost paternal responsibility for this move, describing how he recognised the king's fragility and sent him and his family into the countryside, as if for a holiday.[22] Others have implied that Henry's residence at Hertford was less voluntary and more akin to imprisonment. The arrangements of their residence are unclear but their freedom of movement does not appear to have been restricted. Since 1445, the castle had been in Margaret's ownership, having been granted to her at the time of their marriage, so at least she had control over its governance. The medieval castle no longer stands but a surviving plan drawn up in the Elizabethan period shows apartments grouped around a central courtyard with the great hall to the east, featuring a square oriel window. Another square courtyard to the south of the hall was surrounded on three sides by an open-timbered cloister, and a great chapel on the first floor of a projecting eastern wing. Records of 1327 list a King's Chamber with two adjoining chapels and a hall with two chimneys. Descriptions in 1522 mention the river running past, which served all the offices of the house, and a little garden.[23]

During Henry's residence at Hertford, he was consulted on a number of issues that could not be resolved without his approval. He would have had to approve the appointment of George Neville, Warwick's brother, as Bishop of

Exeter on 8 October, and was aware of Parliament reassembling in November, perhaps even of the rioting erupting between warring families in London and Devon. When York was appointed Protector for the second time, Henry was clearly not in the same debilitated state as he had been in 1453. Whether or not the decision was made by him, or by York, or the Council, it was considered that York, rather than Henry, should once again take the helm. Henry and Margaret passed a quiet Christmas, probably still at Hertford, and the period of calm appears to have done the king good. By the arrival of February 1456, Henry had sufficiently recovered to appear in person in Parliament. York offered his resignation as Protector and was officially removed from the position by an act of Parliament dated 25 February. He left London without waiting for the end of the session, leaving the field once more to Henry.

## II

In the summer of 1456, Margaret was approached by a delegation of noblemen with Lancastrian sympathies. Numbering among them the dead Somerset's son and survivors of St Albans, they warned the queen that Henry's life was in danger from the Duke of York. Whether or not they were correct, Margaret took their fears seriously. As Polydore Vergil reported:

> Henry, Duke of Somerset and Humphrey, Duke of Buckingham, with many other noblemen who held and stood with King Henry, lamenting his adversity, and not ignorant to what end all the Duke of York's crafty courtesy tended, went secretly to Queen Margaret, privately offered her their counsel, and declared that the Duke of York sought to deceive the king, yea, in very deed to kill him unawares.[24]

Writing a generation later, Edward Hall included more detail:

> That venomous worm, that dreadful dragon called disdain of superiority, which hath consumed the blood of so many noble princes ... could not abstain from incensing the hearts [of Beaufort and Buckingham] ... and of other lords and men of authority favouring and following the part of King Henry, whiche not only bewailed and had compassion of the unsure condition and wavering estate of his rule and lordship, perceiving openly, whereunto the cloaked gentleness and subordinate fashion of the Duke of York ... thought it necessary and convenient to pursue for a remedy, or the mischief happened.[25]

As Hall continued though, the lords not only feared for Henry's life, but they made Margaret sensible of the indignity of his situation, and urged her that it must not be allowed to continue:

With open mouthes and fierce courages they came to Queen Margaret, informing her that it was not honourable, but a reproach and infamy to the king, to have one to be a Protector and a governor of him and his realm, as who would say that he was either a child that had need of a nurse to breastfeed him, or an innocent creature which must be ruled by a tutor … [and] that the Duke of York's only intent was, under the colour of this protectorship, suddenly to destroy and depose the king, when he least thought of it.[26]

Margaret was spurred to act in her husband's defence. Hall described her as having 'a wit, more than the common sort of women have', while Vergil stated that she was 'much moved by this warning'. It may be that this occasion predated Henry's return to Parliament in February, prompting the termination of the second Protectorate, or else it occurred soon afterwards. Margaret made arrangements for the movement of the royal households, and that of Prince Edward north, into the heart of Lancastrian territory. Such a move had to be timed carefully, too. In the spring and early summer, their movements had a predictable feel, as they shuttled between Westminster, Sheen, Windsor and Eltham, with visits to Greenwich and, perhaps, to Canterbury. That August, while York was absent, dealing with a threat posed by the Scots, they travelled to the Midlands on the pretext of hunting, staying at Woodstock, then at Kenilworth Castle. A safe hundred miles from Westminster, the red-stone Kenilworth had been extensively rebuilt by Henry's great-grandfather John of Gaunt, to comprise state apartments, great hall, towers and new kitchens. Since then, it had proved a popular residence of the Lancastrian kings, sheltering Henry IV during illness and being chosen by Henry V as the location for a fashionable new garden and banqueting house in the style of a miniature castle set on an island.

From Kenilworth, they travelled on to Lichfield and then to Coventry, where they paused for a month, from mid-September to mid-October, being welcomed by elaborate civic pageantry. Greeted at the city gates by figures representing Jeremiah and Isaiah, Margaret was termed Queen and Empress, and congratulated upon the birth of her son, who was then not quite two. At the gates to the church, she was addressed by saints of personal significance; St Edward the Confessor and St Margaret, as well as St John the Evangelist. The lines spoken by Edward the Confessor stressed her gentleness and referred to his connection with her son, as a result of his birth on the saint's day:

*Model of meekness, dame Margaret, princess most excellent*
*I, King Edward, welcome you with affection cordial.*
*Testifying to your highness meekly my intent*

*For the wealth of the King and you, heartily pray I shall,*
*And for Prince Edward, my ghostly child, who I love principal*
*Praying thee, John the Evangelist, me help therein to be*
*On that condition right humbly I give this ring to thee.*[27]

St Edward continued, welcoming Margaret to the city as the 'most notable princess of women earthly' and the 'chief mirth of this empire'. He urged her, when she was ever 'in any dreadful case' to call upon him for help. This was followed by a pageant of the nine worthies, where her virtues were eulogised and champions promised to fight for her; she was compared to the Queen of Heaven by the performers and presented with silver cups and £100 by the Mayor. At the city conduit, a great dragon had been created, breathing fire, which was slain by an actor representing St Margaret. It must not have been too difficult for the queen to read a national and dynastic symbolism into this scene, with herself responsible for the country's defence against the monstrous threat posed by York.

This occasion was commemorated in a large tapestry now in St Mary's Guildhall, commissioned between 1485 and 1500, featuring portraits of the king and queen. Dressed in a pearl collar and hood decorated with a fleur-de-lys and topped with a crown, Margaret's hands are resting on a missal book as she prays. The folds of her gold dress lie about her on the floor and her sleeves are folded back to reveal their ermine lining. Henry is depicted kneeling and reading from a prayer book. He wears a blue robe embroidered with gold, with a wide ermine collar and lining, and gold chains around his neck. He has removed his magnificent gold crown, which sits beside his book, and replaced it with a simpler, broad red hat, like those worn by the members of his court behind him. His brown hair is worn shoulder-length and his face has a calm, almost beatific expression.

Safe and welcome in Coventry, Margaret persuaded Henry to replace his officials with loyal members of her own household. She gathered around her a new court of young Lancastrians, including the survivors of St Albans and the children of the bereaved; the sons of Edmund Beaufort: his eldest, Henry, who had been wounded in the fight and Henry's young brothers Edmund and John. There was also their sister Margaret's husband, Humphrey, Earl of Stafford and his father, the Duke of Buckingham, John Clifford, son of Thomas, whose father had died in the battle, leaving him the Baronetcy, and now also the Tudor brothers, Edmund and Jasper. For various reasons, the Tudors had previously been allied with York, but now came out firmly on the side of their half-brother Henry VI. The following month, while she and Henry were still at Coventry, James Gresham wrote to John Paston that certain key appointments had changed hands. York's relative, Thomas Bourchier was dismissed as Chancellor in favour of William Waynflete; the second Lord Shrewsbury, son of Margaret's former advisor, was now Treasurer and John Brown was Under-treasurer with Laurence Bothe as Privy Seal. The news of these changes soon reached London, prompting York to head to Coventry. His visit was more of a success with Henry than with Margaret, as he 'departed ageyn in right good conceyt with the Kyng but not in gret conceyt with the Queen'.[28]

It is possible that Henry and Margaret stayed in Coventry's twelfth-century castle, which no longer survives, but probably stood in the city centre, given that its approach was through Broad Gate. There is a good chance though that they stayed at Cheylesmore Manor, which had been used by former monarchs as a hunting lodge. The timbered gatehouse remains in the city's suburbs but the moated manor beyond it, which was present by 1250, has since been demolished. Like Kenilworth, Coventry was to form an important alternative base to London for the Lancastrians. With Westminster now associated with York's Protectorship and the influences of his allies, the physical distance allowed Henry greater confidence in his own autonomy and removed him, as Margaret believed, from potential dangers. With the king in residence, and travelling in the immediate vicinity, it established an alternative capital, to which disaffected Lancastrians could flock. It was also an opportunity for her to make her son more visible, and to present him to the people as the future heir.

After her attempt to take a more political role by launching a bid for the Protectorship, Margaret's queenship during 1456–7 returned to the traditional model she had followed before. It was determined and focused, but largely took place behind the scenes, as she worked to re-establish her husband's authority, exerting her influence as a figure of authority and patronage. As John Bocking wrote to Sir John Fastolf, 'the quene is a grete and strong labourid woman, for she spareth noo peyne to sue her thinges to an intent and conclusion to her power.'[29] Perhaps the most important of her 'thinges' was the future of her son, around whom she was careful to build a loyal base, and whose education continued under the guidance of key Lancastrian figures. A group of four loyal knights was established to manage and administer the prince's estates during his infancy. James Butler, Earl of Wiltshire and fifth Earl of Ormond had replaced York as Lieutenant of Ireland and was the son-in-law of the Duke of Somerset; John, Viscount Beaumont, had served in France and was Lord Great Chamberlain and Steward of the Duchy of Lancaster; John Sutton, Lord Dudley, was a favourite of Henry VI and the family of Thomas, Lord Stanley, had supported the takeover of the Lancastrians in 1399. Edward would have come to know them well, as their job was to authorise his expenditure and supervise his officials. He was also served by Robert Wittingham as his receiver-general, Thomas Throckmorton as his attorney-general and Giles St Lo as the keeper of his wardrobe.[30] That Edward was intended to take a more active role is clear from the licence dated 26 March 1457, enabling him to issue charters and writs, even though he was only 3½.

Margaret's focus on Prince Edward was echoed in contemporary literature which extolled him as, and encouraged him to become, the ideal prince. The anonymous *Knyghthode and Bataile* may have been written by John, Viscount Beaumont, who was appointed chief steward of Edward's lands in 1456. It stresses the divine connection between God and king, referring to the monarch as 'God's son' and the earthly representative of divine order. The chivalric ideal is embodied as a form of worship, moving to the logical conclusion that those who oppose the king were ungodly, and did so at the instigation of the devil:

> *The premynent is first th'almyghti Lord,*
> *Emanuel, that every lord is undir*
> *And good lyver; but bataile and discord*
> *With him hath Sathanas.*[31]

Reading into the troubled times, with this new division opening between north and south, the chronicles also contained warnings for the king. The 1457 *Hardyng's Chronicle* urged Henry to consider the lessons of history, of his 'ancestry in wealth and health reigned of high record that kept peace and law continuously.' He added that former monarchs who 'kept neither law nor peace … were destroyed, right as they had deserved,' and urged the need for strength, because there was no peace in the realm:

> *Misrule doth rise and maketh neighbours war*
> *The weaker goeth beneath, as ofte is seen*
> *The mightiest his quarrel will prefer…*
>
> *They kill your men always by one and one*
> *And who say ought he shall be better doubtlesse*
> *For in your realm justice of peace be none.*[32]

Other poets hoped for peace, such as the pro-Lancastrian author of *The Reconciliation of Henry VI and the Yorkists*, and *The Ship of State*, which used a vessel as metaphor for the Lancastrian kingship:

> *This noble ship made of good tree*
> *Our Sovereign Lord King Henry*
> *God guide him from adversity*
> *Where that he go or ride.*[33]

Prince Edward was the mast of the ship, Henry Holland, Duke of Exeter was the light and Somerset's son Henry Beaufort, was the rudder, but the metaphor illustrated the way that the Lancastrian cause was riding upon tempestuous waves.

Margaret, Henry and Edward remained in the north for a year without returning to Westminster. However afraid they were for Henry's life, regardless of whether there was any justification for this, the move represented a split kingdom in terms of governance. Two centres of authority now existed, that of the Yorkist-held capital and the king's residence, creating something of a rallying cry for both sides, whether intentional or not. It was not unusual for the king to travel, but on those occasions, the royal presence was an extension of his London-based power; he was the embodiment and ambassador of that power, working synonymously with it. By leaving the capital for such a long time, under such circumstances, Henry opened himself to accusations of having escaped or fled, or even deliberately creating a division. Not even while he was ill had he stayed so far away. Historically, London had not always been the absolute centre of government, as parliaments had been called in a number of northern cities, but the long-term establishment of an alternative court, where new appointments were made, was certainly within Henry's remit as king, even essential to the survival of his kingship under the circumstances. Yet it was also problematic and threatened the traditional co-dependence of the court and capital. With authority dangerously divided, the opportunities for lawlessness and civic disobedience were magnified, as incidents of rioting against Italian merchants in London illustrated.

Conscious of the pro-Yorkist sympathies in the capital, Henry and Margaret hoped to widen their support network by undertaking visits through the north, especially around the edges of territories held by the Duke. They spent the autumn of 1456 making their presence felt in Stafford, Eccleshall, Chester, Shrewsbury and Kenilworth again, tracing a wide, geographical semi-circle above the Yorkist centre of Ludlow. The first half of December found them again at Coventry, before they divided the Christmas season between Kenilworth and Leicester. Margaret may also have gone separately to Bristol that year, being received with honour and entertained by the local nobility.[34] Not all was harmonious though, as the young Duke of Somerset, just 20 years old, proved a volatile and potentially violent figure. Having survived significant injuries at St Albans that may have left him disfigured, he struggled to control his anger towards York and those he held responsible for his father's death. Upon his young shoulders rested the hopes of the Lancastrian supporters as an active replacement for the man who had steered politics and advised the king for a decade, but Henry Beaufort had none of the old duke's experience and wisdom. When the Yorkists visited Coventry in October 1456, in an attempt to unite the two sides, a 'great affray' broke out between Beaufort's servants and the town watch, resulting in the deaths of a few locals.[35] This cannot have helped the king's situation and Beaufort would remain an unpredictable figure, his loyalties vacillating between York and Lancaster until his luck ran out in 1464. More trouble arose when Henry's half-brother, Edmund Tudor, Earl of Richmond, was ousted from Carmarthen Castle by Sir William Herbert, York's principal agent in the area, who imprisoned him in the castle dungeons. When Herbert moved to Aberystwyth he left Richmond behind and in the unsanitary conditions the Earl contracted plague and died on 3 November 1456.

Henry and Margaret were back at Kenilworth in January 1457, with security on their minds and the intention to act against Herbert. The royal master of the Ordnance was summoned to join them, where he equipped the castle with twenty-six serpentines, new guns that were intended for use on the field of battle, along with 294lbs of gunpowder, 1,200lbs of sulphur, 1,800lbs of saltpetre and balls of lead and iron. While there, he built an additional three serpentines that were designed to be mobile and were so powerful they could 'subdue any castle or place that would rebel'.[36] At the king's side, Buckingham, Shrewsbury, Wiltshire and other lords had their men at the ready, should Henry require the support of an army. A few weeks later, the king and queen were joined at Kenilworth by the new Earl of Northumberland, Henry Percy, who had also lost his father at St Albans. Being only a few months older than the king, he had been knighted with Henry when they were boys and was a familiar, welcome addition to the royal circle. His brother, Thomas, was also in the king's favour, receiving the Constableship of Dunstaburgh Castle, and other members of his family and household were rewarded for their loyalty. It was inevitable that the ongoing Percy–Neville feud would drive such figures into the Lancastrian court, but the losses at St Albans and what was perceived as the exile of the king established a network in the north upon which Margaret would rely in the future.

At the end of March 1457, the court moved to Hereford, close to the Welsh border, twenty-five miles to the north of Herbert's seat at Raglan Castle. A local Assize court was held there on 28 April, at which many of Herbert's allies and agents appeared; others were tried in London, where they were imprisoned until February 1458. The earl himself kept his distance until Henry issued a promise that his life and goods would be spared, which prompted Pembroke to come to the king and submit, whereupon he received a pardon. This had the advantage of drawing the earl to the Lancastrian side, away from York's influence, but it would not last for long. While they were in Hereford, Margaret's ward, Isabella Ingoldsthorpe, married into the Neville family. The 15-year-old Isabella was the niece of Sir John Tiptoft, Earl of Worcester, now Lord Deputy of Ireland, and had been placed in Margaret's care following the death of her father, although she probably still lived with her mother. On 27 April 1457, she wed the son of the Earl of Salisbury, John Neville, who was then 26 or 27, at Canterbury Cathedral. John paid Margaret a total of £1,000 in ten instalments for the hand of the bride and they went on to have a number of children. Marriage was a traditional way of healing the breaches between warring families and, although historians have variously categorised this as a love match, or a deliberate affront to Margaret, it is likely to have been another means of creating peace in a limited local gene pool. Through that spring and summer, Henry and Margaret divided their time between Coventry and Kenilworth, with visits to Hereford and Worcester in May, Winchcombe in May, Rothwell and Northampton in September. Gathering her allies, and reflecting upon her situation, Margaret decided to deliver York and Warwick a timely reminder about with whom they were dealing.

In the summer of 1457, Margaret appealed to her father, René and her uncle Charles, who influenced Charles VII to plan a full-scale invasion of England. As Hall relates, there were strong historical precedents for the French exploiting English weaknesses. Just as Henry V had cut a swathe through a France weakened by political infighting, so the French desired 'to be revenged of old displeasures and great damages which they had do many years sustained by English people'.[37] A fleet was equipped, 4,000 soldiers embarked and Pierre de Brézé, Seneschal of Normandy, set sail from Honfleur on 20 August 1457. Before long, bad weather drove them back and they did not reach Sandwich until eight days later, where they launched an attack upon the town. Unprepared for the assault, and possibly depopulated by a recent outbreak of plague,[38] the town put up a fierce resistance but could not hold off the soldiers, who proceeded to loot and pillage. One French chronicle estimated that 300 English were killed in comparison with only thirty of his kinsmen.[39] This was probably the success Margaret had intended, hoping that the incident would remind York, and Warwick, then Captain of Calais, that she had the backing of Charles VII and that their actions against the Lancastrian had ramifications on a European stage. If they moved against her or Henry, Margaret hoped they understood that they might trigger a full-scale invasion of England. It may have been the raid upon Sandwich that prompted Henry to travel south, making his first appearance at Westminster on 22 September, and returning for a six-week period from mid-October until the end of November.

In January 1458, Henry summoned all the nobility to a Great Council. By initiating their meeting, he was taking control of the situation and making himself personally responsible for offering a solution. It was a brave, perhaps idealistic move in a volatile climate, but the ongoing situation had to be addressed and resolved. Henry did not shy away from it, he brought all the opponents together to deal with it head-on. York arrived in the capital with 400 men, while Salisbury and Warwick brought slightly more. A constant armed watch patrolled the streets and to prevent outbreaks of violence, the Yorkists were lodged within the city walls and the Lancastrians were housed without. This did not stop Northumberland, Clifford and Egremont attempting unsuccessfully to ambush York and Salisbury as they rode from London to Westminster for a council meeting, one of many skirmishes and narrow escapes experienced by the Yorkists during these years. The pro-York *Short English Chronicle* framed the conflict to suggest that York and Warwick 'lay peaceably' in London while Somerset and his allies arrived 'intending to fight',[40] a sentiment echoed by the English chronicle while, predictably, Lancastrian sources would identify York as the aggressor.

Margaret and Henry had initially been resident at Chertsey and then Berkhamsted, keeping a distance from the two sides in an attempt to achieve impartiality. Henry went to address the nobles in person on 27 January, then retreated while the Archbishop of Canterbury, Thomas Bourchier, acted as a go-between. A settlement was agreed, eventually, after a long and acrimonious dispute, and Henry headed for Westminster, arriving on 16 March, 1458. The terms acknowledged the actions, even the responsibility, of the Yorkist lords in a way that their pardon of July 1455 had failed to do, suggesting a general acceptance that they had been the aggressors on the day. York was to pay Somerset compensation of 5,000 marks, Warwick to play Clifford 1,000 marks and Salisbury to forego certain fines levied on Egremont and Northumberland as part of the Neville-Percy feud. In addition, the Yorkists were to endow the Abbey of St Albans with an annual payment of £45 to fund masses for the souls of the dead. The only Lancastrian to be issued with similar conditions was Lord Egremont, who accepted a 4,000 mark bond to keep the peace with the Nevilles for ten years. The terms were announced on the same day, 24 March, that the parties assembled to make a public show of reconciliation and friendship.[41] An imposing piece of theatre, this personal effort of Henry's to forge a lasting peace, came to be known as the Loveday.

The scene for the spectacle was St Paul's Cathedral, the central and highest point of the city, and a far more public arena than Westminster, indicating that the intention was also to reassure the people. Londoners had been living with outbursts of violence followed by weeks of curfew and armed guards. Henry needed to prove to them, many of whom were sympathetic to the Yorkist cause, that he was demonstrating strong but pacific kingship. Dressed in his robes and crown he led them into a sermon and Mass before they emerged in pairs, holding hands; Margaret and York, Warwick and Exeter, Salisbury and Somerset. A rather optimistic poem written by a Londoner, perhaps Lydgate,[42] who witnessed the procession described the mood between Henry, Margaret and the Lords:

> *At St Paul's in London, with great renown,*
> *On our Lady Day in Lent this peace was wrought*
> *The king, the queen, with lords many a one...*
> *Went in procession, and spared right nought*
> *In sight of all the commonality*
> *In token that love was in heart and thought...*
> *There was between them lovely countenance*
> *Which was great joy to all that there were*
> *That long time hadden been in variance*
> *As friends forever that had been in fear.*[43]

The Loveday was a successful visual spectacle, but it did not acknowledge the key issue, which had been the exclusion of the Yorkists from the heart of government. Perhaps only Henry fully believed that it had settled all the quarrels and grievances of recent years. It certainly upheld Henry as the legitimate king, but the public show of harmony pulled a veil over York's grievances, pushing him to feel he had no recourse to resolve them by legitimate means.

After the ceremony, Henry returned to St Albans for the first time since the battle, staying there from 29 March until 20 April. This was a visit of immense personal significance for the king, who would have passed through the streets where his councillors and friends had died, and no doubt he took the opportunity to pray for their souls in the abbey. Symbolically and literally, the town was the place where his authority had been stripped away, leaving him virtually a prisoner, so it was an important stage of his own recovery that Henry now returned as a reigning king. He revisited St Albans on a high from the Loveday ceremony, optimistic for success and peace, confident in the steps he had taken to be reconciled with his former enemies and reassert peace. While Henry was away, celebratory jousts were held at the Tower of London, presided over by the queen, at which Henry Beaufort and Anthony, Earl Rivers, were the leading participants.

That summer, Henry and Margaret returned to her favourite palace of Greenwich, staying there between 6 May and 5 June and also managed a short progress, spending several weeks in the quiet surroundings of Woodstock. Henry's health still required constant monitoring and a grant made on 20 August rewarded one of his physicians, a John Faceby, with an annuity of 50 marks paid out of the coffers of St Augustine's Priory, Canterbury.[44] On 10 September they returned to St Albans, staying almost a month before the return journey home and a longer residence at Westminster, symbolic of the king returning to claim the seat of his power. Later that autumn, Margaret took steps to replace Warwick as Captain of Calais, with Henry Beaufort. She had already cut off his supplies but reports of his acts of piracy in the Channel prompted her to act again, which was followed by an attack was made upon the earl in London. The *English Chronicle* relates that on 9 November a quarrel arose between Warwick and 'men of the king's household, so that they would have slain the earl had he not escaped to his barge and went soon after to Calais'.[45] Warwick's exile meant the removal of another powerful ally of York's, to the satisfaction of the Lancastrian-loyal Percies.

In October 1458, the visiting Italian, Raffaelo de Negra, wrote a gossipy letter to the Duchess of Milan, describing the impressions of Margaret and her history that he had received from 'an Englishman'. He related the story about Margaret's arrival in England 'without any dowry' and Henry's disguise as a squire, which he employed as a means to see her for the first time. After that, he proceeded to dwell on her 'magnificence' and appearance; she was, in the eyes of this anonymous Englishman, 'a most handsome woman, though somewhat dark' and, of course, 'not so beautiful as your serenity,' the duchess. The Lancastrian leanings of his source is also evident in the reference to Margaret as his 'Mistress', or the queen he served; she was also wise and charitable, with a 'most handsome' son and an income of 80,000 gold crowns. De Negra reported the courtly protocol of women at Margaret's court, all of whom 'go on their knees' before her, when they speak with her, which information would have pleased the duchess as she 'delighted in noble things'.[46] This source confirms the extent to which Margaret was able to inspire loyalty and admiration among her followers. As a recruiter of men to the Lancastrian court, as well as a figure of courtly devotion, her queenship was highly effective at this time.

*Chapter Seven*

# Disaster 1459–1460

## I

The fragile peace of March 1458 did not last. The combatants who had walked hand-in-hand from St Paul's were soon plotting against each other's lives, lying in wait in dark corners of the city with swords drawn. Responsibility for the outbreak of hostilities in 1459 has often been placed firmly by historians with Queen Margaret and her band of followers, but it was not this simple. The Pro-Yorkist *English Chronicle* related how she now 'ruled the roost as she liked' and Benet records that she was the instigator of the Coventry parliament that June, during which York and his allies were declared to be traitors, stripped of their assets and attainted. It was the unavoidable fate of the last Lancastrian family that their immediate successors would judge them harshly. Being on the losing side, on the wrong side of history, they are represented in the surviving chronicles as being deeply flawed; Henry weak and ineffectual and Margaret ambitious and warlike, while their son has been reduced to a blood-thirsty stereotype. Thank goodness, breathed the writers of the York-ruled 1460s and 70s, that the Lancastrians had been prevented from dominating England and establishing their line. It was not until the advent of the Tudors and the reign of Henry's half-nephew, Henry VII, that a reappraisal of Henry VI began, but Margaret would have to wait significantly longer. As a woman taking an active part in a bloody conflict that threatened the throne of her husband and son, Margaret was the convenient scapegoat of contemporary, and subsequent, chroniclers who did not want to place blame for the next phase of war directly on the shoulders of an anointed king.

At the end of 1458 though, in spite of Henry's plans, more new orders of weapons were arriving to swell the royal arsenal against 'certain misruled and seditious people'.[1] On 2 December, 500 leaden clubs, 500 pikes and three 'great serpentines', or guns, arrived into the keeping of John Judde, Henry's Master of Ordnance, so that he was able to 'subdue any castle or place which rebels might try to use against him'.[2] The following May, as if anticipating trouble, the royal pair withdrew again to the north, arriving at Coventry in the middle of the month. Henry personally signed summons that were issued to certain lords to attend upon him at Leicester, with enough supplies to last them for two months' worth of military service. It is likely to have been during this time that Margaret ordered silver badges to be made for her son, in the shape of a swan the device she shared with the prince, and a reminder of the boy's descent from Edward III, who had also employed it. As they travelled in the north, the 6-year-old boy distributed the badges among those who were granted a personal audience with him, with the intention of inspiring their loyalty.

The Council were summoned to meet that June at Coventry but York, Salisbury and Warwick refused to attend through fear that it would lead to their arrests. According to the account given by Abbot Whethamsted, Warwick complained that he had been deliberately excluded from Council meetings and parliaments, nor admitted to any other business, 'as if [Henry] had no faith at all in us nor had he the trust in his heart or mind'. He found the king's advisors 'so bold, almost all of them, and so stiff-necked that they do not fear to disobey royal commands'. Henry's inner circle were a 'group of men without prudence or counsel' and wished they had 'wisdom and understanding, behaving more modestly in their manners and rule'. He no longer felt able to 'approach the king's presence or enter his presence in person to beg for pardon … to prostrate ourselves before [Henry's] feet to beg for grace'.[3] The council met in the last week of June, with Margaret and Prince Edward in attendance, and the queen indicted those who had refused to appear, actions which prompted the conflict which followed that autumn.

By the autumn of 1459, the Yorkist forces were gathering in response to the indictment and their mistrust of the king and queen. One of the catalysts in the escalation in tension was the return of Warwick to England after an absence of ten months. Smarting after his self-imposed exile in Calais, he was determined to make a statement of power and not to be kept at a distance by what he perceived to be the queen's dislike. On 21 September, he marched through London with 500 armed men, and headed north to the city of Warwick, with the intention of meeting with York. The news would have reached Henry and Margaret at either Coventry or Kenilworth, leaving them wondering at Warwick's plans and preparing their own forces to meet any challenge they might mount. Later documents drafted against York suggest they believed he was intending to attack the royal court at Kenilworth. Henry responded by travelling the sixty miles north-east to Nottingham, while Margaret and her son were then staying a similar distance north-west at Eccleshall.

The clash came sooner rather than later. Just two days after Warwick's march through the capital, the Earl of Salisbury was on the move, marching an army of several thousand men from his Yorkshire home of Middleham Castle south-west in the direction of Ludlow, to rendezvous with York and, presumably, to meet the force Warwick was bringing north. Some sources give Salisbury 3,000 men, although the *Davies Chronicle* affords him a more generous 7,000. At Eccleshall, Margaret was situated on the road between Middleham and Ludlow, just fifty miles from the latter. Salisbury was coming dangerously close as she summoned her 8,000-strong army under the leadership of John Tuchet, Lord Audley, sufficiently so for her to fear his intentions. On September 23, Audley intercepted Salisbury's men just ten miles away from the queen at a place called Blore Heath, to the east of Market Drayton. The *Davies Chronicle* paints the Yorkist manoeuvres as a defensive act: the Earl of Salisbury, 'fearing the malice of his enemies and especially of the queen and her company, which hated him mortally', hoped to meet with York 'so that they both together would have ridden to the king at Coleshill in Staffordshire to have cleared themselves of certain articles and false accusations touching their allegiance laid against them maliciously by their enemies.'[4] As Davies continues, 'the queen then lay at Eccleshall, and at once by her urging the king assembled a great power, whereof Lord Audley was chief ... and went forth to a field called Blore Heath'.[5]

Audley established his army in a field or heathland before a stream, and waited for Salisbury to approach. After spotting the Lancastrian banners above the trees, the earl realised that he was walking into an ambush set by a larger force, but decided to deploy his troops and stand his ground. Salisbury had to make the best of a difficult situation, so used wagons to block one side of the approach and feigned a withdrawal to prompt a Lancastrian charge, cutting the enemy down as they crossed the stream. As Hall related,

> Salisbury, [who] knew the sleights, strategies and policies of warlike affairs, suddenly returned, and shortly encountered with the Lord Audley and his chief captains, ere the residue of his army could pass the water. The fight was sore and dreadful. The earl desiring the saving of his life, and his adversaries coveting his destruction, fought sore for the obtaining of their purpose, but in conclusion, the earl's army, as men desperate of aid and succour, so eagerly fought, that they slew the Lord Audley, and all his captains.

The death of Audley hastened the end of the battle, leaving Salisbury to pursue the fleeing Lancastrians, who suffered far greater casualties. Then the Earl marched on to Ludlow to report the matter to York and Warwick. Margaret had clearly believed that she was in danger and prompted the attack in defence of herself and her family. However, because the Lancastrians took the initiative, and because they lost, they appeared to be the initiators of the outbreak of hostilities, making York feel justified in retaliating.

The fact that the attack had been made by Margaret's army, acting upon Margaret's orders, also made the situation worse. As the *Brut Chronicle* related, after Blore Heath 'the Duke of York and the Earls of Warwick and Salisbury saw that the governance of the realm was exercised mostly by the queen and her council' and 'no lord in England at this time dare disobey the queen, for she ruled all that was done about the king, who was a good, simple and innocent man'. But if Margaret did rule in this way, she did so with Henry's permission and in his interests. She could only invoke power in the name of her husband and son, but she was the queen and her aim was to ensure the continuance of their governance and peace in the realm. She acted against York and his allies when they threatened this; from her perspective, they were the antagonists, continually pushing for more power, belittling her husband and undermining her son's inheritance. She was reacting to their threat, but when she did react, she was determined to achieve stability in the Lancastrian name. Far from being the relentless she-wolf that subsequent historians have painted her to be, Margaret usually took a back seat, protective of Henry, distancing him from York's control, hoping the duke would accept the many opportunities for peace. She stepped forward when she felt it was necessary to do so, as her family were under threat. It was York, not Margaret, who relentlessly drove the dissent of the late 1450s; she resisted responding until she had no choice. Edward was too young, and Henry was not capable of the firm kingship that the situation demanded. Margaret had to take the reins and step into the 'masculine' role of leadership and political intrigue. Her active style, coupled with her gender, played to contemporary stereotypes about appropriate female behaviour that her enemies were swift to exploit. The case of Joan of Arc, thirty years earlier, illustrates how a strong woman leader could be lauded or demonised, depending upon which side was heard. Had Margaret been on the winning side, the chronicles would have been lauding her abilities.

In the meantime, Henry did not sit passively waiting for, or weakly avoiding, conflict. He responded with decisive action, marching from Nottingham down through Market Harborough, to Walsall, Coleshill near Birmingham and down to Worcester, gathering troops and support along the way. This aspect of Henry's kingship has often been overlooked, but his visible presence through the midland counties as he marched to defend his crown, offered real leadership. As the chronicler Benet related, York attempted to reach London, but found that Henry had assembled an army of 40,000 near Worcester, blocking his way. After offering prayers in the cathedral there, and sending Henry letters professing his loyalty, York retreated towards Tewkesbury with his 25,000 men, crossing the Severn and heading back home to Ludlow. Benet relates that Henry's army followed in pursuit, making the king active in pursuing the battle.[6] With this situation unfolding, a new parliament was summoned on 9 October, to meet at Coventry, from which the Yorkists were excluded. According to the Brut, York 'saw that the governance of the realm was exercised mostly by the queen and her council, while the great princes of the land were not called to the council but set apart ... it was proclaimed through the realm that these lords should be destroyed utterly'. The chronicle continues that

> the king sent out commissions and privy seals to all the lords of his realm
> to come and await upon him in their most defensible array. So, every man
> came, in such numbers that the king was stronger and had far more people
> ... no lord in England dare disobey the queen, for she ruled all that was
> done about the king, who was a good, simple and innocent man.[7]

On 12 October, 1459 the forces of the king gathered outside Ludlow, overlooking the bridge into the town where York's army were camped, their cannon ranged along the River Teme. Above the hedgerows, Henry's personal banner fluttered in the breeze, visible to York's troops, which not only shattered their morale but provoked a crisis. To fight against the king's evil councillors, or even perhaps the queen, could be legally justified, but to take arms against Henry himself was undeniable treason. According to *Stowe's Chronicle*, York claimed the King was dead and ordered masses to be said for his soul, in an attempt to trick his men into fighting, but if this was true, it was the action of a desperate man. York dug in at Ludford Bridge, in a defensive ditch by a crossing over the river, and erected a barricade of carts upon which he located his cannon. The rumour soon spread around the camp despite York's best efforts. In addition, his force was smaller than that of the king, 'over-weak', according to the *London Chronicle*, while Croyland states that 'the king's party ... got stronger every day with the gathering of great numbers both of nobles and common people'. A later parliamentary account adds that York had assembled a number of people, 'blinding' them with 'wages, promises and other exquisite means', and brought before them 'certain persons to swear that [the king] was deceased' so they were 'less fearful of taking the field'.[8] The tide turned that night, when Sir Anthony Trollope, who had come from Calais with Warwick, at the head of around 600 men, decided to desert York and go over to the king's side. Jean de Waurin states that Trollope's conscience was pricked by a letter from Somerset 'which rebuked him because he was coming to wage war against the king his sovereign lord'. He promised that any lords returning to the king's side 'would receive both great rewards and a pardon for everything.'[9] The same incident is described by the *Croyland Chronicle*, with the addition that the men found themselves ranged against their king 'contrary to their expectations.' Trollope's men were 'received joyously' by Henry, while the Yorkists realised that to engage in battle now would prove a disaster.[10] Under cover of darkness, they fled the scene and went into exile, York and his second son Edmund, Duke of Rutland, into

Ireland, while Warwick, Salisbury and Edward, Earl of March sailed for Calais. It seemed that, finally, the problem of York's inheritance and ambition, had been overcome. No contemporary source places Margaret at Ludlow, or nearby. She was probably waiting with her son, perhaps still at Eccleshall, for the arrival of the messenger. Hearing the news of the bloodless victory, Margaret must have experienced feelings of relief regarding the autonomy of her husband and the future of her son.

The behaviour of the royal army in the aftermath of the Yorkist withdrawal at Ludford Bridge did nothing to help the Lancastrian cause. Although reports may have been exaggerated by hostile sources, the soldiers appear to have run out of control after being let loose in the town, and perhaps further afield. Gregory's chronicle reports that the 'misrule of the king's gallants at Ludlow, when they had drunken enough of wine that was in taverns and other places, they full ungodly smote out the heads of the pipes and hogsheads of wine, that men went wet-shod in wine and then they robbed the town and bore away bedding, cloth and other stuff and defouled many women.' Hearne's fragment adds that 'King Harry rode into Ludlow and spoiled the town and castle,' although this must have been attributed to his men, rather than the king himself. Sometimes this has been used as ammunition against Margaret, but the extent of her influence over the royal army, in her absence, can hardly be established. That the Yorkist armies were better disciplined appears to be a typical factor of the bias reflected in their chronicles.

When the so-called 'Parliament of Devils' met on 20 November at Coventry, punishment of the rebels was at the top of their agenda, as the final stage in preventing further trouble. It opened in the Chapter House of St Mary's Priory with a speech by William Waynflete, Bishop of Winchester, on the theme of peace, but twenty-four individuals were indicted for 'levying war' against the King at Blore Heath and Ludlow, with three more accused of plotting his death elsewhere. Acts of Attainder were passed against the Yorkist lords, detailing the reasons Henry should have expected to rely on his loyalty, and the ways he had abused this kindness and trust:

> Please it your highness to call to your noble remembrance how you had Richard, Duke of York, in his young age, in your most high presence and noble court, and him all that time cherished and favoured; and afterward at greater age for the love, trust and affiance that you had in his person, made him Lieutenant of your realm of France and Duchy of Normandy and created his 2 eldest sons Earls and granted him offices and great benefits … so that it could not be thought a subject of his estate of so little defect, to have had more cause to have had been true, obedient and diligent to serve and love his sovereign Lord than he had.

These benefits and many others that may be rehearsed not withstanding, how falsely and traitorously he hath acquitted himself to your highness, against God, nature, all truth, humanity and, contrary to his Liegaunce ... his false and traitorous imaginations, conspiracies, feats and diligent labours, born up with colourable lies compassed by the most unheard of means that ever subject did to his Sovereign Lord.[11]

It had not been forgotten that during the time of Jack Cade's rebellion in 1450, the men of Kent had cited York as their leader, and the duke had returned from Ireland with a large number of armed men and 'bette down the speres and walles in your [Henry's] chamber, having no consideration to your high presence'. Then, Henry had answered his 'desires and demands' in a way which it seemed to all his 'true subjects' that 'the spirit of Wisdom of God was in' him. After this, in various parliaments, York 'made crafty labours and desires' to the executing of Henry's will so his 'malicious and traitorous' purposes were achieved. He had written many letters to cities, boroughs and towns, and to private individuals, 'coloured under a pretence of a wele [common good] to have made a common insurrection'. York had sworn an oath to keep the peace in 1452 and broken it, continuing in his 'said malicious and traitorous purpose'; he had also broken the peace made after St Albans, when it was agreed that all grievances should be laid before the king and submit to his laws, and that friendship forged at the recent Loveday. In spite of this, York had shown the 'most diabolic unkindness ... wretched envy and ... most unreasonable appetite of such estate', having enriched himself with royal gifts, continued in his treachery against the king, queen and prince.[12] Thus, a sentence of death was passed against York and his allies; their goods, titles and lands were forfeited and their heirs were barred from inheritance, although the duke's eldest son, Edward, Earl of March, was also included in the attainder anyway. At the end of the session, on 11 December, the assembled lords swore an oath of loyalty to the king, queen and Prince Edward. When the royal family arrived at Leicester Abbey in order to spend Christmas, they had good reason to believe they had triumphed over their enemies.

## II

After the battle, Henry retreated from Ludlow, reaching Worcester on 16 October, Warwick on 20 October and from there on to Coventry. If he had not already been reunited with Margaret en route, they would have met again in the city that was rapidly becoming their home. Coventry had become the fourth largest city in England by 1400 and was granted its charter as a separate entity from the rest of the county of Warwickshire in 1451. Located at the point of intersection of important Roman roads, including Watling Street and the Fosse Way, it already had five gates by the fifteenth century and was connected by road to London, Worcester, Leicester and Holywell. Trade formed the basis of its wealth, both locally and beyond the seas, along with the textile industry, whose dyers produced distinctive, unfading colours. In 1377, tax returns show that the city was home to almost 5,000 people, which had risen to 6,601 by 1520.[12] Maps of the time suggest the walled city itself was around half a mile at its widest point and a similar distance from top to bottom, with the River Sherborne and Radford Brook passing through it, powering the city's many mills. The castle was central, with St Mary's and the church of St Michael just above it, while to the south, the Whitefriars and Greyfriars gates indicate the presence of other monastic communities. The Bishop's Palace may have hosted the royal visitors on occasion. Between them, Cheylesmore Gate shows where Henry and Margaret probably stayed, close to the most southern point of the city, and would have allowed access to the large Cheylesmore Park which extends beyond the walls, divided into the Great Park and Little Park. Outside and to the east, Margaret would have known the Spital Moor, associated with the hospital beyond the Gosford Gate and the Hermitage that sat at the fork of the road. To the west, passing out of Spon Gate, parallel with the river, where woodchips for roofs were made, she would have seen the Chapel of St James and St Christopher, perhaps praying for guidance on her travels, before the looming shadow of the leper hospital came into view. With its chapel dedicated to St Mary Magdalene, the hospital had historically belonged to Cheylesmore, so Margaret could well have dispensed charity or patronage to the inmates there.

Twenty-five miles to the north-east of Coventry lay Leicester Abbey, the twelfth-century Augustinian house of St Mary Praxis. After spending Christmas there as the guests of Abbot John Pomery, Henry and Margaret remained at the abbey almost all January. While there, they would have heard the news of distinguish from former one that took place in Sandwich, after an attack was launched by Sir John Dynham, a Yorkist loyalist who had offered his ships to help Warwick to escape to Calais after Ludford. In the early hours of the morning, Dynham's men sacked the town and captured the Lancastrian Earl Rivers and his family, bringing them back to Calais, where they were berated by Warwick, Salisbury and Edward, Earl of March. Such an incident gave Henry and Margaret warning that their enemies were not likely to simply sit out their days quietly in exile and accept their fate. Nor was Henry prepared to tolerate such behaviour. On 28 January, William Paston wrote to John Paston: 'The King comes towards London and, as it is said, raises people as he comes: it is certain commissions have been directed to several shires, every man to be ready, in his best array, when the king sends for him.'[14] It is likely that, given the volatile situation, Margaret remained in the north with their son, perhaps at Coventry or Kenilworth. Two days later, Henry had reached Northampton where, on 31 January, he appointed Henry Duke of Somerset Captain of Calais for twelve years. On 10 February he set out again, heading south to reclaim the Palace of Westminster as his own. The policy of creating an alternative capital in the north had been a shrewd one while York and Warwick held sway in the south, but Henry's power would not be complete until he consolidated what he had achieved in his northern bases with the traditional seat of government and finance in London.

Henry had also been keen to reward those who had been loyal to him through the years of struggle. On 19 December, he made grants of annuities of 20 marks to James Earl of Douglas, Henry Duke of Exeter, Thomas Earl of Devonshire, and four others, for their assistance in resisting the rebellion of Richard late Duke of York, Richard late Earl of Warwick, and Richard late Earl of Salisbury.[15] Some of the rewards involved the redistribution of confiscated Yorkist assets such as the park of Raskell in Yorkshire, forfeited by Salisbury, and given to Edmund Bolton on 13 January, and four other similar posts that went to men in the king's household. Henry's stepfather Owen Tudor, then in his late sixties, was appointed parker of Moylewike, and other places in Denbigh in North Wales on 5 February, while a week later, Humfrey, Duke of Buckingham, was recompensed for his services in Kent against the rebels and Henry's half-brother Jasper, Earl of Pembroke, received goods of the persons within Denbigh Castle, for his services in besieging it. Nor were the bereaved forgotten. Following York's attaintment and exile, he was unable to keep up the payment to the family of Edmund Beaufort, former Duke of Somerset, which had been agreed at the Loveday. On 20 January, Henry set out an annuity of 400 marks to be paid to Beaufort's widow, Margaret's friend, Eleanor, Duchess of Somerset.[16]

Henry was anticipating future assaults from the Yorkist lords because on 22 February he sent a commission to Jasper, Earl of Pembroke, to raise men in Wales to resist Richard, late Duke of York, Edward, late Earl of March, and other rebels. That day he arrived at Bedford, before proceeding to Dunstable where he stayed at the Priory, then on to St Albans between 26 and 28 February. Soon after that, he arrived in Westminster, where he awarded his 7-year-old son, Edward, Prince of Wales, the ability to grant pardons to rebels in Wales and the marches, and an annuity of £1,000. He also gave Sir Thomas Grey, of Rugemond Grey, 100 marks from the possessions of Richard, late Duke of York, and other rebels, in repayment of a loan.[17]

After making an appearance in London, Henry headed north once more, probably passing through St Albans again, before arriving on 28 March at

Royston in Hertfordshire, then on to Cambridge, where he stayed until the end of the month. By 6 April he was in the quiet seclusion of Peterborough Abbey where he remained for two weeks, and issued a commission to Henry, Duke of Exeter, to receive the submission of rebels. By 4 May, he was back at Leicester and then on to Coventry, where he may have been reunited with his wife and son on 6 May. Apart from an interlude of a week spent at Kenilworth, they remained at their Coventry home until mid-June. That he was expecting to hear more from the Yorkists is clear from the powers he gave to Henry, Duke of Somerset, Captain of Calais, on 5 June, to grant pardons to rebels, except a select group including John Dynham and his associates, and the proclamation of 11 June to be made by the sheriffs of Oxford, Berks, Southampton, and Wilts, that 'all persons assisting Richard, late duke of York, Edward, late earl of March, Richard, late earl of Warwick, and other persons attainted of high treason at the late parliament at Coventry, shall be considered rebels [sic]'. Similar proclamations were to be made by the sheriffs of London, Middlesex, and five others and £20 was given to a Nicholas Leveson for his services against the rebels at Blackheath and Blore Heath.[18]

It is likely that Henry learned of a manifesto that was being distributed from Calais, featuring the names of York, Edward, Warwick, Salisbury, and inciting criticism. It listed the failures of Henry's government: the losses in France, abuses in the legal system and the bad advice and greed of the king's favourites who, it was claimed, had planned the Yorkists' attainders in order to benefit from their lands. The criticisms bore the lengthy title of *These be the Points and Causes of the Gathering and Assembling of us, the King's True Liegemen of Kent, the which we trust to remedy, with help of him, the King, our Sovereign Lord, and all the Commons of England.* In a more direct challenge than before, it questioned the nature of kingship and its exercise of power: 'they say that our sovereign Lord is above law and that the law was made but to his pleasure and that he may make and break it as often as him list … the contrary is true'. Henry's 'false friends' also informed him that 'the commons … would bring in the Duke of York to be their king, so by these false men's leasings [rumours] they made him to hate and to destroy his very friends'. The rebels claimed they would be found the king's true men, and the true guilty ones would be found 'by a just and a true inquiry by the law'.[19] Early in June Warwick's uncle, Lord Fauconberg, made another humiliating attack upon Sandwich, destroying the fleet that Henry Beaufort had been rebuilding since Dynham's assault in January. This gave the Yorkists a foothold into England and by the end of the month, Edward, Warwick and Salisbury had joined him there with around 2,000 men.

Francesco Coppini, Bishop of Terni, had been appointed papal nuncio to England in 1459, arriving in the country that June in an attempt to persuade

Henry and Margaret to support the Pope's mission to battle the Turks and collect a tax to aid it. With the current situation so volatile and royal funds famously low, Margaret had informed Coppini this was not possible, no matter what her private feelings on the matter may have been. The Bishop's letters from 1460 reflect his unique position as a witness to unfolding events in England, a nation to whom he was also charged to bring peace. Coppini had been in Calais when Warwick, Salisbury and March set sail and, for varied reasons, had crossed the Channel with them. On 4 July, he reported to Henry that he had found 'almost everything in turmoil, and those nobles all ready to cross to England, declaring that they could not wait any longer in the existing state of affairs'. Attempting to calm them, Coppini elicited,

> a written pledge that they were disposed to devotion and obedience to your Majesty, and to do all in their power for the conservation and augmentation of your honour and the good of your realm. But they desired to come to your Majesty and to be received into their former state and favour, from which they declare they have been ousted by the craft of their opponents, and begged me to cross the sea with them to interpose my efforts and prevent bloodshed, assuring me that they would do anything honourable and just that I should approve for the honour and estate of your Highness and the welfare of your realm.[20]

Coppini remarked how the people were 'flocking to them from a remarkable eagerness for their arrival', due to a desire for 'the reunion of the whole realm', which created 'hindrances and dangers on the way from the concourse of various people'. He reported the actions of those who 'professed themselves devoted to your Majesty and are not',[21] and issued genuine plea to Henry to act at once to prevent imminent bloodshed and chaos in the realm:

> I beg you for the love of God, for the devotion you have always shown, which served for pious and holy things to the extent of its powers, and out of the pity and compassion you should have for your people and citizens and your duty, to prevent so much bloodshed, now so imminent. You can prevent this if you will, and if you do not you will be guilty in the sight of God in that awful day of judgment in which I also shall stand and require of your hand the English blood, if it be spilt. Let your Serenity provide swiftly, before arms are taken up, that I may communicate safely with you about the ways and means to avoid these evils and arrange a union. This is certainly not impossible nor even very difficult if your Serenity will allow yourself to be persuaded and informed with an open mind and judgment.[22]

Coppini urged Henry to listen to the grievances of his opponents before taking up arms:

> Therefore let a safe way be found for your Serenity to hear and communicate with those who are not partisans or suspect in the matter of truth and justice, and I doubt not but that everything will be put straight, to the advantage of all your dominions. If after that experiment your Majesty does not consider the matter thus, you may then justly take up arms, but to do so before, especially after the mediation of a legate and apostolic nuncio would be nefarious, impious, unjust and contrary to the honour, wish and command of God. The means of communicating safely will be found if your Serenity will put aside those who are thus suspect and listen to moderate and neutral men such as all may trust. It is necessary for all this to be done quickly, as the case does not permit delay, and offences, murder and the infinite shedding of Christian blood are prepared. These will rise to the sight of God and cry out against those who hindered remedies, to whom I have referred above.[23]

The bishop knew Henry well, and which arguments would sway him. His letter is significant because it gives an insight into the way Henry saw his kingship as a construct of peace-making, duty and the word of God. He turned to the Bible for guidance and believed himself to be driven by its message, implementing it literally and fearing that he could not save the kingdom. With Coppini advocating himself as God's messenger, the responsibility upon Henry's shoulders, the suffering and damnation if he should fail, would be enough to have completely broken a lesser man. It provides an insight into the kind of rhetoric contributing towards Henry's mental state on the eve of battle:

> I have often written and spoken to your Majesty, calling to mind the Gospel words, A kingdom divided against itself cannot stand. The same thing has been frequently foretold by word and by writing touching the danger and ruin of your state unless you turn to God and ways of piety; your Majesty knows the way. Behold, God scourges them, chastises them that they may arise, come to their senses, be converted and live. But if they close their ears like deaf vipers, woe to them and also to your Majesty, I say it with sorrow, unless you provide peace when you can. You can do so now if you hearken to me and understand that I am the messenger of God, the apostolic messenger, not seeking my own, as your Majesty has long known and all your Council my integrity and fidelity and my attachment to your Crown. If you will not listen to what is right and true I am guiltless before Almighty God and the Holy Apostolic See and all the community, both cleric and lay, by the evidence of this letter, which I have had published, and

I have also sent it by a faithful messenger of your Majesty's household, and so I am guiltless of the blood of your people if it is shed through the fault or negligence of yourself or others, when this could be prevented in the way I have shown. I expect a speedy reply, because the danger is imminent and does not brook delay. May God Almighty bless and enlighten your Majesty for the peace and safety of your people. I commend myself to your Majesty. London, the 4th July, 1460.[24]

Aware of the coming storm, Henry bid farewell to his family, blessing his son and kissing Margaret, urging her to stay away from him until he summoned her by a 'special token' which only they would understand.[25] Gregory's chronicle explains this as being because the Yorkists would try and entice her to London 'for they knew well that all the workings that were done grow by her, for she was more wittier [cleverer] than the king'.[26] Exactly where this took place, and Margaret's subsequent whereabouts, are unclear. It is possible that she remained behind in Coventry, which was only thirty miles away, but other indications suggest she accompanied Henry at least part of the way. Hall has Margaret encouraging the troops and 'promising great rewards to her helpers', taking responsibility for dispatching the royal army once she judged that it was 'able to match with the force of her adversaries'. After that, the chronicler relates that she and Somerset retreated to a safe distance, perhaps into the town of Northampton itself, although other sources place her at Eccleshall Castle.

On 7 July, Henry arrived in Northampton. Marching up from a London which had welcomed them, the Yorkist lords arrived on the outskirts of the city three days later. The king appears to have taken Coppini's advice, as the morning was spent in talks and negotiations, which ultimately proved fruitless. Then, as tremendous rain fell across the fields, the two sides engaged in battle in the grounds of Delapré Abbey, to the horror of the nuns within. As Warwick approached the king's camp, Lord Grey of Ruthin lay down his weapons and allowed the earl access to Henry.

According to Bale's chronicle, Henry's advisors tried to persuade him to wait at Ely, which was more easily defended, but he insisted on remaining near the battle site perhaps bearing in mind the effect of his presence at Ludford Bridge. Other sources place his tent in Hardingstone Field, close to the site of the abbey.[27] A newsletter from Bruges contains the details that:

When the king heard of Warwick's arrival, he betook himself to a valley between two mountains, a strong place. But Fortune, who throughout showed herself favourable to Warwick, willed that it should rain so heavily that they were forced to come out of that place and encounter Warwick.

Without a serious fight or much slaughter, Warwick very soon had the king in his power. He forthwith put to death the Duke of Buckingham, one of the great lords of that country, and the Lords of Beaumont, Egremont and Shrewsbury, all great lords.[28]

Once again Henry was in Yorkist custody but although his enemies afforded him the respect due to his rank, it was a terse and bitter ghost of the ceremony for a puppet king. The Lord Chancellor, William Waynflete, resigned his position and the great seal of office was surrendered to the Yorkists, enabling them to conduct business in the king's name. The *Croyland Chronicle* relates how 'the victorious Earls paid all honours of royalty to King Henry and conducted him to London in solemn procession, Richard Neville, Earl of Warwick, bare-headed, carrying a sword before the king, in all humility and respect'.[29] And the shadow of York loomed large in that duke's absence. The streets of London buzzed with the rumour that 'the Duke of York will descend upon the country with a large number of troops, as well as the King of Scotland with quite 30,000',[30] and that Warwick would 'appoint new offices and arrange the government of the country' or that 'they will make a son of the Duke of York king, and that they will pass over the king's son, as they are beginning already to say that he is not the king's son'. The chronicler was also convinced that in the wake of these events, 'the queen also runs great danger'.[31] News of the battle's outcome, including the death of the loyal Duke of Buckingham, and Henry's arrest, would have had a devastating impact in Coventry, thirty miles to the east. With the victorious Yorkists so close, viewing Margaret as the 'brains' behind Henry's actions, she was indeed in great danger. Hall, Polydore Vergil and William of Worcester have her fleeing north at this point, through Yorkshire and up to Durham.

The Yorkist victory brought national uncertainty. After the rebel lords had taken control of the king, a period of waiting ensued, before the return of the Duke of York would allow him to announce his intentions. Henry was taken south by his captors, afforded the expected outward signs of respect due to his position, and between 16 and 25 July, was resident at the Bishop's Palace in London. Yet Henry must have wondered at his fate and had the words of Coppini, the 'messenger of God', ringing in his ears, in the wake of such bloodshed and defeat. If the indications of Henry's piety and serious character are to be accepted, he can only have been convinced that he was partly, if not entirely, responsible for the state of chaos in his country, and that the victory of his enemies was God's judgement on his own inability. Historians have often commented on Henry's weakness at this point, on his acquiescence to the Yorkist demands and his quiet complicity in the events that followed. It may seem surprising to modern readers that he was apparently passive, failing to resist or rebel, even if he was in fear of his life, but the answer may lie in his character and deep faith. Coppini had established this in the king's mind before Northampton, but the roots of this emotion went deeper, back as far as Henry's illness of 1453, perhaps even further. Far stronger than the locks and restrictions imposed upon him by the Yorkists, the king's pious mind created its own cage: he had been defeated in battle because God willed it. Warwick, Salisbury and March had been victorious because that was God's punishment for Henry's failure. As God's instruments, Henry owed them obedience.

Yet having won their decisive victory, the Yorkist Lords lacked a longer-term plan. Warwick, Salisbury and March had possibly taken the country against even their own expectations. With their implicit questioning of the nature of kingship, the statements in their manifesto suggested they had foreseen more than a simple return to the terms of the Protectorate, although they presented no alternative vision at this point. In the first week of August, Henry was permitted to make the journey to Canterbury, where he stayed for six days, perhaps visiting the shrines in the cathedral. It would seem that Warwick accompanied him to the city as, on 5 August, Henry issued an order to Henry, Duke of Somerset, to deliver possession of the castle of Guisnes into Warwick's hands and on 8 August, the,

> bailiffs and other officers in Jersey and Guernsey are to make a proclamation declaring Richard duke of York, Edward earl of March, Richard earl of Warwick, Richard earl of Salisbury, Alice his wife, and Edward earl of Rutland, are the King's true subjects and friends, and to restore their possessions [sic].[32]

By 23 August, Henry was back at Greenwich, where he remained until news of York's return from Ireland prompted him to travel, or his guardians to take him, to Westminster.

What happened next was the most extraordinary, unexpected coup, in which Henry's dependent position after Northampton was exploited to bypass his successors entirely. Gregory's chronicle records the details of York's return from Ireland, his banners fluttering in the breeze, bearing the arms of England, the sword borne before him as a signifier of his regal status, the pomp and ceremony with which he rode through the streets. The people were confused about his intentions as hitherto he had professed loyalty to the crown, but these symbols expressed a conscious regality which threatened the fragile construct of Henry's existing kingship. Whethamsted wrote that when York returned, there were varied and contrary reports amongst the people ... some said that his arrival was peaceful and that he intended nothing else but the restoration of harmony among the quarrelling lords, bringing peace to the kingdom, and reforming it, by his authority. Yet others, including those who were older and wiser, suspected that he meant to act litigiously against the king for the royal crown.[33]

Once he reached Westminster, York's intentions became shockingly clear. Croyland describes the duke bursting into the presence chamber of the palace where he,

approached the royal throne and claimed the sole right of sitting upon it; he then put forward a genealogy tracing his lineal descent from Lionel, Duke of Clarence, to whose successors, he asserted, the kingdom of England rightly belonged .... He would no longer endure the injustices which the three Henries, who were usurpers, had for so long inflicted on his line.

Whethamsted relates a more regal, formal entrance, but the details are essentially the same. York arrived with

great pomp and splendour and in no small exaltation of mood, for he came with trumpets and horns, men-at-arms and a very large retinue ... he marched straight through the great hall until he came to the solemn chamber .... Made directly for the king's throne, where he laid his hand on the drape or cushion as if about to take possession of what was his by right.

When asked by Archbishop Bourchier whether he wished to see the king, the 'irritated' York replied: 'I do not recall that I know anyone in the kingdom whom it would not befit to come to me and see my person, rather than I should go and visit him.'[34]

After making his dramatic statement in the presence chamber, York then entered the inner rooms of the palace where, as Gregory relates, he 'compelled King Henry to remove to the queen's apartments, and took over the king's apartments himself. Croyland describes him taking a more violent approach, broaching the 'principal chamber of the palace [the king being in the queen's apartments], smashed the locks and threw open the doors, in a regal rather than a ducal manner'.[35] Depending upon the recorder, Henry was either present in the room, or in Margaret's vacant apartments, but he certainly could not have remained unaware of unfolding events for long. Soon he was face-to-face with York, who assumed control of his person. Over the next three weeks, Henry was kept a prisoner, 'by force and strength until, at last, the king, for fear of death, granted him the crown: for a man that has little wit will soon be afraid of death … I trust and believe there was no man that would have done him bodily harm'.[36] With Henry controlled entirely by the Yorkists, perhaps in fear of his life, he had little choice but to acquiesce to the demands they now presented. Perhaps his profound faith and sense of personal failure also led him to believe that they were enacting God's will. If such a thought occurred to Henry, he would not have been able to question their wishes.

First, they insisted upon a reversal of the Coventry attainders passed against the Yorkist lords. This was to be expected as they sought scapegoats, blaming,

> several seditious and evil disposed persons, having no regard for you most noble person and realm, sinisterly and importunely begged your highness to call a Parliament to be held at Coventry [on 30 November 1459] for the sole intention of destroying certain of the great, noble, faithful and true lords of your blood.[37]

They argued further, that the parliament had not even been legal, with lords called to attend it 'without due and free election, some without any election, against the king's laws and the liberties of the commons, by the means and labour of these seditious persons'. Thus, the parliament held at Coventry was declared to have been no true parliament, and 'all acts, statutes and ordinances made by its authority be reversed, annulled, repealed, revoked, and no force or effect'. Next, York forced through the Act of Accord on 24 October 1460, which named the duke as Henry's heir to the exclusion of Prince Edward. It is an indication of the duress under which Henry found himself, that he was not able to prevent his son's inheritance from being taken, or the completely broken state of his pious mind:

> Richard, Duke of York, tenderly desiring the weal, peace and prosperity of this land, and to set apart all that might be trouble to the same, [considering that] King Henry the Sixth [has] been named, taken and reputed King of England and of France [during] his natural life [agrees] without hurt or prejudice to his own right and title, [to] take, worship and honour him [Henry VI] for his sovereign Lord …. It is accorded, appointed and agreed that Richard, Duke of York, be entitled, called and reputed from henceforth, very and rightful heir to the crowns of England and France and, after the death of Henry VI, the duke and his heirs shall immediately succeed to these crowns.[38]

Waurin suggests the act was an unpopular move, even among York's supporters, while the Earl of Salisbury 'disclosed how the lords and people were unhappy at his desire to strip the king of the crown.'[39] Croyland places Queen Margaret and

Prince Edward in the north, probably at Coventry, where 'the queen's northern supporters found Parliament's decree both odious and execrable, the people and nobles of those parts rose up with the aim of altering it'.[40] On 1 November, the lord processed to St Paul's to mark the occasion, with Henry wearing his crown. York walked with him and Edward carried the royal train. That night, Henry was removed, 'against his will'[41] from Westminster to the Bishop of London's Palace, where Gregory's chronicle relates that he received an unwelcome visit from York, who 'came to him that same night by torchlight, behaving as if he were king, and said in many places that "this is ours by every right"'. Henry was either terrified, and in fear of his life, or believed that God was speaking through York, as another 'messenger of God'.[42]

The Act of Accord posed a direct threat to the identity, and perhaps even the life, of Margaret's son. It was a dark time for the queen, as even her flight to safety was fraught with terror, according to various accounts. Gregory's chronicle relates that as she travelled into Wales, her money was stolen by one she believed she might rely upon: 'one of her own servants, whom she had created an officer of her son the Prince, plundered and robbed her, and put her in doubt of her life and her son's also'.[43] This story may be apocryphal, as it appears in different versions, dated to different moments in 1460 and 1463, but the essence could be true, indicating that Margaret was robbed at least once as she tried to reach safety. If so, it was a terrifying and humiliating experience for a young woman used to being afforded the dignity and respect of a queen. William of Worcester names the thief as a John Cleger, who was in the service of Lord Stanley, and the *Davies Chronicle* puts the sum stolen at a substantial 10,000 marks. Historians have been divided over whether these accounts are the conflation of two separate incidents or differing reports of the same one, but Margaret did survive whatever ordeal she underwent and arrived, perhaps considerably poorer, at Harlech Castle in Gwynedd. Finally in loyal Lancastrian territory, she was given 'many great gifts and was greatly comforted, of which she had need', before she went into hiding with her brother-in-law, Jasper, Earl of Pembroke. The terms of the Act of Accord were intolerable to her. In secret, she began to plan a lasting, permanent revenge.

## Chapter Eight

# Civic Chaos 1461

## I

One hundred and thirty miles to the north-east of Coventry, Hull represented an even greater geographical and symbolic distance from Westminster than Margaret's former base. It was also a major port on the river Humber, giving access to the North Sea, and potential escape routes across the North Sea into to Scotland, the Baltics or the Netherlands. Hull already had a tradition of supporting the Lancastrian dynasty and its allies; its first mayor in the fourteenth century had been a de la Pole, in 1451–2 it had made gifts of wine to leading Lancastrian lords, it lent Henry £100 in 1454 and sent him fifty archers in 1457. When Margaret established her new household in the city, late in 1460, she sent summons to the Duke of Somerset and Earl of Devon to join her, along with a number of other Lords. The *English Chronicle* stresses that this was done with great secrecy, and the numbers swiftly mounted:

> This matter was not delayed but very secretly done, and she sent letters to all her chief officers that they would do the same, and that they should warn all those servants that loved her or meant to preserve and encourage her royal office, to wait upon her at Hull by the day she appointed. All these people were gathered and conveyed so secretly that they were assembled to the number of 15,000 before any man would believe it; so that if any man said, or told, or talked of such a gathering, he would be disgraced. [1]

Margaret was wary of approaches coming from London, reputedly in the name of her husband, recalling his final words to her and aware of how valuable a prize she would be to York:

> Counterfeit tokens were sent to her as though they had come from her most revered lord ... however they were not of his sending [but] forged things, for that they brought were of the king's house, and some of the prince's house, and some of her own house, and warned her beware of the tokens, so she gave them no credence ... For the [Yorkist] lords would have liked to have got her to London, for they knew well that all the arts that were done were encouraged by her, for she was more intelligent than the king. [2]

While Margaret was mustering her forces at Hull and with Henry virtually under house arrest at the Bishop's Palace, York was busy in Westminster Palace, acting, to all intents and purposes, as king. The tenants of Middleham Castle were ordered to pay their rents and services to Richard, Earl of Salisbury, 'who is the King's faithful subject' and Edward, Earl of March, York's eldest son, was appointed Constable of Bristol and keeper of various forests.[3] At the beginning of December, when reports finally reached London about the army gathering in Hull, York took action. He sent March west to confront the troops being raised there on Margaret's behalf by Jasper Tudor, left Warwick in charge of Henry in London and marched north with his second son, Edmund, Earl of Rutland and the Earl of Salisbury. It was clear that a decisive encounter was imminent and, unwilling to risk the life and liberty of her son, her husband's only heir, Margaret made the decision to take Edward to the safety of the Scottish court. In Edinburgh, they were received by the newly widowed regent, Mary of Guelders, who was ruling for her infant son James, upon whose mercy Margaret cast herself. Apart from the shelter and sympathy on offer, Mary's situation must have provided Margaret with a vision of exactly what she had hoped to achieve in England.

A letter to the city of London composed on Edward's behalf that December objects to the actions of the Duke of York in the strongest possible terms. York was 'a fals traitour that ceasith not his said malice but utterly entendith the distruccion of my lord and of my lady and the disherityng of us'. He was acting in self-interest, not for 'the wele of this my lords reaulme and the seurete and welfare of his subgettes to the same' and had rejected the prince's 'rightful and lineal' descent and place in the succession. Edward vowed to free his father from captivity in a way that protected the city from harm and any who threatened its stability and peace would be punished.[4] What Edward offered, even as a 7-year-old boy whose literary skills were unlikely to have been equal to such a composition, was hope. The most likely author was his mother, Margaret.

At the end of 1460, Margaret and Prince Edward were staying with Mary of Guelders at Lincluden Abbey, in Dumfries. Now a series of picturesque red stone ruins, the abbey occupied a good defensive position, having been built upon the foundations of a former castle on the site. Their host, the Dutch-born Queen Mary, was a couple of years younger than Margaret but shared the experience with her of marrying into a foreign dynasty and being forced to take over the reins of government for the sake of their child. As the year came to a close, they would have had the opportunity for worship and reflection. With the speed of travel, the new year would have arrived by the time a messenger had covered the 170 miles to the abbey from Wakefield in Yorkshire. Such men had previously delivered sad tidings, of loss and defeat in the aftermath of battles and meetings but, on this occasion, Margaret may have asked for confirmation, scarcely able to believe the account that she was hearing. On 30 December her army, under the leadership of Henry Beaufort, Duke of Somerset, had encountered York's forces at Sandal Castle, just outside Wakefield. After a fierce clash of arms, York and his second son Rutland had been killed at the scene, while the Earl of Salisbury had been beheaded shortly afterwards. The man who had caused Margaret a decade of trouble, was finally dead.

The details of exactly how the battle unfolded, later became the cause of antagonism between the two sides, but it appears that York's party were taken unawares. The *Annales Rerum Anglicarum* claims the queen's men had agreed to an embargo on fighting over the Christmas season, which the duke celebrated at Sandal. Technically, at this time the festive season lasted from 25 December through to Epiphany on 6 January, with new year often being considered the most significant day, so that Christmas itself took a more sombre, reflective tone, and the light-hearted elements appeared at the end, on twelfth night. The *Annales* has York's men coming out of the safety of Sandal Castle and roaming about the countryside in search of victuals on 30 December, when they may have still believed themselves not to be in danger from the queen's army, stationed nearby at Pontefract. The duke was waiting for reinforcements to arrive from his eldest son, Edward, Earl of March, before engaging, but as Waurin and Hall recount, Beaufort concealed a portion of his army in the woods, so the Lancastrian numbers appeared significantly less. Defecting from his brother-in-law to fight under the king's banner, John Neville may have displayed the arms of the Earl of Warwick, hoping to lure York out in the belief that the earl had arrived or that he himself was offering support. Waurin also suggests that Sir Anthony Trollope from Calais, who had previously defected at Ludford Bridge, sent messages to York indicating his willingness to return. However it happened, the Yorkists were caught in a pincer movement made by Beaufort's army and cut off from returning to the castle. Hall relates that the duke was 'environed on every side, like a fish in a net, or a deer in a buckstall'.[5]

Margaret was not present at the Battle of Wakefield. She was not riding among her troops on a white palfrey, encouraging them to die for her cause as narrated by the chronicler Waurin, or in a position to order the decapitation of York or relish his head being placed upon Micklebar Gate, topped with a paper crown, as some historians have claimed. In Scotland, she heard the news as it was gradually spread by word of mouth and in letters. What she *was* doing, was sitting in talks lasting over a week with Mary of Guelders, discussing terms for a Treaty of Lincluden, by which she agreed to cede the border town of Berwick to the Scots and possibly to marry her son to a Scottish princess in return for military aid against York. In response to victory at Wakefield, she headed south, wearing the crimson and black badge of the Prince of Wales featuring a plume of white feathers, yet as some sources relate, the unruly antics of her Scottish army instilled fear into her subjects. At York, where a counsel of twelve Lancastrian lords met, it was decided to march with all possible strength to London and rescue King Henry from the hands of his enemies.

Prospero de Camulio, Milanese Ambassador, heard that Henry was 'much moved' when he heard the news about Wakefield 'although, the ambassador added, the Duke of York seems rather to have been slain out of hatred for having claimed the kingdom than anything else'. The account was also related to the Duke of Milan by Antonio de la Torre, who was travelling through England at the time, and composed his letter in Sandwich. Having discharged his duties, and poised to leave, Torre was aware that 'some very important events occurred' and chose to 'stay on for some days in order to see the end'.[6] He reported that 'some of the lords of the queen's party' had been rendered desperate by the victory of the Yorkists that summer, so 'assembled a force in the northern parts … to come and attack their opponents'. His account continues:

> Accordingly, the Duke of York, with his son and Warwick's father, the Earl of Salisbury, went out to meet them. And it came to pass that, although they were three times stronger, yet from lack of discipline, because they allowed a large part of the force to go pillaging and searching for victuals, their adversaries, who are desperate, attacked the duke and his followers. Ultimately, they routed them, slaying the duke and his younger son, the Earl of Rutland, Warwick's father and many others. This news caused great alarm in these parts, although it seems Warwick was not there.[7]

On 9 January, in response to rumours that he was close to the Yorkist lords, Coppini felt obliged to defend his position and declare his loyalty to Margaret, in terms that echoed those in the letter he had sent to Henry the previous summer. His dramatic offer to be flayed alive or torn asunder to prove his devotion echoes the terms of battle, but his advice to Margaret was that she should not become 'too arrogant' over such a 'trifling victory'. The rapid timescale of spring 1461 would ultimately prove Coppini correct:

> Owing to manifest causes and dangers … we cannot proceed in person to the queen and the lords with her, as you know. First and foremost, as the basis of everything, we require you to declare and offer on your own behalf, that should it ever be found that we have excommunicated or cursed any one assisting her Majesty or being with her, or if we have ever committed or consented to such things, we will gladly be flayed alive or torn asunder, for we excommunicated no one, cursed no one and wronged no one at any time

in this kingdom, but we shall be ready to do all these things and more still, if we are called upon to do so for her Royal Highness and for her wellbeing and obedience …. That we love and revere her Majesty as much as any man living she herself knows, and she has seen and experienced that we did not abandon her when she was in difficulties, and for her cause and wellbeing we are ready to suffer anything in this world.

Tell those lords, and especially the Duke of Somerset, whom we admire for his character and because we believe that he loves the queen and her estate as we do ourselves, that if they do not attend to our advice they will bring desolation upon the whole realm and the estate and wellbeing of his Majesty. They must not be arrogant because of the trifling victory they won, owing to the rash advance of their opponents, because we have seen and know full well that all the people are incensed and in the worst possible humour against those who do not desire peace. There are two reasons for this: firstly, the countless acts of cruelty related of them, whereas those here were not cruel, but received into favour those who wished to come; secondly, because they recognise and know that his Majesty and the lords with him and ourself with them are really disposed to an honest and honourable peace, salutary for both parties. Therefore if your influence with them does not suffice, their cause will be in the worst possible case, because the feelings of the people are incredibly incensed against them, and they will see more than two hundred thousand desperate men rise against them, who are constantly assembling, offering to devote their goods and their persons in such an honest and just cause.[8]

Then, while all parties were considering their next move, Edward, Earl of March, clashed with Jasper and Owen Tudor at Mortimer's Cross on the Welsh borders. On 2 or 3 of February, the eldest of York's sons won a resounding victory, pursuing their adversaries for miles, seeking retribution for the duke's death. Jasper escaped but Owen was captured and taken to Hereford, where he was led to the marketplace and beheaded, despite believing until the last that his life would be spared. As Gregory's chronicle relates, his final words were 'that hede shalle lie on the stocke that was wonte to lie on Quene Kateryns lappe' and his head was set upon the market cross where a madwoman combed his hair, washed the blood off his face and set more than a hundred candles to burn around him. Camulio attempted to estimate the numbers involved, writing that 'on the 3rd inst. the Earl of March won a battle against two of the princes of the island, who support the queen; 8,000 men fell in that battle, including, they reckon, 200 and more knights and noble squires'.[9] After Mortimer's Cross, Edward marched his armies north in search of the queen, reputedly increasing his forces as he went, although Richard Beauchamp's estimation that he had a following of 200,000 may have been exaggerated.[10] Warwick was still in London with Henry, when reports reached him of Edward's victory and Margaret's impending return to the capital. He readied himself at once to join March and intercept her, leaving with a significant Yorkist force drawn from the southern counties. Until this time, Henry had still been resident at the Bishop's Palace, but now he was instructed to be ready to leave. On 12 February, the earl set out with 60,000 men, taking the king with him.[11] Potentially, the difficult situation faced them that the 'king's' army could come face-to-face with that of the queen, as Camulio outlined:

> They are to the effect that the king is going with all the forces of England against the queen, and he has 120,000 men, of whom the Earl of Warwick is chief and leader. He is going against the queen, who is towards the part of the island which faces French Britanny. On this account he has provided a fleet at sea, so that she may not escape that way. He has arranged this great multitude in three divisions: the first of 20,000, the second of 40,000, and the third of 60,000. The queen, however, is in a strong place, and they say she has some 30,000 combatants. The issue is expected within a fortnight; it will involve much cruelty, and decide many things, whatever be the event.[12]

True to Camulio's prediction, the second clash occurred a fortnight after the Yorkist victory at Mortimer's Cross. Warwick expected Margaret's army to approach London through St Albans, so set himself up in a defensive position to the north of the town, using cannon, obstacles and earthworks. There, he awaited the arrival of the queen. Margaret, though, had a spy in the earl's household, who informed her of the preparations that had been made, allowing her to move her army to the east, to capture Dunstable on 16 February, and avoid all the traps that Warwick had made. Unaware of this, the earl continued to wait, as Margaret manoeuvred her troops through the night to attack St Albans at dawn, from the west. She and Prince Edward were in the vicinity on this occasion, although not at the site where the fighting took place, as Henry had been in 1455. This time the conflict continued for hours, hampered by damp conditions, as Warwick struggled to regroup the resources he had already committed. As night began to fall, the earl realised that he was outnumbered and made a tactical withdrawal. Not only was this a victory for Margaret, it was also the means by which she was reunited with her husband, from whom she had been parted since Northampton the previous July.

Much has been made of Henry's mental state after this battle, when he was reputedly found sitting in a field, singing to himself, a description that deliberately frames him as the madman, and plays to Yorkist narratives about the need for a new king. For Henry, the cumulative effects of his humiliations and guilt since Northampton came to a head when he witnessed the bloodshed at this second battle of St Albans, feeling powerless to prevent it and, possibly, that this was another manifestation of God's disapproval. His actions make more sense in the context of the account given by the *Davies Chronicle*, which states that 'whanne the kyng herde that they were so nyghe hym, he went oute and took hys felde besyde a lytelle towne called Sandryge, nat fer fro Seynt Albonys, in a place called No-mannes land, and there he stoode and sawe his peple slayne on bothe sydes'.[13] Seen in this light, Henry's actions are less mad than pious and cautious. After his narrow miss with an archer's arrow in 1455, he would have been advised to keep away from the action and find a suitable, safe place to wait, and as the hours passed and he witnessed the slaughter, it would have been in keeping for the king to recite Biblical passages or even to sing hymns for the passing of the souls of soldiers. His focus would have been far more on the spiritual than the martial side of the day. This was what defined Henry's character, but it also set him in stark contrast to the military leadership shown by the Yorkist lords.

Yet the descriptions of Henry's reputed weakness or insanity were inseparable from the implementation of justice afterwards. Camulio described him as being 'placed' under a tree a mile from the battle, suggesting manipulation and 'when the defeat of the Earl of Warwick was reported,' he was fearful and 'detained upon his promise the two princes who had been left to guard him'. After Somerset arrived, he received him 'in friendly fashion and went with them to St Albans to the queen, and on the morrow one of the two detained, upon his assurance, was beheaded and the other imprisoned.'[14] Other sources relate how the two men set to guard him were sentenced to death, and this decision is frequently attributed to Queen Margaret, overriding the king's former promise. She is reputed to have asked her 8-year-old son Edward what their fate should be, and he condemned them to death.[15] According to Waurin,

> the king was taken under a great oak, where he was laughing greatly at what had occurred, and he begged those who came to him that they should do no hurt to the person of Monsieur Kyriel [his captor], which they promised, but Lovelace, the disloyal traitor, led the king, Sir Thomas, and his son to the queen, who was right glad to meet the king.

Waurin relates that Margaret encouraged her son to order and witness the executions of their enemies,[16] and Henry VI's formidable biographer, Professor Griffiths, accepts and repeats this incident.[17] If Edward was encouraged to witness Lancastrian acts of justice, it was to put his legal commission into perspective and, modern sensibilities aside, must be seen within the context of threats to his realm and future kingship. The prevalence of death in the fifteenth century would have made it far more of a reality for a child, than a single traumatic event. Any scruples might also have been lost in the euphoria of success.

This volte-face of royal justice was designed to underscore an increasing impatience with the king that was now rushing towards its conclusion. George Neville, Bishop of Exeter, informed Coppini of the Yorkists' defeat, apologising that 'the details of which would be equally painful and lengthy to narrate, and everyone who heard of it must have been much astonished'. The letter reveals a marked change in tone towards Henry, who is now 'that puppet of a king', and 'that statue of a king', who 'turned his face towards the North'.[18] The king's instability and the ease at which he could be manipulated, formed a central part of Yorkist rhetoric in the months ahead.

There is no doubt that Henry was relieved to be reunited with Margaret after the battle had been won. Gregory gives Henry the more active role in the meeting, as 'in the myddys of the batayle Kynge Harry wente unto hys Quene and for-soke alle hys lordys, ande truste better to hyr party thenne unto hys owne lordys',[19] while others present him more passively awaiting the arrival of Beaufort. The *Davies Chronicle* briefly describes the moment which must have been far more emotionally charged after so many months of uncertainty:

> Whan the kyng sawe his peple dysparbeled and the feeld broke, he went to his quene Margarete that came wyth the Northurmen, and hyr sone Edward; for thay of the North sayde that thay came for to restore the kyng to the quene his wyfe, and for to delyuer hym owte of pryson; forasmeche as seth the batayle of Northampton he had be vnder the rewle and gouernaunce of the erles of Warrewyk and Salesbury, and of other.[20]

That night, after the battle, Henry dubbed his son Edward a knight. As Gregory relates, the 'king blessed his son the Prince and Dr Morton brought forth a book that was full of orison, and there the book was opened and blessed that young child and made him knight'. Edward was dressed in purple velvet decorated with beaten goldsmith's work and he, in turn, made many more knights, including Sir Anthony Trollope, who had one of Warwicks's caltraps (a spiked metal device), embedded in his foot.[21]

A letter in the Milan papers to a member of the Arnolfini family in Bruges, highlights the widespread fears of contemporaries that the royal troops would run wild. The writer was grateful that 'the queen and prince have not descended in fury with their troops', and so might be admitted peacefully to the city, which was probably London, because 'the least lack of control would ruin everything'.[22] Richard Beauchamp felt that 'many thousands' did not feel safe, anywhere, and that a 'general dread prevailed of the destruction of cities, of rapine without respect of persons, sex or place' and that the nobles were being betrayed by the 'treachery of the common people', who thought they could 'procure peace for themselves by the heads of such great men'.[23]

Whethamsted, who had reported the disturbance after Ludford Bridge, described the progress of the queen's army down from the north, as they 'robbed, plundered and devastated, and carried off with them whatever they could find or discover, whatever clothing or money, herds of cattle or single animals, or any other thing whatsoever, sparing neither churches nor clergy, monasteries, chapels nor chaplains'.[24] The *Davies Chronicle* contains a similar detail, with the royal army 'robbing all the country and people as they came, spoiling abbeys, houses of religion and churches, and bearing away chalices, books and other ornaments, as if they were pagans or Saracens and not Christian men'.[25] Croyland describes the men 'like so many mice rushing from their holes and everywhere devoted themselves to pillage and plunder … in their unbridled and frantic rage', as they despoiled the churches and, worse still, 'broke open the pixes in which were kept the body of Christ and shook out the sacred elements from them'.[26] Clearly, fear of the behaviour of the victorious 'heathen' soldiers was real, even justified, by prior experience of the Lancastrians. That Henry and Margaret's troops were not issued with instructions to curtail such behaviour, or suffered the consequences of ignoring such instructions, was a serious oversight on their part, and a failure in their responsibility towards their subjects.

A second letter from the same group in the Milan papers, relates how a delegation of four aldermen and three sympathetic women was dispatched from London, leaving almost as soon as the victory had been reported. Margaret and Henry received the widowed Lady Buckingham, Lady Scales and Jacquetta, Countess Rivers, whose role was to offer them the city 'provided they were guaranteed against pillage'.[27] The women were back in London on 20 February, with the message that 'the king and queen had no mind to pillage the chief city and chamber of their realm, and so they promised, but at the same time they did not mean that they would not punish the evildoers'.[28] In anticipation of Henry and Margaret's return, a proclamation was issued that 'everyone should keep fast to his house and should live at peace, in order that the king and his forces might enter and behave peacefully'. Logically and militarily, it was the path that made most sense, for Henry to return to Westminster as a victor and to the exclusion of the Yorkist lords who had dominated the city. However, within an hour of the proclamation, rumours were circulating that Warwick and March were returning with thousands of men to protect Londoners against the king's army, sending the place into 'uproar'.[29] Giving the appearance of retreat, Margaret then dispatched two bands of soldiers to attempt to break through the city gate at Aldgate. It was an unexpected move that changed the direction of the conflict, as they found the gates closed and barred against them, and any remaining sympathies of the city were lost.

For whatever reason, Henry and Margaret did not march to London. On 19 February, they were at Dunstable, which left the way clear for Warwick and March to re-enter the city. Neville recorded that plunder did take place. Henry 'turned his face towards the North, pillaging in the country, and at length the wife, with her husband, arrived at York, glorying in their very bloody victory.'[30] Gregory's Chronicle confirms this, adding that,

> there were not 5,000 men that fought in the Quenys party, for the moste parte of Northeryn men fledde a-way, and some were take and spoylyd owte of their harnysse by the way as they fledde. And sum of them robbed ever as they yede, a pityfful thynge it is to hear it.[31]

He believed they had not followed through an earlier intention to go to London, because 'the Northern men would have been too cruel in robbing if they had' and 'by the advice of Dr Morton, they sent certain knights and men' south, 'but they might not be suffered to entry into the town.'[32] The decision made by the Lancastrians not to enter London may have made sense to them at the time, given the city's fears and their own established power base in the north but, with hindsight, it is difficult not to see this as a turning point. Edward, Earl of March and Warwick marched into the capital and claimed it as their own.

On 1 March, 1461 Warwick's brother George Neville, Archbishop of Exeter, addressed a group assembled at St John's Field in Clerkenwell, explaining Edward's claim to the throne and listing the ways in which Henry had broken his promises. The crowd were then asked if Henry should remain king and the response was a predictably resounding denial. Edward was proclaimed king instead. The *London Chronicle* adds that 'it was demanded of the people whether Henry was worthy to reign as king any longer or not. Whereunto the people cried hugely and said Nay, nay. And after it was asked of them whether they would have the Earl of March for their King, and they cried with one voice, Yea yea.'[33] Three days later, a Nicolo Darabatta wrote to Coppini that the Earls arrived with an army of 5,000, whereupon 'a great crowd flocked together and with the lords, who were there, they chose the Earl of March as their king and sovereign lord'. After that, they 'celebrated the solemnity, going in procession through the place amid great festivities'. It remained to see, continued the letter, 'how King Henry, his son, the queen and the other lords will bear this, as it is said that the new king will shortly leave here to go after them'.[34] Another of Coppini's correspondents estimated that Edward was in command of 200,000 footmen and was still recruiting more,[35] while George Neville put the figure at 30,000.[36] Camulio was even more specific about the crowning ceremony Edward underwent and his intentions for the Lancastrian royal family;

I also wrote how the people of London, the leaders of the people of the island, together with some other lords, full of indignation, had created a new king, Edward, son of the Duke of York, known as my lord of March. From what we have heard since, he was chosen, so they say, on all sides as the new king by the princes and people at London. By the last letters they say that his lordship accepted the royal sceptre and staff and all the other ceremonies except the unction and the crown, which they have postponed until he has annihilated the other king and reduced the island and the realm to a stable peace, and among other things, exacted the vengeance due for the slaughter of his father and of so many knights and lords, who have been slain of late.[37]

It is difficult to imagine the mixture of emotions that news of this event elicited in Henry and Margaret, when it reached them in York. Anger, no doubt, at March's presumption; frustration, at his persistence and horror, at the affront this offered to God, by attempting to usurp an anointed king. If Henry ever doubted his own position and God's intentions for him, Margaret never did, fighting both for herself and her son.

Edward's unofficial succession angered Margaret's family too. On 10 March, it seemed that René of Anjou was planning to go and help his daughter, as a letter to the Duke of Milan related that,

a courier coming from Nice and Provence and going to Rome [reported] that King Rene is preparing a large force to go to help the Queen of England, and from what the courier says it seems that the English are much strengthened by means of the Duke of Burgundy. The King of France is said to be making great preparations for the future.[38]

The traditional rivalry between France and Burgundy meant that Burgundian overtures of friendship towards the new Yorkist regime served to galvanise the French in Margaret's favour, but in the end no such invasion force arrived. When Margaret's uncle, Charles VII, died that July, help for the Lancastrian cause seemed even less likely, as his successor, Louis XI, was keen to make peace with Edward.

Less than a week later, bizarre rumours circulated around Europe that Henry had abdicated in favour of his son, after which Margaret had given him poison. Heartlessly, Camulio spread the story that 'at least he [Henry] had known how to die, if he did not know what to do else', clearly believing that the king's weakness was the primary responsibility for the country's chaos. Camulio added, somewhat euphemistically, that it was said 'the queen will unite with the Duke of Somerset', which may have been intended to imply a personal connection now that, as he believed, the king was dead. Even Camulio was unsure of the veracity of this, though, wondering if these were 'the words of common fanatics, such as they have at present in that island'.[39] More substantial facts were related by George Neville, close enough to the action to be able to report with accuracy that his brother, Warwick, had set out for the west country on 7 March, in order to collect more troops, while March left London five days later, to seek out Henry and Margaret.[40] Camulio summed up their respective chances:

> Those who support the claims of Edward and Warwick say that the chances in favour of Edward are great, both on account of the great lordship which he has in the island and in Ireland, and owing to the cruel wrongs done to him by the queen's side, as well as through Warwick and London, which is entirely inclined to side with the new king and Warwick, and as it is very rich and the most wealthy city of Christendom, this enormously increases the chances of the side that it favours. To these must be added the good opinion of the temper and moderation of Edward and Warwick. Some, on the other hand, say that the queen is exceedingly prudent, and by remaining on the defensive, as they say she is well content to do, she will bring things into subjection and will tear to pieces these attacks of the people, who, when they perceive that they are not on the road to peace, will easily be induced to change sides, such being the very nature of the people, especially when free, and never to let things go so far that they cannot turn.[41]

The simultaneous existence of two kings in the country could not be allowed to continue. Waiting in York, Henry and Margaret understood that one must defeat the other in such a decisive way as to silence the alternative claimant. This meant a fight to the death or, at least, to another period of exile. Gathering their resources, accounts arrived of the progress of three separate armies, under Warwick's uncle, Lord Fauconberg, followed by a second wave led by Warwick himself, and a third branch that travelled up from the east, under the Duke of Norfolk. At this point, it must have been difficult to estimate how many men were fighting on York's side, or where the armies would converge. Until now, Henry's kingship had provided an essential trump card, placing any opposition army in fear of the charge of treason, but now, with two armies fighting under the names of two kings, that advantage was lost. On 28 March, the Yorkists came across a group of Lancastrians rebuilding a bridge at Ferrybridge, just outside Pontefract, and routed them. The following day, Palm Sunday, a huge battle was fought between the villages of Saxton and Towton, ten miles to the north.

Amid driving snow, what may have been as many as 100,000 men were deployed on a plateau of agricultural land, bound in on one side by the winding river Cock Beck. Henry and Margaret awaited the outcome in York, as Somerset, Trollope, Exeter and Northumberland led their armies against the combined forces of March, Salisbury, Norfolk, Warwick and Fauconberg. George Neville relates that the fighting began with the rising of the sun 'and lasted until the tenth hour of the night', while Vergil later related that it lasted ten hours. As Camulio stated, 'the combat was great and cruel, as happens when men fight for kingdom and life', with fortune seeming to favour the Lancastrians before the tide began to turn in favour of Edward. Early estimates suggested that around 28,000 had been killed, including Northumberland, Clifford and Sir Anthony Trollope, with many others drowning in the river as they tried to flee, or being cut down by their pursuing victors, over a radius of many miles. The Battle of Towton was one of the bloodiest and most terrible in English history, as recent excavations at the site have revealed but, if nothing else, it was decisive. Henry, Margaret and Prince Edward fled to Newcastle, 'full of sorrow and heaviness'[42] and Edward, Earl of March, underwent a formal coronation in St Paul's Cathedral as Edward IV.

*Chapter Nine*

# Royals in Waiting 1461–1470

## I

In the spring of 1461, Henry's formal tenure of kingship came to an end after almost forty years. With power shuttling back and forth between the two sides since 1453, the advantage had not favoured Lancaster or York for long before illness, battle or rebellion had destabilised any fragile truce or rule. The decisive defeat at Towton brought an end to that in a way that must have been recognisable as significant and lasting at the time. Margaret and Henry still clung to hope, with the queen launching herself into plans to raise money and arms, but the pair surely recognised that they faced a far greater struggle this time. The greatest problem was not so much that Edward had won the country by right of conquest, but in the contrasts between him and Henry, in terms of personality and ability.

A significant factor in contemporary perceptions of Henry VI's weakness was his inability to play the part convincingly, in terms of his behaviour and appearance. He favoured plain and simple clothing over ermine and cloth of gold and his preferred lifestyle was ascetic rather than luxurious; he would wear a rough hair shirt next to his skin on the occasions of feast days. As John Blacman recorded, after the king's death:

> Further of his humility in his bearing, in his clothes and other apparel of his body, in his speech and many other parts of his outward behaviour, it is well known that from his youth up he always wore round-toed shoes and boots like a farmer's. He also customarily wore a long gown with a rolled hood like a townsman, and a full coat reaching below his knees, with shoes, boots and foot-gear wholly black, rejecting expressly all curious fashion of clothing.
>
> Also at the principal feasts of the year, but especially at those when of custom he wore his crown, he would always have put on his bare body a rough hair shirt, that by its roughness his body might be restrained from excess, or more truly that all pride and vain glory, such as is apt to be engendered by pomp, might be repressed.[1]

Sir John Fortescue's treaty, *De Laudibus Legum Anglae* or *The Governance of England,* had exhorted Henry to dress the part, in 'rich clothes and rich furs ... rich stones and other jewels and ornaments ... rich hangings and other apparel for horses'. Henry was a model of piety, but not of kingship. Edward had a regal appearance; he was athletic, broad-shouldered, handsome, unusually tall at almost 6ft 4in, and was half Henry's age: the very image of medieval kingship. In character, Henry was gentle and pacific, pious and ascetic, and although he had made concerted efforts to present strong leadership, it could only represent a shadow of Edward's military abilities. Quite simply, Edward's sphere was warfare; he was a talented, even gifted general, dynamic, brave and active. Henry's 'softer' qualities, his compassion and mercy, as well as his religious devotion, suited him more to a life of pious retirement than the realpolitik of medieval warfare. Blacman related examples of his charity and mercy:

> First; once when he was coming down from St Albans to London through Cripplegate, he saw over the gate there the quarter of a man on a tall stake, and asked what it was. And when his lords made answer that it was the quarter of a traitor of his, who had been false to the king's majesty, he said: 'Take it away. I will not have any Christian man so cruelly handled for my sake.' And the quarter was removed immediately. He that saw it bears witness.
>
> Again, four nobles of high birth were convicted of treason and of the crime of lèse-majesté and were legally condemned therefor [sic] by the judges to suffer a shameful death. These he compassionately released, and delivered from that bitter death, sending the writ of his pardon for their delivery to the place of execution by a swift messenger.
>
> To other three great lords of the realm who conspired the death of this king (or conspired in the king's troubles) and assembled an innumerable host of armed men, aiming ambitiously to secure the kingly power, as manifestly appeared afterwards, the king showed no less mercy: for he forgave all, both the leaders and the men under them, what they had maliciously designed against him, provided they submitted themselves to him.[2]

Henry's naïve hope in organising the Loveday of 1458 underlines his style of kingship, while Edward's abilities came to the fore at Towton. Both kings could act out of character, as inconsistent as they were human, and both had flaws that interfered with the exercise of their roles but Edward's skills were a more successful match with the expectations of medieval kingship than Henry's. Edward won followers through his military record and the recent, relentless pursuit of the throne by his father. Henry's followers adhered to him for his personal qualities and his birthright as the son and heir of Henry V, but he was also widely criticised, his reign not being considered a success, with rebellion at home, losses abroad, financial disaster, unpopular favourites and a lack of strong leadership. By the end of August, when Count Dallugo spoke to Lord Rivers, 'the lords adherent to King Henry [were] all quitting him, and come to tender obedience to this king', and Rivers believed Henry's cause to be 'lost irretrievably'.[3]

With the Yorkists in the ascendant, the only option for the Lancastrian royal family was flight again. From Newcastle, Margaret and Edward rode at speed to the border town of Berwick, then on to Linlithgow Palace, where Mary of Guelders provided them with lodgings at Falkland. Henry made his way to join them separately, which was probably a precaution against the king and the heir both being captured, before staying at Linlithgow Palace, then at the Dominican Priory in Edinburgh. Henry Beaufort, Lord Roos and other Lancastrian survivors of the battle also made the Scots capital their safe haven. They were soon followed by a delegation sent by Edward IV, requesting that Mary surrender 'Harry, late usurpant King of our said Realm, Margaret his wife and her son', a request that was backed by Edward's allies, Philip of Burgundy and the Valois Dauphin Louis. Edward described them as 'traitors and rebels ... Henry, late usurpant king of our said realm, Margaret his wife and her son', and as 'late called king' and 'our great traitor and rebel'.[4] He also wrote letters to be circulated, explaining to the people the terms of agreements Margaret had made at Lincluden, which he judged would not be popular. On 1 June, Coppini wrote to the Pope that Henry and Margaret had ceded Berwick to the Scots, as outlined in the Treaty of Lincluden, so that it was 'suspected on all sides, that something fresh is in preparation ... and that these Scots are about to break into England with Henry, his son and wife, to recover the realm'.[5] Henry travelled south to Durham, as Margaret still had in her possession a handful of castles in the area, but was repelled by an army led by Lawrence Booth, Bishop of Durham, who had formerly been Margaret's Chancellor and now went over to the Yorkist side. Such betrayals cannot have been easy for the exiled Lancastrians to bear.

Margaret's nationality, and the old alliance of France and Scotland, was a dual edged sword for the queen. Her 'Frenchness', with all it represented in terms of English losses, gave her xenophobic subjects a cause for suspicion, but now it also offered the royal family a potential route of salvation, if they were able to harness the support of the Valois and Angevin kings. René and Charles were outraged to hear of the overthrow and exile of Margaret and her husband. One contemporary believed that 'the French also will assist, and render support both by land and sea, because they also are inflamed against the English, especially under these new conditions'.[6] Camulio heard that a force of 20,000 Frenchmen had left Normandy, to sail past Bristol and assemble an army in Wales, but because it was 'not easy to navigate' in that area and 'owing to a tide that lasts six hours', it was thought 'they cannot get any nearer to Scotland from that direction'.[7] The French army would arrive in due course, but only after Margaret had gone in person to request it. For the time being, she dispatched the Duke of Somerset, Lord Hungerford, Robert Whittingham and other Lancastrian Lords to France but, upon landing at Dieppe that July, they were arrested by the new king, Louis, and informed of the death of Charles VII. As Hungerford wrote to Margaret, to reassure her:

> Madam, fear you not, but be of good comfort, and beware that ye adventure not your person ne My Lord the Prince, by the sea, till ye have other word from us; in less than your person cannot be sure there, as ye are, and that extreme necessity drive you thence. And for God's sake, the King's Highness be advised the same for, as we be informed, the Earl of March is into Wales by land, and hath sent his navy thither by sea. And, Madam, think verily, we shall not sooner be delivered, but that we will come straight to you, without death take us by the way, the which we trust he will not, till we see the king and you peaceable again in your realm.[8]

By October 1461, as Henry Windsor wrote to John Paston, most of Wales had fallen to the Yorkists. The Duke of York and Earl of March had traditional ties with the country, especially through their associations with the administrative centre of Ludlow, but Henry's half-brother Jasper was half-Welsh so although Windsor might report that 'all the castles and strongholds in South Wales and North Wales are given and yielded up into the king's hand', Harlech remained a Lancastrian bastion until 1468. The letter also reported that 'the Duke of Exeter and the Earl of Pembroke are flown and taken to the mountains, and several lords with great power are after them, and the most part of gentlemen and men or worship are come unto the king, and have grace, of all Wales'.[9]

On 4 November, Edward's first parliament convened at Westminster and declared Henry to be a usurper, as a result of his grandfather, Henry IV, taking the throne from Richard II, whose heirs were the York/Mortimer family. Previous parliamentary action taken against Edward and his father was revoked and an Act of Attainder was issued against Henry, Margaret, Prince Edward and 140 leading Lancastrians.[10] Henry's reign was decried as a lawless, ungoverned period, where under 'the usurped reign of your said adversary Henry, late called King Henry VI, extortion, murder, rape, effusion of innocent blood, riot and unrightwiseness were commonly used in your said realm without punishment' so that the country had descended into 'misery, wretchedness, desolation, shameful and sorrowful decline'.[11] Unsurprisingly, Henry was accused of treason towards the Duke of York, as he had 'continued in his old rancour and malice, using the fraud and malicious deceit and dissimulation against truth and conscience ... with all subtle imaginations and deceitful ways and means to him possible, intended and covertly laboured, excited and procured the final destruction, murder and death of the said Richard.'[12] It appears that Edward was considering putting Henry on trial for murder, as Warwick was appointed to oversee the proceedings.[13] Although this never came to fruition, it was a serious threat against Henry's life and an affront to his birthright and anointed kingship. Whether or not Henry and Margaret knew of this is unclear.

Edward was heading to Scotland to negotiate a peace with Mary, when a more dangerous threat was exposed in the heart of his court. The loyal Lancastrian, Sir John de Vere, Earl of Oxford, had been attempting to avoid the new regime, feigning illness so as not to have to come to peace with Edward, as Lord Rivers and others had done. In his fifties, de Vere had a long history of loyalty to Queen Margaret. The exact nature of the plot is only known in outline, with chroniclers focused more on the outcome than the plan, but the intention appears to have been Edward's murder, and the restoration of the Lancastrian line under Henry. A letter written by Warwick and de la Torre to Coppini suggests that de Vere intended to travel with Edward's army into the north, fall back and attack them from behind once the Lancastrian army appeared. Henry was to lead troops down from Scotland, Somerset was to bring troops from Bruges and Pembroke from Brittany. In addition, Warwick adds,

> some priests and others also have been taken, because so they say, they wrote some notices over the doors of the churches in which they stated that the supreme pontiff had revoked all that your lordship had done in this kingdom, that he gave plenary absolution to all those who would be with King Henry and excommunicated those who were with our king.[14]

Had all those elements come together as planned, they might have proved devastating for the new regime.

Yet the planned rebellion did not succeed as, reputedly, Edward was saved by divine intervention, when 'God sent the king himself knowledge of these treasons'. Hearne's fragment states that de Vere was accused by his own son, Aubrey, who was then arrested with him. However, this has largely been discounted by historians, in favour of Warwick's assertion that one of the messengers passing between de Vere and Margaret suffered from a guilty conscience in a Yorkshire church and, instead of continuing to the queen, surrendered his missive to Edward. A Thomas Howes wrote to John Paston that 'hit was leten me wete in right secret wise that a puissance is ready to arrive in three parties of this land, by the mean of King Henry and the queen that was, and by the Duke of Somerset and others', landing their forces up the River

Trent, in the Channel Islands and in Wales. Howes had heard that 120,000 men were involved, but this must be an over-exaggeration.[15] An alternative version, in the *Brief Latin Chronicle* suggests that Somerset and Oxford were intending to land an army on the coast of Essex.[16] Between 12 and 20 February, John de Vere, his son Aubrey, Sir Thomas Tuddenham and William Tyrell underwent a trial in the Tower, officiated over by John Tiptoft, Earl of Worcester, who condemned them to death. Their executions on 26 February were especially violent, leaving Tiptoft with a reputation he would never lose, which would catch up with him at the Lancastrian restoration in 1470.

A year after she had been displaced as queen, Margaret set sail for France, determined to return at the head of an invading force. Leaving Henry behind at the Scots court, she sailed with her son from Kirkcudbright and landed in Brittany on 8 April 1462. Abbé Prevost, relating her life in the early eighteenth century, recorded that she was 'entirely destitute of money', and so, was 'indebted for the means of performing this voyage to the gratitude of a French merchant who, in her early days she had rendered an important service at her father's court at Nancy'.[17] Margaret headed to Touraine to meet with her cousin Louis, who was also a grandchild of Yolande of Aragon. The reunion took place at the Chateau de Chinon, on the bank of the Vienne, situated in the forest between Tours and Angers. It was the first time the queen had returned home since her marriage at the age of 15. Then, she had departed on a high, amid celebrations, to become a queen; now, in her early thirties, she was back as an exile, named as a traitor by her subjects, pleading for assistance on behalf of her son. Overlooking the river, the royal apartments of the chateau were made from a clean, white local stone. Some sources state that Margaret was welcomed by Louis, who 'expressed the greatest concern for her misfortune', but Agnes Strickland's account of the meeting assumes the opposite, that Louis was 'callous to her impassioned eloquence' in spite of the pair having been attached as children. Louis did see an opportunity to profit from Margaret's distress, as the treaty they signed on 28 June contained a clause whereby she would hand over Calais, although in turn, he would give her 2,000 men led by Pierre de Brezé and a loan of 20,000 livres:

> Margaret, Queen of England, being empowered by the King of England, Henry VI, her husband, acknowledges the sum of twenty thousand livres lent to her by the King Louis XI, to the restitution of which she obliges the town and citadel of Calais, promising that as soon as the king her husband shall recover it, he will appoint there as Captain his brother Jasper, Earl of Pembroke, or her cousin, Jean de Foix, Count of Candale, who will engage to surrender the said town to King Louis XI within one year as his own,

or pay to the said King Louis XI, forty thousand livres. Sealed at Chinon, Juin 1462.[18]

De Brezé was the Seneschal of Normandy who had fought with Yolande of Aragon and been formerly Seneschal of Anjou, knighted by Charles of Anjou, Margaret's uncle. According to Villaret, de Brezé was more willing to help than Louis, because he 'entertained for the queen more tender sentiments than pity and compassion'.[19] While Margaret was at Chinon she stood as godmother to Louis, son of the Duke of Orleans, to whom the king, his namesake, was godfather.

By July, 1462 hopes were cautiously rising in England, when Thomas Playters wrote to John Paston that 'King Harry and his adherents in Scotland shall be delivered … the queen and the prince have been in France [and persuaded] many people to come to Scotland, where they trust to have succour, and then to come into England.'[20] That October, Margaret left France with de Brezé and an army that some sources put at 6,000 soldiers, perhaps swelled by Pierre's Norman troops. They endured a 'tedious and tempestuous passage' before attempting to land at Tynemouth on the Northumberland coast. According to Prevost and Holinshed, the garrison there pointed its guns at her fleet, so they put to sea again, heading north when they were caught in a storm and many of her ships were stranded near Bamburgh Castle. Gregory relates that this was seven days before the great All Hallows tide, so weather conditions were terrible. The *Great Chronicle* adds that she landed there 'with a small army, came out of France into Scotland and, enjoying the aid of the King of Scots, crossed the border into England and made sharp war'. Edward headed north to respond, but she had advanced warning, and fled back to Scotland at such speed that she suffered losses:

> She was so sharply pursued that she was forced to take a carvel and, with a small number of supporters, sail to some coast for her safeguard. Not long after, such a tempest arose that she had to abandon her carvel and take a fishing boat; by this means she was preserved and able to land at Berwick, for shortly after the carvel was sunk and, with it, much of the queen's riches. Shortly after, about 400 Frenchmen of her retinue were, by the force of this tempest, driven ashore near the castle of Bamburgh … and afterwards, rode to an island off Northumberland, [Holy Island] where they met a squire named Manners and the Bastard of Ogle who … skirmished with the Frenchmen, and took and slew most of them.[21]

De Brezé was one of the few who managed to escape and joined Margaret in Scotland.

Henry had been waiting, in hiding, at Harlech Castle, and was now reunited with his wife and son. With Prince Edward safely stowed at Berwick, they spent the coming months battling to keep control of the border in the face of raids led by the Earl of Warwick. Bamburgh Castle on the Northumberland coast had been held by Somerset, Pembroke, Roos and Percy, and a garrison of around 300 men, but it fell to the Yorkists after a nine-month siege, and the persistent bombardment of their superior artillery. Eighteen miles to the south, the Captain of Alnwick Castle, who had been appointed by Edward IV, was betrayed by the sympathetic Sir Ralph Grey. He handed the property back to the Lancastians, an act for which he would pay with his life, when he was executed by Yorkists in the summer of 1464.[22] Dunstanburgh Castle was also returned to Margaret under similar circumstances by Sir Ralph Percy, who switched sides after being granted custody of it by Edward. Norham Castle, near Newcastle, had been held by the Yorkists but in 1463, De Brezé laid siege to it for eighteen days until Warwick and his brother, Lord Montagu, arrived to alleviate the soldiers inside. Warwick and his armies then went on to ravage the borderlands. It must have felt as if Henry and Margaret were continually fighting in the attempt to stem an interminable tide.

Events of the following spring were to prove decisive for Henry and Margaret, largely due to the vacillations of one man. From being the 'hope of the Lancastrian party' in the years following the first battle of St Albans, Henry Beaufort, Duke of Somerset, had made efforts to befriend the triumphant Yorkist king, even becoming a close personal friend. Having been attainted on Edward's accession, he surrendered Bamburgh Castle at the end of 1462 and received a royal pardon the following spring. Yet the son of York and the son of Somerset, between whose fathers there had been so much enmity, would never have a comfortable relationship. Their attempts to forge a peace sounds intense, even claustrophobic, with Edward keeping Henry close, perhaps through the affection that developed, perhaps through mistrust. Reports suggest they were in each others' company night and day, a similar age, and similar characters, hunting, fighting tournaments together, with Henry being afforded the honour of being the bodyguard who, as the custom dictated, shared the king's bed. In the autumn of 1463, when the pair were at Northampton, an unsuccessful attack upon Beaufort led Edward to send him to Chirk Castle for his safety, where he appears to have had a change of heart and returned to the Lancastrian fold. Evading attempts to arrest him, he hastened to join Henry VI who was then at Bamburgh. The following April (1464), Beaufort launched a surprise attack upon Montagu's army at Hedgely Moor, but the death of Sir Henry Percy scattered the Lancastrian effort. Montagu pursued the fleeing rebels, to catch up with Beaufort and Hexham Bridge in May, where the young Duke was defeated and killed. This bad news was shortly followed by the information that Edward had signed the Treaty of York with James III of Scotland, the son of Mary of Guelders, who had been ruling for himself since the death of his mother the previous December. Thus, Henry and Margaret lost significant members of their party, allies and their safe Scottish haven.

Margaret's nineteenth-century biographer, Mary Ann Hookham, dates the incident of Margaret being robbed to the aftermath of Hexham. With the poetic but dubious claim that 'her adventures that night were so romantic as to raise the tone of history', Hookham describes how the queen was 'wandering, with her little son, in the darkness of the night', when she met a band of 'ruffians' in the woods who, 'unawed by her rank and untouched by pity for her sex or situation, they seized her, stripped her of her jewels, and would have treated her with even greater indignity' had they not quarrelled about the division of their spoils. She escaped while they fought, carrying Edward through the forest, 'oppressed with fatigue and hunger, and almost overcome with terror and anxiety', before encountering a man with a knife. According to Hookham, 'the great soul of Queen Margaret would never succumb under any accumulation of misfortunes', so she approached the man with confidence and presented her son, saying 'here, my friend, I entrust to your care the safety of your king's son'. Whereupon, fairy-tale-like, he turned out to have been outlawed for his 'adherence' to the Lancastrian cause and led her to shelter in a nearby cave.[23] Such a story is a colourful embellishment to the narrative of Margaret's life but there is no evidence for it, beyond the existence of a cave and a legend. However, it may contain something of an emotional truth regarding the queen's character and determination. It also fits with the mood of May, 1464, when her fortunes were at their lowest ebb.

## II

Soon after Hexham, Margaret made the decision to leave England again, to seek foreign aid. Gregory relates that it was the losses at Hexham that prompted her to flee 'wythe alle hir counsel' incuding her son, de Brezé and Beaufort's brothers Edmund and John, taking a ship for Sluys in Flanders. However, the chronicle adds the detail that she 'lefte Kyng Harry that was behind ... and all her horse and her harnesses', because they were 'so hasted by my Lord of Warwick'.[24] Gregory's account make it seem almost accidental, even careless, that Henry was left behind, but there are likely to have been sound reasons for this. It may have been essential for Henry to remain in order to see any necessary business in England, while his wife was busy abroad, but also on a symbolic level, considering that the king was seen to be the embodiment of his country, he may have seen his flight as an admission of failure too far. For all his flaws in providing consistent leadership, Henry was committed to the welfare of his country. If Margaret could take an entourage of around 200 with her abroad, including a number of leading knights and ladies, plus their households,[25] the omission of Henry was no accident. There is no doubt that the king was pursued closely after Hexham, losing some of his entourage, but he made no move to follow Margaret abroad once he had got free. Instead he went into hiding, possibly heading to Harlech.

Margaret's intention was to petition Duke Philip of Burgundy for assistance. After landing on the coast near Sluys, her party travelled to Bruges, where she was given an honourable reception, and left a section of her party behind, including Prince Edward. From there, she travelled fifty miles south, over the French border to the city of Lille, and on to Bethune, where she was met by Philip's son Charles, Count of Charolais, later to succeed his father as Charles the Bold. Charles was then aged 30, just three years younger than Margaret, 'the most magnificent prince of his age',[26] but they also had in common their connection to the Lancastrian line, as Charles's grandmother, Philippa, had been a daughter of John of Gaunt. Another tie was established by his father Philip the Good, Duke of Burgundy, who was an uncle of Henry's by marriage. In his youth, Philip had been married to Michelle of Valois, a daughter of Charles VI, and sister to Henry's mother Catherine during his youth, making a connection with both the worlds in which Henry and Margaret had inhabited as children. By 1463, Philip was 67, and had married three times, fathered four legitimate children and at least eighteen illegitimate ones. During his long reign he had presided over a magnificent court, the seat of the Order of the Golden Fleece, which he had founded, based in Lille, Brussels and Bruges. He created a world of chivalry and extravagance in clothing, feasting, pageantry, art and spectacle, setting a style that, ironically, Edward IV would seek to emulate in England.

While Margaret was in Bethune, being entertained by Charles, Philip was at St Pol, but he dispatched an armed escort to ensure her safety and arranged for her to be lodged with the Carmelite nuns. Margaret was again welcomed and, when the Duke arrived, proceed to relate her circumstances. However, she found Philip less than sympathetic towards Henry's predicament, he had already allied himself with the Yorkists and in four years' time, his son Charles would marry Edward's sister Margaret. Yet on a personal level, as one ruler to another, Philip understood Margaret of Anjou's predicament and was generous in offering her 2,000 gold crowns for her current expenses, along with 1,000 to de Brezé and 100 to each of her ladies.[27] He instructed the escort he had granted Margaret to accompany her to the Duchy of Bar, then held by her brother John, Duke of Calabria. Six years older than his sister, John could sympathise with her predicament, dedicating his time to efforts to regain the family territory of Naples.

At some point soon after her return home, Margaret was reunited with the father she had not seen in two decades. René of Anjou was in his mid-fifties when she arrived, still presiding over a court of cultural splendour, although he had signed over the governance of Lorraine to his son John, and had remarried. Margaret's mother, Isabel, had died in 1453 and the following year René had married Jeanne de Laval, daughter of Guy, Count of Laval. Revisiting her childhood home at Angers, Margaret met this new step-mother who was three years her junior and probably went to visit the tomb erected to her mother in the cathedral. During this time, René was devoting himself to artistic pursuits, writing letters, poetry, painting and composing his magnum opus, his *Tournament Book*, which explored the history of the combat known as the mêlée, and offered new ideas to be used in planning future entertainments. It may have been based on a series of tournaments held at Angers in the 1460s, possibly some witnessed by Margaret, and was included in an inventory that listed 202 books in the ducal library in 1471. He was also still hosting spectacular masques and performances, including mummeries and Moorish dances, in which some of his grandchildren took part, although the identities of which ones is unknown. In 1464 or 65, René made his exiled daughter the offer of a pension of 6,000 French crowns and the residency of Chateau Koeur-la-Petite, lying four miles to the south-west of Saint Mihiel-en-Bar, near a bend in the River Meuse, in the Duchy of Bar, in Lorraine. It was to be her home for the next seven years, the most permanent and significant home that the young Prince Edward would know.

The two villages of Koeur-la-Grand and Koeur-la-Petite sit about a mile apart, looking, to all appearances, to be typical small settlements of the area. The Voie des Koeurs, which connects them, reveals flat lands on both sides, with a handful of square, beige houses lining the route, and most landmarks including the church, small square and pond, dating to a later period than the one Edward would have known. Much of the village was destroyed in fighting during the First World War but two surviving postcards show images of an 'ancien Château' and 'vieux Château', clearly the same building, in existence shortly before this time. The two images are taken from a similar perspective, showing a building of substantial size, with a long wing of two storeys, flanked by seven large decorative archways containing smaller windows. At the far end it abuts a taller section with three storeys and on the near end, closest to the photographer, another part contains a small doorway up three steps and a shuttered window. One photograph shows that the building is constructed of old, substantial stones at the foundation level. Children sit on the step, a broom leans against the wall and local people stand on the path before it, alongside a small piece of grass and a tree. It may well be that this was the place where the Lancastrians stayed, repaired and improved by later generations, or else this building was erected on the foundations of the original. The existence of a Ruelle de Chateau, midway between the main road and a tributary of the river suggests its original location, although the building there is listed as dating to the first part of the eighteenth century. Here, or near here, the exiled queen and prince established their own Lancastrian court.

Around her, Margaret gathered a court of exiled Lancastrians. Possibly the most influential was Sir John Fortescue, a veteran of English law, and loyal servant of Henry VI, whom Margaret appointed as tutor to the 10-year-old Edward. Born 1394, Fortescue was an MP and chief justice, the king's Lord Chancellor in exile, although this was technically invalid as he was not in possession of the great seal, the essential ingredient to make the matter legal. In France, Fortescue composed a number of works on subjects including the nature of law and the law of nature, on the differences between an absolute and a limited monarchy, on England's constitutional framework and the conceptual and political basis of English law. As Edward's tutor, he wrote *De Laudibus Legum Angliae* around 1468–71, as a manual to assist a future monarch. It takes the form of a dialogue between tutor and pupil, with Fortescue proposing certain areas of study and the prince making his reply.

Margaret took the education of her son seriously. While in exile from their kingdom, he became the focus of their hopes, a future king in training, whom she hoped would avenge the indignities forced upon his father. The poet George Ashby, a former Keeper of the Signet to Henry VI, who arrived at the castle in 1464, had either just been released, or had escaped from the Fleet Prison in London, perhaps having been incarcerated there by the Yorkists. His poem *The Active Policy of a Prince* is dedicated to 'your highnesse Edward by name, trewe son and heir of the high majestie of oure liege lorde Kynge Henry and dame Margarete, the Quene' and drew heavily on the boy's lineage and right to rule. It was written in the anticipation that he would continue the legacy of his Lancastrian forebears 'aftur the statues autorised by noble kynges your progenitours', with particular focus on eradicating the threats of traitors: 'suppresse youre false conspiratours, aftur the lawe and constitucion, established ayenst opyn traitorous'.[28] The poem offers the child a model of kingship that would have been complementary to his mother's respect for the dynasty and active approach to dealing with potential challenges to it. It echoes many of the instructional manuals of the day with its emphasis on finding a middle path, not being too hasty or too slow, too lofty or too simple, but to choose clever servants, act wisely, subdue rebellion, heed the lessons of the French wars and to show traitors no mercy 'if th'offence touche the subversion of the realm'. Broken into three sections representing the past, present and future, it exhorted him to live within his means and not make the same mistakes as his father. He praised Edward for his circumspection, for living without funding from Parliament, choosing his advisors carefully and listening to them, paying debts, being quick and decisive, and staying in charge. The Prince should remember the recent conflicts as well as those of the past, and think carefully before beginning fresh conflict:

> *I would fain you keep in remembrance*
> *The be right well advised by good sadness*
> *By discreet prudence and faithful constancy*
> *Before you begin a war for any riches,*
> *Or out of fantasy or simplicity.*
> *For war may be lightly commenced*
> *The doubt is how it shall be recompensed.*[29]

There were other figures in Koeur-la-Petite who influenced the growing youth. Along with the ever-present Margaret was a group of her chaplains, headed by a Thomas Bird, Bishop of St Asaph, who had formed part of the queen's entourage upon her entry to England in 1445.[30] She also gave a home to about fifty members of the exiled Lancastrian court, including the Dukes of Exeter, Edmund Beaufort, the new Duke of Somerset and his brother John, the Earls of Ormond and Devon, Edward's receiver-general Sir Richard Wittingham, his chamberlain Sir Edmund Hampden and his chancellor, John Morton. Jasper Tudor, the King's half-brother, was in France during the first winter of the prince's exile and may have travelled the 170 miles east to report on his efforts to raise funds from Louis XI. Their resources were stretched but, through her prudence, Margaret used her income to sustain them. As Sir John Fortescue wrote to the Earl of Ormonde, who was then in Portugal, 'we are all in great poverty, but yet the Queen sustaineth us in meat and drink, so we be not in extreme necessity. Her highness may do no more than she doth.'[31]

Early in 1465, rumours reached Margaret's little court that fractures were appearing in the formerly close friendship between Edward IV and Richard Neville, Earl of Warwick. The queen was quick to recognise that if her enemies fought among themselves, they were vulnerable to attack from the Lancastrians. On 6 February, Maletta, the Milanse Ambassador in France, described how Margaret wrote to Louis XI that she was advised that King Edward and the Earl of Warwick,

> have come to very great division and war together. She begs the king here to
> be pleased to give her help so that she may be able to recover her kingdom

or at least allow her to receive assistance from the lords of this kingdom who are willing to afford this, and if he will not take any one of these courses, she writes that he will take the best course that she can.[32]

However, having come to terms with Edward himself, Louis remarked upon the arrogance of the letter, commenting, 'look how proudly she writes'.[33] Nothing came of this opportunity, but it was an indicator of change to come.

As that summer arrived at Koeur-la-Petite, Margaret heard about an event that had taken place in London, which she cannot have chosen to accept. In secret, Edward IV had married a young widow, Elizabeth Woodville, whose husband Sir John Grey was killed fighting for the Lancastrians at the second Battle of St Albans. As his wife, and as the daughter of Jacquetta, Baroness Rivers, Elizabeth may well have been known to Margaret, possibly even having met her, although there is no truth in the claims that the younger woman served her queen as lady in waiting. With the Woodville family making their peace with Edward and this marriage, further old ties were broken, although Margaret was probably shrewd enough to realise that many of these new alliances were concessions made through necessity to prevent conflict with the new regime. What was most difficult though, was that at the end of May 1465, Elizabeth Woodville underwent a magnificent coronation in Westminster Abbey, almost exactly twenty years to the day since the same ceremony had been performed for Margaret.

Then, in July, King Henry was captured again by the Yorkists. Having spent the last year in flight, trying to avoid his enemies, Henry had made himself a base of sorts at Bamburgh Castle in Northumberland. The account of his confessor, John Blacman, was written in indignation that 'after the horrid and ungrateful rebellion of his subjects had continued a long time and after these rebels had fought many hard battles against him, [Henry] fled at last with a few followers to a secret place prepared for him by those that were faithful to him'. He might have remained there in safety except, in 1465, he had attempted to re-enter England. Blacman blames the king's 'madness', stating that 'as he lay hid there for some time, an audible voice sounded in his ears for some seventeen days before he was taken, telling him how he should be delivered up by treachery'. Other sources suggest he was tricked into accepting hospitality from his enemies and taken hostage in Lancashire,[34] from whence he was led south, tied to his saddle. Vergil relates that the king may have been 'past all fear or driven deeply to some kind of madness' to enter England in disguise, while Gregory adds that he proceeded as far as Furness Fells, seventy miles over the Scottish border before he was recognised. He was several times sheltered by a John Maychell of Crackenthorpe, who was later pardoned by Edward for this, but was captured at Waddington Hall near Clitheroe, the home of Sir Richard Tempest, as he was having dinner.[35] He briefly escaped again, but was recaptured in Clitherwood by Sir Richard and his brother John, who were rewarded with the lands formerly owned by Henry's carver, Sir Richard Tunstall.[36]

Blacman says Henry experienced a vision, a 'revelation from the Blessed Virgin Mary and Saints John Baptist, Dunstan and Anselm', which foresaw how he was brought to London 'without all honour like a thief or an outlaw, and led through the midst of it', having to endure 'many evils devised by the thoughts of wicked men'. The vision strengthened him 'to bear with patience these and like trials' as he was carried to London, his feet bound to his stirrups.[37] On 24 June, Warwick met him at Islington and conducted him on an ignominious ride through the streets of the capital before he was committed as a prisoner to the Tower of London. With his father no longer at liberty, a greater burden fell upon the shoulders of young Prince Edward in France, who represented the hopes for the Lancastrian dynasty: from this point, if not before, his thoughts and preparations must have been dominated by the idea of regaining his kingdom. Having lost so many of her close friends, Margaret must have feared for her husband's life in Yorkist custody after the act of attainder passed against him in 1461.

Very little information survives about Henry's captivity. Blacman's hagiographical work claims he underwent severe trials; abuse, mockery, starvation, in order to draw a parallel with Christ's suffering, but there is no evidence surviving to support this. It is most likely that he was given a quiet, simple regime as 'Henry of Windsor' in the Wakefield Tower, in a first floor octagonal room with stone vaulted ceiling, containing chapel and an alcove for a bed. He was attended by five key members of Edward's household, with as many as twenty-two members of staff, including guards, and his weekly maintenance cost 5 marks. A priest named William Kymberley celebrated mass for him daily, he wore clothes made from velvet from the royal wardrobes and drank wine from the royal cellars.[38] Most significantly, it was a passive existence, which removed from Henry the need to make decisions or take action, reducing him to a symbolic rather than an active role in the conflict. While he remained in Yorkist hands, his captivity validated their rule and, although it provided a motive and figurehead for Lancastrian attempts to free him, the security of the Tower made this unlikely. Unless it was brought about by an insider. And that is exactly what would happen.

The indication of dissention among the Yorkist ranks that had surfaced in 1465 took a step closer to completion in 1467. Warwick had not approved of Edward's secret marriage, having been encouraged by the king to arrange a match for him with Bona of Savoy, Louis's sister-in-law. When the king was forced to announce his actions, it left Warwick looking a fool and further conflict developed as Edward's pro-Burgundian policy came into conflict with Warwick's commitment to France. That February, Margaret's brother John, Duke of Calabria, accompanied Louis on a pilgrimage to Bourges, and their talk over the dinner table turned from hunting and hawking to the earl. Naturally, John spoke vehemently against Warwick, in defence of his sister, denouncing him as a traitor and 'would not say or suffer any good to be said of him'. Calabria outlined how he 'only studied to deceive, he was the enemy and the cause of the fall of King Henry and his sister the Queen of England'. He advised Louis that he 'would do better to help his sister to recover her kingdom than to favour the Earl', an attitude which the ambassador described as 'exaggerated' and 'opprobrious'.[39] Louis defended Warwick, as he had 'always been a friend to his crown and had advised against making war on his realm'. On the other hand, Henry had proved 'a mortal enemy and had waged many wars against him', so the friendship of the earl was 'worth preserving'. This led Calabria to suggest that as Louis was so fond of Warwick, he should incite him to 'try and restore his sister in that kingdom', and spoke with passion on the topic demonstrating, perhaps, a similar kind of personality or temperament to his sister. The first glimmers of a restoration plan were born that night:

> The king asked what security they would give or if they would offer the queen's son as a hostage. This boy, though only thirteen years of age, already talks of nothing but of cutting off heads or making war, as if he had everything in his hands or was the god of battle or the peaceful occupant of that throne. The king also asked, supposing they promised, if the security would be observed. At this the duke in a [rage] said that if his nephew promised at his instance and did not keep his word, he would have to reckon with him and with others, and they would fly at him and tear out his eyes.
>
> After some further discussion the duke began to complain about his Majesty without any respect, saying he had never loved their house; to which the king retorted that the House of Anjou had given him reason for this. Thus, half joking, they said very sharp things to each other during the dinner.[40]

In late April or early May, Margaret welcomed a visitor to her exiled court. The 18-year-old Nicholas, Marquis of Pont-à-Mousson, was her youngest nephew, the son of her brother John. The vigilant Milanese ambassadors reported that he had left his home in Nancy 'and gone to visit the late Queen of England', and that she had been invited by Louis 'to come and stay at the court here … the king has sent the Count of Vaudemont to fetch her, and she should soon be here'.[41] It appears that Margaret never went, though. The reason may appear in the Ambassador's letter of four days later, which reports that Louis was on his way to Rouen to meet the Earl of Warwick: 'there has been talk of treating with the Earl of Warwick to restore King Henry in England'.[42] Sensing that she was being summoned to comply with the French King's plan to unite her and the earl, the exiled queen may have refused. Margaret was not yet ready to sign a deal with her mortal enemy; three more years would pass before it would take place. Alternatively, she may have offered terms that the earl rejected, or she rejected his, as the letter commented on 9 May that 'the ambassador of the old Queen of England is already here'.[43] It may also have been that Prince Edward was ill during this time, which prevented their departure. Apparently, that year he recovered from a serious malady, after which his mother undertook a pilgrimage to the shrine of St Nicholas de Port, the patron saint of Lorraine, to give thanks for his recovery.

However Warwick had planned to assist Louis and Margaret failed to translate into anything practical that year, but the intention was there. French ambassadors travelled to England that summer, where they found the earl 'unable to effect what he had promised on his departure' because he had met with 'many opponents to his plan', so no 'positive arrangement was made'. They did, though, find King Edward 'very averse to France', and 'constantly at strife' with Warwick, which helped push the earl into the arms of the Lancastrians. The Milanese Ambassador reported uprisings in Wales on behalf of Henry, to where Jasper Tudor had been dispatched, with additional followers sent by Margaret 'to make their party take the field if possible'.[44] Louis was expressing dissatisfaction with Warwick that September, but through the winter and into 1468, he warmed more to the idea of supporting the earl against Edward. This meant that Margaret became a viable potential ally and by October that year, Louis was saying 'that he means to help the old Queen of England [and] favour her in that enterprise as much as possible'. A factor that further committed the French king against the Yorkist regime was the marriage of his traditional enemy, the Duke of Burgundy, to Edward's sister Margaret of York.

It has been claimed, by Abbé Prevost, that Margaret visited England in 1467, wearing a heavy disguise, in the train of the Archbishop of Narbonne, Antoine du Bec-Crispin. This was an important embassy sent by Louis in response to deteriorating Anglo-French relations in an attempt to gain concessions from Edward. The named ambassadors were the Bastard of Bourbon, the Bishop of Laon, John Popaurcote and Oliver Rous, who remained at the English court for four months, receiving gifts of dogs, collars and horns from the king. It seems a bizarre and unlikely suggestion that Margaret may have been among them, unrecognised, but the rumours were fuelled by such comments as made by William of Worcester, that various individuals were arrested and condemned, on suspicion of having carried letters for her. Holinshed relates that one of her agents, a man named Hawkins, implicated others when he was under torture with the result that a London alderman, Thomas Cook, was fined 8,000 marks and a shoemaker suffered a painful death for reputedly facilitating her correspondence.

In the summer of 1468, in response to threats by Edward IV to invade France, Louis funded a Lancastrian army of 200 ships which landed close to Harlech on the North Wales coast.[45] Led by Jasper Tudor, who was 'devoting himself to gathering as many of his partisans there as he can', they reputedly 'had some 4,000 English put to death'.[46] This figure may be hugely exaggerated, but the source was correct that Wales had 'always been well affected towards' the Lancastrians, and that this year would prove decisive for Tudor's forces there. Harlech Castle, where both Henry and Margaret had formerly sought shelter, which had held out against Yorkist assaults since Henry's deposition, was a significant symbol of the dynastic struggles and the widening breach between Warwick and Edward. The previous October, the Yorkist Earl of Herbert had intercepted a messenger on the way to Harlech carrying letters from Margaret to Tudor, which implicated Warwick. Tudor captured Denbigh, and held court there in Henry's name but, on the occasion of his absence, a double-sided attack upon Harlech by Herbert led the castle to surrender.

With Warwick's dissatisfaction simmering, problems arose between Edward and his brother George, Duke of Clarence, who was then aged 19. Following on from the prestigious match between his sister and the Duke of Burgundy, George hoped that he would be provided with a wife of international importance, requesting that his brother match him with the duke's heiress, Mary of Burgundy, which would have brought him considerable wealth, lands and titles. Edward though, for reasons of his own, did not favour the marriage, perhaps feeling that it would bring the volatile Clarence too much power that he was ill-equipped to deal with. In response, George rebelled against his brother, allying with Warwick and sailing for Calais. There, in an act of defiance against Edward, he married the Earl's elder daughter, Isabel Neville, on 11 July 1469. Warwick and George returned to England almost at once, leaving behind the Countess of Warwick, Isabel of Clarence and her younger sister Anne Neville. There was already discontent in the north, either stirred up or exploited by the earl, who circulated rumours that Edward was illegitimate and Clarence, his new son-in-law, was the true Yorkist claimant to the throne. At the end of July, the two sides clashed at Edgecote Moor, with Warwick capturing Edward for his own 'protection', a tactic that sounds very much like that formerly employed against Henry. Warwick sent his ambassador to Louis 'to make an understanding', and the messenger returned 'very satisfied'.[47] Although the situation came to nothing at this point, with the brothers reconciling and Warwick 'allowing' Edward to escape from Middleham Castle, this development presented Margaret with hope that another opportunity of weakness would arise, which she might exploit. If the Earl of Warwick was powerful enough to overthrow Edward in 1469, he may be persuaded to do so again on behalf of the Lancastrians. Strickland relates that at the end of the year, Margaret's family, including King Louis, her father René, her brother John, her elder sister Yolande and her brother-in-law Ferri de Vaudemont, gathered at Tours 'to hold a council on the best means of improving the momentous crisis for the cause of Lancaster'. Margaret and her father 'embraced with floods of tears[48] and even the French king 'betrayed unwonted tokens of sensibility'.

## Chapter Ten

# Readeption 1470–1471

In the summer of 1470, Margaret prepared to set aside all the accumulated years of bitterness and dislike she felt towards the Earl of Warwick, and went to meet her former enemy. It was a difficult step for the proud Lancastrian queen, for whom the earl had been the cause of so much heartache and loss. Parted from her husband for seven years and raising her son in exile, outcast from the kingdom she had been anointed to rule, Margaret must have wrestled with her conscience before agreeing that, in the interests of her son, she would forge a deal with the devil. Equally, Warwick was uneasy about coming face to face with the woman he had deposed as queen, not wishing to be present when she arrived, hoping that Louis would 'shape matters a little with her' before he provided the 'finishing touches'.

A second attempted rebellion against Edward had been defeated at the Battle of Losecoat Field (Battle of Empingham), where Warwick and Clarence's allegiance had been discovered, forcing them to flee the country. Taking a boat to Calais, they found their entrance to be blocked by Edward's command, and were forced to seek an alternative place to land. Tossed by storms, Isabel, Duchess of Clarence, lost her first child, before they could reach a safe haven down the coast. Far from being in charge of the country, with 'the tart [being] divided between them',[1] they were now traitors and had nothing to lose by entering into a deal with their former enemies. Upon his arrival in France, the earl made his way to the Chateau of Amboise, to meet with Louis. There, they were 'closely closeted and in secret councils' which gave the king 'plenty to think about', although he did not yet show 'any inclination to help him in his kingdom'. Instead, according to the Milanese Ambassador, Louis urged Warwick 'by every means in his power ... to return to England, and has sent to offer him ships and troops to fight'. It was rumoured that the earl would indeed soon return, taking with him 'the Prince of Wales, son of King Henry, and [would] take the part of that king to see if, in that way, he will enjoy better success than he did in the other'.[2]

On June 25, Edward and Margaret arrived at the Chateau of Amboise, on the Loire, 300 miles to the west of Koeur-la-Petite. They were received 'in a very friendly and honourable manner' by Louis, who spent 'every day in long discussions with that queen to induce her to make the alliance ... and to let the prince, her son, go with the Earl to the enterprise of England'. Initially, Margaret showed 'herself very hard and difficult' and would 'on no account whatever' allow Edward to go with Warwick 'as she mistrusts him'.[3] Instead, it was suggested that the prince remain behind and Jasper Tudor take his place at Warwick's side, but the symbolic presence of Edward could not be overlooked and it is likely that the young man urged her to let him go, so a compromise was reached. The Milanese Ambassador summed up the progress that had been made by Louis' negotiations, no doubt fuelled by the Burgundian support sent to Edward:

> The Queen of England, wife of King Henry, has been induced to consent to do all that his Majesty desires, both as regards a reconciliation with Warwick and the marriage alliance. The said queen and Warwick are expected here in a day or two, to arrange everything finally, and then Warwick will return to England without losing time. The Prince of Wales will not go with him this first time, but one of his uncles will go, a brother of King Henry, who is here. If matters go prosperously, then the prince will go back immediately, otherwise he will not set foot there.
>
> The Duke of Burgundy, with all his power, has sent assistance in ships and troops to King Edward, in order to prevent Warwick from descending again upon England, but it is thought he will not be able to prevent it because Warwick will go to land in the country of Wales, where it is presumed he will be gladly received, because all the men of that part are thorough-going partisans and servants of King Henry and his brother, and these last months they have already been in rebellion against King Edward and when that monarch sent one of his captains with men at arms the better to secure that country and put the bridle upon it, they all rushed to arms and went to fight this captain, so that there perished more than six hundred of his men, from what we hear, and the captain was very glad to turn back.[4]

On 22 July, Margaret finally met the outlawed earl in person, after he was conducted to her childhood home of Angers. Warwick knelt before her 'with great reverence' and 'asked her pardon for the injuries and wrongs done to her in the past'. Initially, Margaret was,

> right difficile and showed to the King of France, being present with the Duke of Guienne and many others, that with the honour of her and her son, he, neither she, might not, nor could not, pardon the said Earl, which hath been the greatest causes of the fall of King Henry, of her, and of their son, and that never of her own courage she neither might be contented with him nor pardon him.[5]

She also explained that it would be 'a thing greatly hurting and prejudicial [as she] had certain parties and friends which they might lightly lose by this mean, and that should be a thing that greatly might grieve them'. In response, Warwick gave the 'excuse and justification' that 'King Henry and she by their false counsel had enterprised the destruction of him and his friends in body and in goods, which he never had deserved against them':

> And [to] him seemed that for such causes, and the great evil will that they have showed him, he had a righteous cause to labour their undoing and destruction, and that therein he had not done that but which a nobleman outraged and impaired ought to have done. Also he said over that, and well confessed that he was the causer of the upsetting of the King of England that now is, but now, seeing the evil terms that the king hath kept with him, and cast him out of the realm, and as much as he hath been with him in times past, now will he be as far contrary, and enemy unto him hereafter.[6]

Margaret, advised by Louis and the servants of her father, 'graciously forgave him', but not before she had kept him waiting on his knees for fifteen minutes, while he 'did homage and fealty' to her, swearing his loyalty to Henry, Margaret and Edward 'as his liege lords unto death'.[7] The marriage between Margaret's son and Warwick's daughter was not discussed on that occasion, although it was 'considered as good as accomplished', and that they only awaited the arrival of Duke René to make it official.[8] René must have arrived soon afterwards, as the formal betrothal between the 16-year-old Edward and the 14-year-old Anne Neville took place on July 25, 1470 at Angers Cathedral, with oaths sworn on fragments on the 'true cross'. Warwick promised 'that without change he shall always hold the party and quarrel of King Henry, and shall serve him, the queen and the Prince, as a true and faithful subject oweth to serve his sovereign lord'. King Louis and his brother, Charles, Duke of Berry, then promised to 'help, bear and sustain to their power the said Earl of Warwick holding the said quarrel of Henry'. Finally, it was the turn of Margaret, who made her oath 'to treat the said Earl as true and faithful to King Henry here, and the Prince, and for the deeds passed, never hereafter to make him reproach'.[9] It was agreed that:

> [the] daughter of the Earl of Warwick shall be put and remain in the hands and keeping of Queen Margaret, and also that the said marriage shall not be perfected [until] the Earl of Warwick had been with an army over the sea into England, and that he had recovered the realm of England in the most part thereof for the King Henry.

Everyone knew it was a deal made out of necessity. Warkworth described it as a last resort; 'they could find no remedy but to send to Queen Margaret and make a marriage … written, indented and sealed between Queen Margaret and the prince her son on the one part and the Duke of Clarence and the Earl of Warwick on the other.[10] Yet, at the time it was being discussed, Margaret produced a letter from England, in which she was offered the hand of Edward IV's eldest daughter, the 4-year-old Princess Elizabeth, as a bride for Prince Edward, and she hinted that it might be a more profitable marriage.[11] However, if this had been a true offer, which Margaret was considering, she did not choose to take it. Shortly after the engagement, Warwick, Clarence, Tudor and de Vere, the new Earl of Oxford, set sail for England 'in the name of St George', as they 'did not wish to lose time in waiting'.[12] Margaret, Edward, Anne and her mother, the Countess of Warwick, were to follow as soon as the Earl had made progress towards Henry's restoration.

Watching Warwick depart, Margaret may have doubted the future, wondering whether this latest alliance was a triumph of hope over experience, and if the earl could really be trusted. He landed in Devon on 13 September, first at Dartmouth, then at Plymouth, where his forces split in two, with Tudor heading for Wales and Warwick joining his brother Montagu, who had been gathering troops in the north. Marching east, word of their arrival spread and Lancastrians who had hidden their old allegiance, or accepted the Yorkists out of self-preservation, flocked to join them. London capitulated upon their approach, with the Mayor and aldermen taking control of the Tower on behalf of the earl, to await his instructions. By 12 October, reports reached Europe that the earl had 'pursued his enterprise with spirit and has practically the whole of [England] in his power'. After closing in upon Edward unawares when he was occupied with rebels in the north, Warwick seized the momentum, forcing Edward to flee the country. The Bishop of Novara observed that 'King Edward is a fugitive and in hiding, his whereabouts being unknown',[13] but in time it became clear that he had taken a boat from the east coast and sought shelter with his allies in Burgundy. Nine years after Edward had been crowned he had been ousted from the English throne. It must have seemed that Margaret's prayers had been answered. Soon, the years of privation, danger and indignity would be at an end. The Queen of England was coming back to claim her crown.

The first that Henry was aware of any change to his routine could have been as early as the end of September or start of October 1470. It is difficult to know the degree to which news penetrated his monk-like cell in the Tower, whether he had guards, or friends, who kept him informed of news or rumour, or whether he understood any such reports, or gave them credence. On Sunday 30 September, as Warwick and Clarence approached London, a sermon was preached by Dr William Goddard at St Paul's cross, in the grounds of the cathedral, to the effect that the citizens could have no loyalty to an absent king, and proclaiming Henry's reinstatement. On 3 October, Henry was visited by Bishop Waynflete and the Mayor, Sir Richard Leigh, and relocated from his room in the Wakefield Tower to the newly furnished royal apartments that Elizabeth Woodville had prepared for her imminent lying-in. Elizabeth and her daughters had fled, days before, to the sanctuary of Westminster Abbey, and now Henry occupied their splendid rooms, with every comfort available to a king. Two days later, Lord Montagu entered the city followed, on 6 October, by Warwick and Clarence. In a state of almost complete passivity, or bewilderment, Henry was led from the Tower after five years in confinement, through the London streets in state, although Warkworth commented that he was not 'honourably arrayed' or 'cleanly kept as should be such a Prince'. He was taken 'from his keepers ... newly arrayed ... and [they] did to him great reverence, and brought him to the Palace of Westminster, and so he was fully restored to the crown again, [of which] all his good lovers were full glad, and the more part of the people.'[14] His new lodgings were at the Bishop's Palace.

On 13 October, which was both his son's birthday and the feast of the translation of St Edward the Confessor, Henry was led in procession to the cathedral. There, a formal crown-wearing ceremony took place, with Warwick holding the king's train and John de Vere, thirteenth Earl of Oxford, carrying his sword. Henry was 'proclaimed through all the town of London with the Earl of Warwick to celebrate the greatest festivities and triumphs', one ambassador related, 'so that it seems a miracle or a dream, yet it is so'.[15] According to Croyland, 'you might then have come across innumerable folk to whom the restoration of the pious king Henry was a miracle and the transformation the work of the All Highest'.[16] All laws were now 'enacted in Henry's name', while Warwick was appointed Chamberlain and King's Lieutenant, and all the other positions were reassigned to create a new royal household. Henry's reign was redated to wipe out the rule of Edward, as 'the forty-ninth year of the reign of Henry VI and the first year of his readeption to royal power'. A parliament was summoned in Henry's name on 15 October, drawing the surviving Lancastrian lords back to Westminster in time for the state opening on 26 November. Edward IV was declared a traitor and usurper, with all lands his confiscated and Clarence was named as the old Duke of York's heir, meaning that in the case of Henry dying without surviving issue, he would be king. The Lancastrian lords who had been attainted under Edward, including Jasper Tudor and John de Vere, Earl of Oxford, were restored to their former positions and George Neville, Lord Montagu, was given the seals as Lord Chancellor. One of the main casualties of the restoration was John Tiptoft, Earl of Worcester, who was tried and executed for having presided with particular cruelty over the deaths of Oxford's father and brother, and other Lancastrians in 1462. Also hastening to the capital in order to offer their loyalty were Margaret Beaufort, widow of Edmund Tudor, and her young son Henry, then aged 13, and a nephew to the newly restored King.

Queen Margaret and her party were still at Angers when the news arrived, which must have created a mood of near-euphoria in the castle. Louis was undecided about how to proceed though, having taken his 'leave of them some days ago for them to return to England', then changing his mind, so it was 'thought that he will detain them until a reply has come from his ambassadors, who have gone to England … it is thought that they will leave immediately the reply comes'.[17] Yet Margaret delayed her return to England, perhaps on the advice of Louis, or others, or preparations to be made, or perhaps due to reasons known only to herself. On 13 December, the marriage took place of Prince Edward and Anne Neville, in Angers Cathedral, bringing the 14-year-old girl into the Lancastrian royal family. In spite of her pedigree and inheritance, Anne was not the bride that Edward and Margaret had once anticipated. As a future King of England, the prince could have sought a princess of royal blood, and previous suggestions had included daughters from the Valois and Burgundian houses. There was also the advantage that a foreign alliance could have brought a new player into the York–Lancaster dynamic, a potentially powerful backer for Margaret's cause, had she looked beyond the triumvirate of England, France and Burgundy. The marriage to Anne was made of necessity, reflective of the dynasty's humbled state but also their investment in Warwick and his potential to restore them to power. A few days later, Margaret learned of the death of her brother, John, Duke of Calabria, at the age of 45, whom the chronicler Commines described as one of the greatest commanders of his time.

After the marriage had taken place, it was reported that 'the Queen of England and the Countess of Warwick, with the prince and princess their children, have left and returned to England, to the unspeakable satisfaction and content of his said Majesty' (Louis), but still Margaret did not leave. The French ambassadors received a warm welcome at Henry's new court:

> words fail them to express the honourable and noble way in which they have been received and welcomed, so they state in their letters to the king, both by the king there and the Earl of Warwick principally, and then by all the other lords and the people of England, with a marvellous demonstration of love and affection towards his Majesty.[18]

The readeption parliament went on to negotiate a peace with France and began to raise troops to help Louis in his campaign against Charles, Duke of Burgundy, who was sheltering Edward IV.

On 16 February, 1471 Warwick signed a peace treaty with Louis, by the terms of which Margaret and her party were to return to England. Sir John Longstrother, newly appointed as Treasurer, and the leading Knights Hospitaller in the country, was charged with the task of conducting her safely back to England. It was not until the following March, 1471 though that the newly restored queen finally set sail after the arrival of her escort, only to be beaten back by bad weather. She was fortunate in having missed the trouble that erupted in the channel days later, between Louis's ambassadors and a fleet of Breton ships, who were 'waging a very bitter war at sea against the English and ... take and plunder whoever falls into their hands without caring whether they are French or anyone else'.[19] Warkworth relates that 'the wind was so contrary to them for seventeen days and nights they could not come from Normandy [whereas] with a wind they might have sailed it in twelve hours'.[20] Another report dated to 9 April may be reflecting a second crossing attempt, which failed, before Margaret finally managed to make the crossing with what the Milanese ambassador estimated to be around 8,000 troops. She landed at Weymouth in Dorset on 14 April.

On 10 April Henry, Warwick and George Neville, Archbishop of York, rode through London from the Bishop's Palace along Cheap and Cornhill, Candlewick Street and Watling Street, and "desired the people to be true" to the king, in a carefully stage-managed event. Neville held him by the hand all the way, with his sword borne before him and a man behind carrying a pole with two foxes' tails tied to it.[21] The author of the *Great Chronicle* commented that it was 'more like a play than the showing of a prince to win men's hearts, for by this means he lost many and won none or right few, and ever he was shown in a long blue gown of velvet, as though he had no more to change with'.[22] Before the show had finished, Edward IV's 'foreriders had come to Shoreditch', to warn of his impending arrival. As darkness fell, the civic dignitaries ordered everyone to return home, either for the sake of the peace, or in awareness that Edward was approaching. According to Warkworth, once it was dark and quiet, 'during dinner time, King Edward was let in', and hurried to the Bishop's Palace 'and there took King Harry and the Archbishop of York and put them in prison'.[23] The *Great Chronicle* has that Henry was alone, Neville having left him, and Edward commanded him to his presence. When he marched north the next day to meet Warwick's army, Edward took Henry 'secretly after him' wearing the same blue gown, as a key pawn in the game that was approaching its conclusion and being unwilling to trust that he would not be released or recaptured in his absence.

After his period of confinement, the troubled king may not have been fully aware of the nature of the changes taking place, either by confusion, illness or lack of information, but the claim made by Mary Ann Hookham, that 'his natural weakness of mind caused him to view with less anxiety, the difficulties and dangers which another of more energy and spirit would have, doubtless, regarded with more alarm'[24] underestimates his sensitivity. Henry would not have relished returning to the battlefield, and may have even been beyond entertaining hope for the reunion of his family, depending upon his mental state. Few reports survive about the king at this point in his life and those that do draw attention to his appearance, while making brief reference to his confusion. The *Great Chronicle* contains the longest description of his personal response to the situation, that

> after long imprisonment and many injuries, derisions and scorns sustained by patiently of many of his subjects, [he was] restored unto his right and regality, in which he took no great pride but meekly thanked God and gave all his mind to serve and please him, and partook little or nothing of the pomp or vanities of this world.[25]

It is entirely possible that, returning to restore Henry to the throne in 1470, Warwick found him to be unwell, or incapable of ruling. Of course, this is not something that would have been expedient for the earl to admit, but secrecy in this eventuality could have helped his cause, as it may even have made his manipulation of the king easier. In effect, it made Warwick king.

Blacman's account relates a conversation he had with Henry during his confinement which underlines his focus on the divine:

> When he was imprisoned in the Tower of London, a certain chaplain of his asked him, about the time of the feast of Easter, how his soul agreed at that most holy season with the troubles that pressed upon him and so sprouted forth that he could by no means avoid them. The king answered in these words: 'The kingdom of heaven, unto which I have devoted myself always from a child, do I call and cry for. For this kingdom which is transitory and of the earth I do not greatly care. Our kinsman of March thrusts himself into it as is his pleasure. This one thing only do I require, to receive the sacrament at Easter, and the rites of the church on Maundy Thursday with the rest of Christendom, as I am accustomed.'[26]

He also reported how Henry had reputedly saved a child's life, as

> when the king was shut up in the Tower he saw a woman on his right hand [or out of his window] trying to drown a little child, and warned her by a messenger not to commit such a crime and sin, hateful to God; and she, rebuked by this reproof, desisted from the deed she had begun.[27]

Blacman also discussed the circumstances of Henry's imprisonment with him:

> Also, when this king Henry was asked during his imprisonment in the Tower why he had unjustly claimed and possessed the crown of England for so many years, he would answer thus: 'My father was king of England, and peaceably possessed the crown of England for the whole time of his reign. And his father and my grandfather was king of the same realm. And I, a child in the cradle, was peaceably and without any protest crowned and approved as king by the whole realm, and wore the crown of England some forty years, and each and all of my lords did me royal homage and plighted me their faith, as was also done to other my predecessors. Wherefore I too can say with the Psalmist: The lot is fallen unto me in a fair ground: yea, I have a goodly heritage. For my right help is of the Lord, who preserveth them that are true of heart.'[28]

Around 150 miles east from where Margaret had landed, across the south downs and on the other side of London, the Earl of Warwick set up his standard at Gladsmore Heath, near Barnet. Edward IV had returned from Burgundy to England on 14 March, being favoured by far better weather conditions than the French ships waiting to cross the Channel. Landing at Ravenspur on the east coast, he had effected an entry to the city of York by stating that his desire was to reclaim its duchy, before marching south for London, gathering supporters as he went. On the night of 13/14 April, as Margaret was in the Channel, Edward's army approached the place where Warwick's men lay in the darkness and mist, before launching a dawn attack. Amid the confusion it was sometimes unclear who was attacking whom, causing the Earl of Oxford to turn on the back of Montagu's forces. After several hours of fighting, during which Montagu and Warwick were both killed, the victory went to the returning Edward IV. With Henry, he returned to London, where the former king was once again incarcerated in the Tower. His sixth months of freedom were over.

After five years' absence, Margaret cannot have found the England she knew to have significantly changed. As she disembarked, travelling through the rolling green hills of Dorset, towards Exeter, her feeling was more likely to have been one of hope, of the belief that she had returned to a land which was her own, rather than despair. She does not appear to have learned about the terrible defeat at Barnet until her party arrived at Cerne Abbas, or Abbey, where she was informed of the loss by Edmund, Duke of Somerset. The news of her father's death also had to be broken to Anne Neville, perhaps by Edward or Somerset, or it may have been a task that fell to Margaret. Fleetwood's fragment, which contains details of this part of Margaret's life, states that she learned of the battle on 15 April 'and was therefore right heavy and sorry'.[29]

Under the roof of the Benedictine Abbey at Cerne, she reassessed her situation, leaning towards the desire to return at once to France, until Prince Edward persuaded her to stay and fight. Hookham relates a possible tension between her concern to restore the Lancastrian dynasty and her maternal fears, which made her 'apprehensive of the unhappy consequences of an unsuccessful enterprise'.[30] The Yorkists were aware of her arrival and, as a Milanese letter relates, 'King Edward has set out with his power to look for the queen and the prince', while many considered the queen's 'prospects favourable, chiefly because of the death of Warwick, because it is reckoned she ought to have many lords in her favour, who intended to resist her because they were enemies of Warwick'.[31] Fleetwood suggests she was aware of this, 'and that for that loss, their party was never the feebler, but rather stronger'.[32] When this was pointed out to Margaret, it may have swayed her decision to stay, although she may instead have been labouring under false hope. In a letter that she wrote to Louis, Margaret expressed the possibility that 'the Earl of Warwick was not dead, as reported, but had been wounded in the fight ... and had withdrawn to a secret and solitary place to get well of his wounds and sickness'.[33] The same letter related that Prince Edward had a 'very large following of men and with the favour and assistance of the greater part of the common people and citizens',[34] but the ambassador relating the news second-hand was incorrect in stating that the prince had reached London. Edward never reached London: by the time the letter reached Louis, he was already dead. Any optimism Margaret retained over the survival of Warwick must have been punctured by reports that his dead body, along with that of his brother Montagu, had been displayed in public at St Paul's. The newly arrived Lancastrians were truly alone, but they decided to take their chances nevertheless.

Marshalling her forces, Margaret set out for Wales. Tudor separated from her to hurry ahead to gather troops, extracting a promise from Somerset that the young duke would not engage with the enemy until his return. Warkworth relates how they 'made out commandments in the queen's name and the prince's, to all the west country and gathered great people' around them[35] and Croyland echoes her support in the area, as there were many in the 'western parts who preferred King Henry's cause to the claims of all the others'.[36] By 27 April, as many as 40,000 men may have come to assist the queen[37] keen to restore her to power, hopeful of the advantage her patronage would bring. Three days later, she had covered the fifty miles to Bath, but when she learned that Edward's army was only fifteen miles away, at Marlborough, she quickly pressed on to Bristol, where she paused to gather supplies. A brief skirmish ensued at Sodbury Hill between her men and the Yorkist scouts, but instead of engaging, she drew her forces north. Her intention was to cross the River Severn and head north through Wales, collecting Tudor's men, before swinging east again into Cheshire where she had been promised a group of archers. At all costs, she wished to avoid engaging with the enemy before she was fully equipped. On 2 May, Margaret's forces reached Berkeley Castle, a secure location, but not an auspicious one, as the rumoured location where the deposed Edward II had been murdered in 1327. Edward learned, or guessed, that she would try to cross the Severn at Gloucester, so he sent troops ahead to refuse her entry to the city on 3 May. Thus deterred, Margaret and her army moved north to the town of Tewkesbury, where her exhausted army rested from the long march and the fiercely hot weather.

Margaret may have stayed in a house nearby called Gobes Hall but early the following morning, after saying goodbye to Edward, she installed herself not far from Tewkesbury Abbey in 'a poor religious house … for the security of her person'.[38] Hookham has her riding through her troops in person impressing upon them the need for valour, but this cannot be verified, although verbal messages may have been sent. With the presence of the Yorkists looming, the 17-year-old prince could no longer hold off preparing for battle before the additional forces of Jasper Tudor could arrive. He installed his men in the field leading up to Tewkesbury Abbey, with the Avon and Severn behind him. The divisions were led by the Beaufort brothers, Edmund, Duke of Somerset and his brother John, Marquis of Dorset, John Courtenay, Earl of Devon, who had been with Edward in exile, and the veteran soldier Lord Wenlock, who had defected from the Yorkist side. The Lancastrians had the slight advantage of numbers, but in spite of earlier reports of an army of 40,000, they had around 6,000 men at Tewkesbury, compared to the Yorkists' 5,000. They also had the advantage of arriving first, enabling them to position themselves as best they could, meaning that their enemy found it difficult to advance upon them and resorted to their archers first. Against them were the three York brothers, Edward, George and Richard, with William, Lord Hastings. Edmund Beaufort launched an attack but was beaten back and driven into the way of 200 Yorkist spearmen who had been concealed in the trees. His flank scattered and headed for the river, where they were cut down in 'bloody meadow'. Beaufort then turned on Wenlock, accusing him of not coming to his aid and, reputedly, attacking and killing him. Lancastrian morale collapsed as the army scattered and headed towards the river, where many of them were drowned.

It was inevitable, as Margaret feared, that in the event of Lancastrian failure, her son would lose his life. Exactly how this came about, though, is still a matter of disagreement. The author of the *Great Chronicle* believed Prince Edward had been brought into the victorious king's presence, where he appealed to his brother-in-law Clarence, but his 'impertinent' comments provoked his death.

Weeks after the battle in 1471, the Milanese ambassador reported that the Yorkists had 'not only routed the prince but taken up and slain him, together with all the leading men with him'.[39] The *Arrivall* described how Edward, 'called Prince', was put 'to discomfiture and flyght' and 'was taken, fleinge to the town wards and slayne in the fielde'.[40] It also contained a miniature depicting the execution by axe of Edmund Beaufort shortly after the fighting, with Edward IV looking on: the prince may have met a similar end. Two years later, a French chronicle, the *Historie de Charles, dernier duc de Bourgogne*, claimed that Edward had been surrounded by his enemies and killed in cold blood.[41] Polydore Vergil, the Italian Historian of Henry VII, who first visited England in 1502, based his account of the battle on primary sources which have now been lost. He described a scene where Edward IV questioned the prince about his opposition, whereupon the 'excellent yowth' replied it was to free his father from oppression and regain the usurped crown. The Yorkist then reputedly struck him in the face with a gauntlet and waved him away for execution.[42] A similar story was included by Robert Fabyan, a London chronicler and sheriff writing before 1512, in which the king 'strake him with his gauntlet upon the face, after which stroke, so by him received, he was by the King's servant incontinently slain'.[43]

Edward's remains were buried in the choir of Tewkesbury Abbey. A brass memorial plaque in the floor of the choir records the event in Latin, which broadly translates as: 'Here lies Edward, Prince of Wales, cruelly slain while but a youth. Anno Domini 1471, May 4. Alas, the savagery of men. Thou art the sole light of thy Mother, and the last hope of thy race.' It seems unlikely that Edward was ever given anything more in terms of a tomb or memorial, although in 1873 Mary Ann Hookham observed a large slab at the entrance to the choir, which used to have brasses attached. His mother was not in a position to insist upon it, nor to finance it, and the Yorkists would have been reluctant to erect such a monument to the last Lancastrian prince, as a potentially dangerous reminder for his supporters. It would have been in keeping for Edward IV to order masses to be said for the youth's soul, as a violent death was considered significant in the individual's experience of the afterlife. Following the battle, the abbey was closed for a month and re-consecrated as a result of the bloodshed and the violation of sanctuary; it may by that this process also included arrangements for Edward's bodily and spiritual remains.

In the aftermath of the battle Margaret was captured by William Stanley, husband of Margaret Beaufort whose family connection may, therefore, have made him a sympathetic figure, yet Jacob Abbott describes him as 'one of her most inveterate enemies'.[44] Hookham dramatically relates that she was 'discovered in a chariot half dead', but the more prosaic likelihood is that Stanley learned her place of refuge and went to apprehend her there. Either before this, or as a result of it, she sent word to Edward IV that she was 'at his command'. It was the complete submission of a broken woman, with no fight left in her. On 11 May, she came face-to-face with Edward at Coventry, her former home, in the full knowledge of her defeat and the terrible loss of her son. It cannot have been easy for the former queen. Abbott describes her as being 'in a continued state of the highest excitement, being almost wild with grief and rage ... she uttered continual maledictions against Edward for having murdered her boy and nothing could soothe or quiet her'.[45] Milanese letters from June related that Edward has 'taken the queen and sent her to London to keep King Henry company, he also being a prisoner there,'[46] while the *Arrivall* states that 'Queen Margaret herself was taken and brought to the king and, in every part of England where any commotion was begun for King Henry's party, they were rebuked, so that it appeared to every man ... that the [queen's] party was extinct and repressed for ever, without any kind of hope of revival'.[47] Margaret was committed to the Tower, but it is unlikely that she was lodged anywhere near Henry, or that he was even aware of her presence. She certainly was not there to 'keep [him] company', as the ambassador had hoped.[48] The death of her son forced Margaret to recognise that her quest had come to an end. Yet there was still one more blow to come.

On the night of the 21 and 22 May, 1471 Henry VI died in the Tower of London, probably in the Wakefield Tower. The *Arrivall*, the instrument of Yorkist propaganda, claimed that his end had come about through 'pure displeasure and melancholy', but few believed it at the time, with consensus leaning more towards Blacman's presentation of Henry as a victim of murder, suffering 'a violent death of the body'. The Croyland chronicler did not shy away from expressing the view that he had been murdered:

> I shall pass over in silence the fact that, at this time, King Henry's lifeless body was discovered in the Tower of London: may God have mercy upon and give time for repentance to the person, whoever it might be, who dared to lay sacrilegious hands on the Lord's anointed! And so, let the perpetrator merit the title of tyrant and the victim that of glorious martyr.[49]

Word of his death soon spread abroad, eliciting the same response:

> King Edward has not chosen to have the custody of King Henry any longer, although he was in some sense innocent, and there was no great fear about his proceedings, the prince his son and the Earl of Warwick being dead as well as all those who were for him and had any vigour, as he has caused King Henry to be secretly assassinated in the Tower, where he was a prisoner. They say he has done the same to the queen ... He has, in short, chosen to crush the seed.[50]

It was Polydore Vergil, writing after the significant watershed of 1485, who recorded that Henry had been 'put to death' and that the 'continual report is that Richard, Duke of Gloucester, killed him with a sword, whereby his brother might be delivered from all fear of hostility'.[51] The 18-year-old Richard was in the Tower on that night, along with most of the other members of Edward's court, but there is no evidence to suggest he was responsible. Far more evidence survives to indicate the need of the Tudors to vilify their predecessor. Henry's murder was more likely to have been ordered by Edward IV, as an essential step to prevent further attempts to restore him to the throne.

Edward was aware, though, that rumours would arise about Henry's death, particularly the cause and the certainty of it. As Croyland relates, 'the body was put on view for a few days at St Paul's church in London and then carried along the Thames, in an illuminated barge solemnly equipped with torches for the purpose, to the monastic church of Chertsey … fifteen miles from the city, for burial'.[52] The *London Chronicle* records the 'silent witness of the blood that welled from his fresh wounds upon the pavement gave an indubitable token of the manner of his death.'[53] Indeed, rumours circulating that the body bled afresh on the pavement belong to the start of the king's cult, imbuing the body with a mythical status that would be developed in later years by pro-Lancastrian chroniclers. The source also loudly proclaims that he was the victim of a murder. After St Paul's, Henry was displayed in an open coffin at Blackfriars, where masses were said for his soul. Edward would not have run the risk of displaying the body had it borne any visible signs of violence, which could provoke an outcry and lose him sympathy, but he needed to prove Henry's demise to prevent future reports that he had survived. After it had been displayed, the body was treated with respect, although Vergil contradicts the earlier account of Croyland by claiming he was transported 'without any honour'. However, the *Issues of the Exchequer* recorded the payments made for the preparation, burial and memorial of the former king:

> To Hugh Brice. In money paid to his own hands, for so much money expended by him, as well for wax, linen, spices, and other ordinary expenses incurred for the burial of the said Henry of Windsor, who died within the Tower of London; and for wages and rewards to divers men carrying torches from the Tower aforesaid to the cathedral church of Saint Paul's, London, and from thence accompanying the body to Chertesey. By writ, &c, —15l. 3s. 6 1/2d.
>
> To Master Richard Martyn. In money paid to him at different times; viz., at one time to his own hands 9l. 10s. 11d., for so much money by him expended for 28 yards of linen cloth from Holland, and for expenses incurred, as well within the Tower aforesaid, at the last valediction of the

said Henry, as also at Chertesey on the day of his burial; and for a reward given to divers soldiers from Calais guarding his body, and for the hire of barges, with masters and sailors rowing the same on the river Thames to Chertesey aforesaid; also at another time 8l. 12s. 3d., for so much money paid by him to four orders of brethren within the city of London; and to the brethren of the Holy Cross therein; also for other works of charity; viz., to the Carmelite brethren 20s., to the Augustine Friars 20s., to the Friars Minors 20s., and to the Friars Preachers, to celebrate obsequies and masses, 40s.; also to the said brethren of the Holy Cross, 10s.; and for obsequies and masses said at Chertesey aforesaid, on the day of the burial of the said Henry,—52s. 3d. By writ, &c,—18l. 3s. 2d.[54]

Henry was buried in the Lady Chapel of the Benedictine Abbey at Chertsey in Surrey, a building that appears in contemporary sketches as squat and long, with a central tower. It was sufficiently removed from London that might allow for his memory to fade away. In 1484, though, Richard III removed the remains and had them reinterred in St George's Chapel at Windsor which, ironically, had been built by Edward IV. Henry's final resting place was just a stone's throw from where Edward had been buried the previous year.

In 1910, Henry's remains were exhumed and studied. The skull still had hair attached, which an observer W. H. St John Hope described as 'brown in colour, save in one place where it was much darker and apparently matted with blood', although this was not based in any scientific testing, only what could be observed to the naked eye by a bystander. A report about the condition of the body was made by a professor of anatomy, containing the detail that 'the bones of the head were unfortunately most broken', but no reference to hair or blood.[55] It could not be established, however, when these breakages occurred, whether they had been the cause of death or took place post mortem, perhaps during the translation of the bones from Chertsey to Windsor. Until such time as Henry's remains are examined again, the results of the exhumation cannot be considered at all conclusive. At present, Henry rests in the south quire aisle under a black marble slab bearing his name.

*Chapter Eleven*

# The Prisoner 1471–1482

Tewkesbury marked the end of Margaret's active life. The rest of her years were passed in quiet seclusion and mourning, whiled away in castle strongholds, a broken woman. Hookham describes her as being 'overcome by melancholy' with 'her heroic spirit, which had braved every danger and sustained such great trials, no longer bore up under the pressure of misfortune'. The news of her husband's death would have been broken to her soon after the event; as a resident of the Tower, she had been almost within reach of him, but there is no indication that they were ever reunited or communicated with each other during that brief window. The report by the Milanese ambassador that Edward had killed her along with Henry could have been a believable conclusion to her story, which Margaret herself might have feared, but this was not Edward's way. Remarkably, in spite of all the barriers and taboos that had been broken through the shedding of cousins' blood, the chivalric code remained intact, whereby the aristocratic combatants drew the line at harming their women. Edward had benefited from it during his absence of 1470–1, when the sanctity of Elizabeth Woodville had been respected, and butchers and doctors allowed to attend her in Westminster Abbey. Margaret might have been an anointed queen but, alone, without her husband or son, she had no claim to the throne and no one to fight for. Her party had been decimated, her family and friends killed. She recognised when she had been defeated and, far from behaving like the harridan created by Shakespeare, adopted a passive approach, simply living out the remainder of her days in anticipation of a heavenly reunion.

Initially, Margaret remained a prisoner in the Tower of London, with all its negative connotations. Before long, though, she was moved to Windsor and then to Wallingford, perhaps, as is suggested by Hookham and Strickland, as the result of an intercession by Elizabeth Woodville. A letter among the Paston collection, dated 9 July, contains the information that 'as for Queen Margaret, I understand she is removed from Windsor to Wallingford, nigh to Ewelme, my Lady of Suffolk's place in Oxfordshire'.[1] Alice, Duchess of Suffolk, was a former friend of Margaret's youth, the widow of the duke who had been a father figure to her from the first days of her marriage, who had suffered attainder, exile and an ignoble death in 1450. By now, Alice was in her late sixties and although her main residence was at nearby Ewelme, as Paston states, she was official custodian of Wallingford Castle. Once an important medieval castle situated on the Thames in Oxfordshire, Wallingford had been largely a defensive structure, used to hold out against siege, but was later renovated into luxury accommodation and became a favourite with royalty. The surviving remains suggest a large structure surrounded by three thick walls, with an inner courtyard containing a range of apartments on the riverside, formal gardens, service range and original motte and bailey, with a busy outer courtyard containing more buildings and part of the moat, ringed by a third, empty yard. A possible Queen's Tower, close to the gate which gave access to the river, might suggest Margaret's lodging place for the next three years. She was allocated five marks a week for her upkeep and that of her servants, living quietly until until Alice's death, on 20 May 1475. Margaret might have attended her funeral at nearby St Mary's Church in Ewelme, admiring or being moved by the cadaver tomb that depicted her rotting remains. Her loss raised the question of what was now to be done with the former queen.

Later the same year, Edward led a successful campaign against France. By the terms of the Treaty of Picquigny, which he signed with Louis in November, Margaret's return to France was negotiated. Louis paid a ransom of 50,000 gold crowns and in return, Margaret agreed to renounce any claims she had to a marriage portion, jewels, or anything resulting from her marriage to Henry. Louis also promised that he would never make any future demand in her favour, putting the final end to any hopes of a return, not that Margaret was harbouring any by this stage. She was probably glad to leave England, thirty years after her arrival, considering it a country that had not served her as well as she had tried to serve it.

Margaret was formally freed on 29 January, 1476. She said her farewells and left Wallingford in the custody of Sir Thomas Montgomery, whose job it was to conduct her to Sandwich, and from there across the Channel to Dieppe and through France to Rouen. She had a small retinue, of around three ladies and seven gentlemen, for protection and to serve her needs. Margaret's journey home would prove to be a colourful one. Jacob Abbott relates that she intended to visit Louis in Paris, to thank him for his kindness but, on hearing of her plan, Louis sent word that she had better not come. Then, as she was travelling home to Anjou, she encountered some exiles from Normandy who had been evicted by the English and, blaming her, as a former Queen of England, for their misfortune, the mob attacked her so that her gentlemen had to fight them off. After this, she accepted a bodyguard sent by Louis to conduct her safely to Rouen. At Rouen, she was handed over to Louis's men, John de Hangest, Sieur de Jenlis and John Raguenet, Receiver-General of Normandy. A report reached Lausanne at the end of April 1476 that,

the King of France has bought, for 24 or 30,000 crowns, Queen Margaret of
England, daughter of King René, widow of King Henry and prisoner of King
Edward in England, and has fetched her to France, it is supposed in order to
get her to give up her claims to Provence as the daughter of King René.[2]

Margaret's feelings about her return home are not known, but she fulfilled the
terms of the bargain that had been struck with Louis. On 1 March 1476, she
ceded to the king all her claims to her father's properties in Anjou, Lorraine, Bar
and Provence, and in return she accepted an income of 6,000 crowns a year from
Louis, which was intermittently paid. Strickland, however, has this occurring
later, after Rene's death, with the paperwork being signed on 19 November 1480
at the Castle of Reculée. More of the events of her final years are difficult to
place exactly in term of dates and locations. Her biographer of the 1970s, Jock
Haswell, has her writing to her father soon after her return, asking to live out
her years in the sunshine of Aix.[3] He cites a nineteenth-century letter published
by French historian Villeneuve Bargemont, which purports to be written by
René of Anjou to his daughter, although its provenance is unknown:

My daughter! May God assist you in your counsels, for we should rarely
expect the help of man under the reverses of fortune! When you desire to
alleviate your misfortunes, think of mine! They are great, my child, and yet
I offer you consolation.[4]

Strickland, though, believes that this letter was written earlier, in 1471, and
sent to her by her father when she was a prisoner in the Tower of London.
From her arrival home in 1476 to the death of her father in 1480, Margaret
may have moved between her family's properties but some sources, such as the
early account of Baudier, place her in the town of Aix-en-Provence, where René
was living in his palace, while others claim she retired to La Reculée, between
Angers and Saumur, a location where she had been happy as a child.

The castle at La Reculée sat on the bank of a river with a pretty garden and a
gallery of sculptures and painting to which Margaret's father was always adding.
Other biographers suggest she passed her days reading the stories composed for
her by George de Chastelain, about 'the ruin of certain unfortunate great ones'.
In the 1460s, he had dedicated his *La Temple de Boccace* to Margaret and his
*Déprécation* to Pierre de Bréze, another old friend whom Margaret lost, killed in
the Battle of Montlhéry in 1465. Villeneuve states that she rarely left the castle
and that in her final years she suffered from leprosy which made her skin scaly
and disfigured, and subsequent biographers repeated the story.

René of Anjou died at Aix on 10 July 1480, aged 80. In his will, he left 'one
thousand crowns in gold to his daughter Margaret, Queen of England, and if

she remains in a state of widowhood, an annuity of two thousand livres and the chateau of Queniez for her abode'.[5] He wrote to Louis, asking him to look after Margaret but, on his deathbed, he committed her to the care of a close friend Francis de Vignolles, Lord of Morains, who took her to the castle of Dampierre-sur-Loire, on the outskirts of Saumur, about twenty-five miles further up river. An Edwardian postcard depicting a castle which claims to be Margaret's last home shows a typical Loire-style fairy-tale building with turrets, sloping roofs and dormer windows, but on a small scale, projecting out of the rocks that form part of it. Windows and doors in the rock face hint at the secret defences that lie behind the pretty façade. Now known as the Chateau d'Anjou in Souzay, Souzay Chateau and the Chateau de la Vignole, it stands on the Rue de Chateau, overlooking the Loire.

If Margaret had been suffering from leprosy, as Villeneuve suggested, she may have already been ill by the time she arrived in Dampierre-sur-Loire. Her last days were spent quietly, reduced to the simple routines and rituals of prayer, meals, bed times. Perhaps she sat looking out over the rushing Loire and the fields beyond, observing the cycle of the seasons change, with the labours of the month unfolding before her eyes: the woodcutting and planting, the hunting and hawking of summer, the harvest and slaughter of animals. In the rural French countryside, little had changed since the creation of the *Très Riches Heures de Duc de Berri* just before her husband's birth. As her strength faded, she may have watched the young aristocrats out riding in their colourful clothes (May), the peasants outside the city walls, mowing the hay (June), the golden corn being gathered and the sheep shorn (July) and, finally, the falconers riding past, as the peasants swim in the river, under a wide blue sky, (August).

Margaret died two years after her arrival, on 25 August 1482, at the age of 52. She was buried in Angers Cathedral in the vault of her father, without a memorial except for her image in a stained-glass window. Her annual memorial, held on the feast of Souls, and involving a procession around her tomb, continued until the French Revolution.[6] Less than a year after her death, the man who had replaced her husband, King Edward IV, died at the age of 40, plunging England into chaos as his sons were pronounced illegitimate and displaced by their uncle, Richard, Duke of Gloucester, who was crowned as Richard III on 6 July, 1483. Margaret did not survive long enough to see how the Yorkists unravelled themselves.

It is possible, but unlikely, that before her death, news penetrated Margaret's retreat regarding the posthumous reputation of her husband. She may even have heard some of the rumours before she left England. Miracles had been recorded by the dean of St George's as early as 1481, after pilgrims had appealed to the dead king, and continuing until as late as 1500, by which time 174 had been recorded. They included individuals being reprieved from hanging, saved from fatal stab wounds, injuries healed, ailing horses revived, ships saved at sea, people protected from fire, the blind healed, children rescued and healed, and lost items found. Visitors flocked to his tomb at Chertsey but he was also commemorated in other parts of the country, with Kent, London and Sussex proving the most popular areas where miracles occurred, but some also being recorded in Calais, Wales, Cornwall and Durham. Prayers to King Henry appeared in the Prayer Books and Primers of the day, with one version in a Norfolk book as early as 1480. In 1484, two years after Margaret's death, Henry's body was removed from Chertsey Abbey to Windsor by Richard III, as a result of the profusion of miracles that were being reported, either as a celebration of the former king, or to control the rapidly growing cult before it got out of control – or a cynical attempt to rehabilitate Richard's own reputation.

His former confessor, John Blacman, produced a hagiographical life, which would do much for the king's future reputation, and was completed around 1510. In words that could scarcely be more hyperbolic, Blacman described the former king as

> being like a second Job, a man simple and upright, altogether fearing the Lord God, and departing from evil … a simple man without any crook of craft or untruth, as is plain to all. With none did he deal craftily, nor ever would say an untrue word to any, but framed his speech always to speak truth.

The lengthy praise continued:

> He was both upright and just, always keeping to the straight line of justice in his acts. Upon none would he wittingly inflict any injustice. To God and the Almighty, he rendered most faithfully that which was His, for he took pains to pay in full the tithes and offerings due to God and the church: and this he accompanied with most sedulous devotion, so that even when decked with the kingly ornaments and crowned with the royal diadem he made it a duty to bow before the Lord as deep in prayer as any young monk might have done.
>
> A diligent and sincere worshipper of God was this king, more given to God and to devout prayer than to handling worldly and temporal things, or practising vain sports and pursuits: these he despised as trifling, and was continually occupied either in prayer or the reading of the scriptures or of chronicles, whence he drew not a few wise utterances to the spiritual comfort of himself and others. So to every sort and condition and age of men he was a diligent exhorter and adviser, counselling the young to leave vice and follow the path of virtue; and admonishing men of mature age and

elders (or priests) to attain the perfection of virtue and lay hold on the prize of eternal life, with those words of the Psalm 'Go from strength to strength; hence shall the God of gods be beheld in Sion.'

In church or chapel he was never pleased to sit upon a seat or to walk to and fro as do men of the world; but always with bared head, at least while the divine office was being celebrated, and hardly ever raising his royal person, kneeling one may say continuously before his book, with eyes and hands upturned, he was at pains to utter with the celebrant (but with the inward voice) the mass-prayers, epistles, and gospels. To some clerics also he used to address letters of exhortation full of heavenly mysteries and most salutary advice, to the great wonder of many.

Moreover, wherever this king was, he always showed himself a venerator and most devout adorer of the Holy Cross and of other symbols and holy things of the Christian religion. When engaged in such devotion he went always with bared head, even when riding on a journey: so that many times he would let his royal cap drop to the ground even from his horse's back, unless it were quickly caught by his servants. So too he preferred a row of signs of the Holy Cross to be set in his royal crown rather than any likenesses of flowers or leaves, according to that word of the wise: 'A crown of gold was upon his head marked with the sign of holiness.' He would be at the divine office quite early, nay at the very beginning: nor did he ever grow weary at the lengthy prolonging of it, even though it were continued until after noonday.

Moreover he would never suffer hawks, swords, or daggers to be brought into church, or business agreements or conferences to be carried on there: even his great men and nobles he enjoined to give themselves frequently to prayer, according to the word of the Saviour 'My house is a house of prayer': and they obeyed him devoutly.

Blacman also had much to say about Henry's marriage, his chastity and his relations with Margaret:

This king Henry was chaste and pure from the beginning of his days. He eschewed all licentiousness in word or deed while he was young; until he was of marriageable age, when he espoused the most noble lady, Lady Margaret, daughter of the King of Sicily, by whom he begat but one only son, the most noble and virtuous prince Edward; and with her and toward her he kept his marriage vow wholly and sincerely, even in the absences of the lady, which were sometimes very long: never dealing unchastely with any other woman. Neither when they lived together did he use his wife unseemly, but with all honesty and gravity.

It is an argument of his watch upon his modesty that he was wont utterly to avoid the unguarded sight of naked persons, lest like David he should be snared by unlawful desire, for David's eyes, as we read, made havoc of his soul. Therefore this prince made a covenant with his eyes that they should never look unchastely upon any woman.

Hence it happened once, that at Christmas time a certain great lord brought before him a dance or show of young ladies with bared bosoms who were to dance in that guise before the king, perhaps to prove him, or to entice his youthful mind. But the king was not blind to it, nor unaware of the devilish wile, and spurned the delusion, and very angrily averted his eyes, turned his back upon them, and went out to his chamber, saying: Fy, fy, for shame, forsothe ye be to blame.

At another time, riding by Bath, where are warm baths in which they say the men of that country customably refresh and wash themselves, the king, looking into the baths, saw in them men wholly naked with every garment cast off. At which he was displeased, and went away quickly, abhorring such nudity as a great offence, and not unmindful of that sentence of Francis Petrarch 'the nakedness of a beast is in men unpleasing, but the decency of raiment makes for modesty.'

Besides, he took great precautions to secure not only his own chastity but that of his servants. For before he was married, being as a youth a pupil of chastity, he would keep careful watch through hidden windows of his chamber, lest any foolish impertinence of women coming into the house should grow to a head, and cause the fall of any of his household. And like pains did he apply in the case of his two half-brothers, the Lords Jasper and Edmund, in their boyhood and youth: providing for them most strict and safe guardianship, putting them under the care of virtuous and worthy priests, both for teaching and for right living and conversation, lest the untamed practices of youth should grow rank if they lacked any to prune them. Not less diligence did he use, I am told, towards others dependent on him, advising them to eschew vice and avoid the talk of the vicious and dissolute, and to lay hold on virtue.[6]

The Croyland chronicler explained the cult of Henry as the result of his saintly character: 'the miracles which God has performed in answer to the prayers of those who devoutly implored his intercession bear witness to his life of innocence, love of God and of the church, patience in adversity and other remarkable qualities'. When his nephew, Henry Tudor, son of Edmund, became King in 1485, he not only avenged the Lancastrian line, but also promoted the cult of his uncle. It was religiously and politically expedient to stress the tenuous continuity of the new line with that of the old and this process began early, with Henry's coronation pageantry referencing the king's death as a 'martyr by great tormenting'. At some point before 1492, Henry VII appealed to the Pope for his uncle to be canonised, but the process was slow, or the Vatican reluctant, and by the advent of the Reformation, the necessity for Lancastrian validation had lessened. Yet even the ravages of iconoclasm could not erase all trace of the cult, with images of Henry surviving in churches in Norfolk, Manchester, Devon, Hampshire, Cambridge and Northumberland.

Six centuries after their deaths, the nature of Henry and Margaret's characters, their rule and context, still fascinate and raise questions. The events of the Wars of the Roses, and the fates of those involved, are well known, but their motivation and their feelings remain elusive. Peeling back the layers of chroniclers' accounts, unwrapping the trail of historiography that has helped shaped their reputations, it becomes increasingly clear that the bias of certain sources, coupled with changing cultural contexts for gender, have distorted interpretations of Henry and Margaret. Henry was essentially an anachronism, a man in the wrong place at the wrong time. He was born into circumstances from which he could not escape and his personal values clashed with the expectations of medieval kingship. He made concerted, but erratic, efforts to provide strong leadership, but this came at the cost of his mental health. Mary Ann Hookham, paraphrasing statements by Whethamsted, Hearne and Blacman, commented that 'such a king in more peaceable times would have been a blessing to his country, but in those turbulent days, when personal prowess was considered the first of virtues, it is not to be wondered, that he should have been looked upon almost in the light of an idiot'.[8] Yet it seems that only his enemies were that harsh in their judgements, and only occasionally, when his inability to offer strong leadership resulted in him being eclipsed by his councillors. One poem of the age, *God Amend Wicked Counsel*, makes a fictional Henry admit that many men were slain because his 'own brain held nowth my lords under awe'.[9] He may have had a 'natural weakness, totally unfitting him to govern' and 'yielded himself up to the guidance of others'[10] but his contemporaries still found much to admire in his character. Had his Lancastrian adherents thought to exploit these qualities during his first reign, presenting him as a divine figure, pre-empting the cult that followed, they may have been able to preserve him as a symbolic figure whose will they interpreted. But Henry also suffered from the strength of his relentless opposition. Hookham stated that his deficiencies were balanced by his qualities, being so 'chaste, temperate, meek and holy, and so good and amiable, that he was beloved by his people, and even by his enemies', but while this was true on a personal level, as a political figure, as a king, 'the weakness of his understanding made him at times appear contemptible in the eyes of those who ought to have reverenced his authority, the purity and innocence of his life preserved their affection for him'. His saintly nature was put to the test repeatedly, as 'the conduct of King Henry when deprived of his crown was exemplary, and when reduced to the level of his subjects, he bore his misfortunes with such meekness and patience, as totally disarmed his successor'.[11]

If Henry was unable to reconcile his personal self with his public role, Margaret suffered from no such difficulties. The problems that led to her failure, and the subsequent vilification of her name, were her nationality and her gender. She was a woman with qualities suitable to kingship but the wrong gender to exercise them, as the rejection of her Protectorship demonstrated. A number of contemporary poems expose the attitudes she was faced with. The 1462 'A Political Retrospect' asserts that it is no wonder that England has been an unhappy country, as 'it is right a great abusion/A woman of a land to be regent,' before launching a particular attack upon Margaret's ambition:

*She and her wicked affinity certain*
*Intend utterly to destroy this region*
*For with them is but death and destruction*
*Robbery and vengeance with all rigour.*[12]

The poem 'God Amend Wicked Counsel', dated to 1464, is narrated by a figure who had reputedly overhead Henry VI lamenting the influence of his wife:

*Sum tyme lords of this land set me at great price*
*Such a prince in this realm was there never none*
*I wedded a wife at my device*
*That was the cause of all my moan.*
*The all her intend said I never nay*
*Therefore I mour and nothing am merry.*[13]

Her early experience of factional politics and strong female leadership did not find the same welcome in England as it did in her native France, where her exceptional strength and talents were more greatly appreciated. Circumstances forced Margaret into a very difficult situation, where to admit defeat would be to relinquish the claims of her husband and son. Instead, she chose to fight. Until that point, her queenship had been conventional, as she took a background role to her husband, channelling her energies through patronage, intercession and modelling ceremonial leadership. Had the crises of the early 1450s not destabilised the country, and her husband, she may have continued this existence, but she was forced to change as circumstances did.

Far from being the masculine, war-like caricature depicted by later authors as revelling in the blood of her enemies, Margaret deserves to be remembered by new generations of historians as stepping up to an almost impossible challenge and sticking it out to the end. That she gambled all she had and lost is not a reflection of her abilities, but rather specific circumstances over which she had limited control. Margaret of Anjou, Queen of England, singlehandedly took on the salvation of the Lancastrian dynasty with great heroism, loyalty and resolve. She lost everything she had: her husband, son, her status, wealth, respect and eventually, her life. She deserves that history should honour her for it.

# Notes

## Introduction

1. Wolffe, Bertram Henry VI Yale University Press, 1991
2. Ibid
3. Dockray, Keith Henry VI, Margaret of Anjou and the Wars of the Roses Fonthill 2000
4. Lewis, Katherine Kingship and Masculinity in Late Medieval England Routlege 2013
5. Kehler, Dorothea Shakespeare's Widows Palgrave Macmillan 2003

## Prologue

1. Allmand, Christopher *Henry V* Yale University Press 2014
2. Monstrelet, Engerrand de (trans Thomas Johnes) *The Chronicle of Enguerrand de Monstrelet* Henry G Bohn, London 1853
3. Matusiak, John *Henry V* Routledge 2012
4. Monstrelet
5. Ibid

## One: Henry 1421-44

1. Urlanis, BTS *Rost naseleniiav Evrope: opyt ischisleniia* Population Growth in Europe (in Russian). 1941 Moscow: OGIZ-Gospolitizdat
2. https://www.royalcollection.org.uk/visit/windsorcastle/about/who-built-the-castle
3. Ibid
4. Capgrave, John, Book of the Illustrious Henries (trans F.G Hingeston) Longman, Brown, Green, Longmans and Roberts, London, 1858.
5. Gairdner, James (ed.) Gregory's Chronicle: The Historical Collections of a Citizen of London in the Fifteenth Century Camden Society, London, 1876
6. Calendar of Patent Rolls 1422-29 Henry VI, Volume 1
7. Griffiths, R.A., The Reign of King Henry VI Ernest Benn 1981
8. CPR

9.  Griffiths
10. CPR
11. Griffiths
12. Ibid
13. Kingford, Charles Lethbridge, (ed.) Chronicles of London Clarendon Press 1905
14. Ibid
15. Devon, Frederick, (ed.) Issues of the Exchequer J. Murray 1837
16. Ibid
17. Ibid
18. Stowe, John, (ed.) Three Fifteenth Century Chronicles with Historical Memoranda Camden Society, London 1880
19. Exchequer Rolls
20. Stowe
21. Gregory
22. Ibid
23. Ibid
24. Wolffe, Bertram Henry VI Yale University Press, 1991
25. Gregory
26. Ibid
27. Monstrelet
28. Ibid
29. Gregory
30. Wolffe
31. Watts, John Henry VI and the Politics of Kingship Cambridge University Press 1999
32. Halliwell-Phipps, James Orchard, Letters of the Kings of England, Volume 1 H. Colbourn 1846

## Two: Margaret 1430–1444

1.  Haswell, Jock The Ardent Queen: Margaret of Anjou and the Lancastrian Heritage Peter Davies 1976
2.  http://www.mousson.com/index.php?page=templates-and-stylesheets
3.  Rohr, Zita Eva, Yolande of Aragon 1382-1443 Family and Power: The Reverse of the Tapestry Palgrave Macmillan 2016
4.  Hookham, Mary Ann, The Life and Times of Margaret of Anjou, Queen of England and 1872
5.  Ibid
6.  Ibid

7. Ibid
8. Staley, Edgcumbe, King René d'Anjou and his Seven Queens John Long, London 1912
9. Ibid
10. Ibid
11. Ibid
12. Brooke, C. N. L. and V. Ortenberg, 'The Birth of Margaret of Anjou' Journal of Historical Research Volume 61 Issue 146 p357-8 October 1998
13. Hookham
14. Haswell
15. Ibid
16. Staley
17. Ibid
18. Rohr
19. Kekewich M, The Good King: René of Anjou and Fifteenth Century Europe Palgrave Macmillan 2008
20. BL Egerton MS 1070
21. Ibid
22. Anjou, René d', The Book of the Love-Smitten Heart (1457) Routledge 2011
23. Ibid

## Three: Marriage 1444–1445

1. Staley
2. Abbott, Jacob, History of Margaret of Anjou, Queen of Henry VI of England Harper and Brothers 1861
3. Seward, Desmond, *The Hundred Years' War* Constable and Company 1978
4. Ibid
5. Hookham
6. Griffiths
7. Hookham
8. Ibid
9. Ibid
10. Weir, Alison Lancaster and York: The Wars of the Roses. Vintage 2009
11. Abbott
12. Ibid
13. Ibid
14. Hookham
15. Ibid

16. Myers, A. R. Crown, Household and Parliament in Fifteenth Century England Continuum 1985
17. Abbott
18. SLP Milan 1385-1616 26
19. Wolffe
20. Abbott
21. Griffiths
22. Ibid
23. Hall
24. Rymer, Thomas, *Feodera* London 1739-45
25. Ibid
26. Kendall, Paul Murray, *Richard III* (1955) W W Norton 2002
27. Abbott
28. Thomson, Richard, *Chronicles of London Bridge* Smith, Elder and Co, 1827.
29. Ibid
30. Ibid
31. Fabyan, Robert, *The New Chronicles of England and France in two Parts.* (ed. Henry Ellis) F.C and J. Rivington, London 1811
32. Hookham
33. Thomson
34. Rymer
35. Ibid
36. Hookham
37. Gairdner, James, (ed.) Gregory's Chronicle: The Historical Collections of a Citizen of London in the Fifteenth Century Camden Society, London, 1876

## Four: The Young Wife 1445–1453

1. Griffiths
2. Hall, Edward, *Hall's Chronicle of England* (ed. Grafton, Richard) J. Johnson et al., London 1809
3. Dockray
4. Blacman, John, Henry the Sixth: A Reprint of John Blacman's Memoir Cambridge University Press 1919
5. Hall
6. Ibid
7. Ibid
8. Lancelott, Francis, *Queens of England and their Times* D Appleton and Co, New York, 1859

9.  Griffiths
10. Monro, Cecil, (ed.) Letters of Queen Margaret of Anjou and Bishop Beckington and Others Camden Society 1863
11. Ibid
12. Ibid
13. Ibid
14. Griffiths
15. Hookham
16. Ibid
17. Wolffe
18. Haswell
19. Hall
20. Dockray
21. Fabyan
22. Hall
23. Griffiths
24. Haswell
25. Ibid
26. Griffiths
27. Ibid
28. Ibid
29. Scattergood, V. J., *Politics and Poetry in the Fifteenth Century* Blandford Press, London 1971
30. Griffiths
31. Wolffe
32. Exeter City Archives, Hooker Bk 51, fols 309 v-310, 317v
33. Wolffe
34. Platts, Beryl, *A History of Greenwich* Procter Press, London 1973
35. Griffiths

## Five: Madness 1453-5

1.  Gairdner, James, *Paston Letters* Cambridge University Press 1898
2.  Griffiths
3.  Storey, R. L., *The End of the House of Lancaster* Barrie and Rockliff 1966
4.  Giles, John Allen, The Chronicles of the White Rose of York J. Bohn 1845
5.  Storey
6.  Giles
7.  Ibid
8.  Hookham

9.  Ibid
10. Blacman
11. Dockray
12. Griffiths
13. Johnson, P.A., *Duke Richard of York 1411–1460* Oxford Historical Monographs, Clarendon Press 1988
14. Ibid
15. Gairdner, Paston Letters
16. *Rotuli Parliamentorum* Volume 5 pp288-9 London 1783
17. *Rotuli Parliamentorum* Volume 5 pp241-2
18. Ibid
19. Ibid
20. Hookham
21. Johnson
22. Scattergood
23. Rotuli Parliamentorum Volume 5 pp280-1

## Six: War 1455–1458

1.  Wolffe
2.  Gairdner
3.  Davies, John Silvester, (ed.) An English Chronicle of the Reigns of Richard II, Henry IV, Henry V and Henry VI Camden Society, London 1856
4.  Dockray
5.  Ibid
6.  Davies
7.  Griffiths
8.  Abbott
9.  Griffiths
10. SLP Milan 23
11. Vergil, Polydore, *The History of England 1534*
12. Wolffe
13. Rymer
14. Wolffe
15. Gairdner
16. Rotuli Parliamentorum Volume 5 p282
17. Vergil
18. Milan 184
19. Chancery Patent Rolls 1452–61
20. Ibid

21. Eyre and Spottiswoode
22. Abbott
23. Victoria County History Hertfordshire
24. Vergil
25. Hall
26. Hall
27. Hookham
28. Dockray
29. Milan 184
30. Griffiths
31. Milan 191
32. Scattergood
33. Ibid
34. Hookham
35. Griffiths
36. Storey
37. Hall
38. Ibid
39. Hookham
40. Giles
41. Griffiths
42. Hookham
43. Scattergood
44. Rymer
45. Davies
46. Milan *26*

## Seven: Disaster 1459–1460

1. Wolffe
2. Ibid
3. Giles
4. Davies
5. Ibid
6. Dockray
7. Ibid
8. Ibid
9. Ibid
10. Ibid
11. Rotuli Parliamentorum

12. Ibid
13. Victoria County History Warwickshire
14. Gairdner
15. Rymer
16. Griffiths
17. Ibid
18. Ibid
19. Ibid
20. Milan 37
21. Ibid
22. Ibid
23. Ibid
24. Ibid
25. Gregory
26. Ibid
27. Hookham
28. Milan 38
29. Croyland
30. Milan 38
31. Ibid
32. Rymer
33. Giles
34. Dockray
35. Croyland
36. Gregory
37. Rotuli Parliamentorum
38. Ibid
39. Dockray
40. Croyland
41. Gregory
42. Ibid
43. Gregory

## Eight: Civic Chaos 1461

1. Davies
2. Ibid
3. Rymer
4. Lewis, Katherine, *Kingship and Masculinity in Late Medieval England* Routlege 2013

5.  Hall
6.  Milan 54
7.  Ibid
8.  Milan 52
9.  Milan 74
10. Milan 79
11. Milan 62
12. Milan 74
13. Davies
14. Dockray
15. Ibid
16. Ibid
17. Griffiths
18. Milan 78
19. Gregory
20. Davies
21. Gregory
22. Milan 64
23. Milan 79
24. Giles
25. Davies
26. Croyland
27. Milan 65
28. Ibid
29. Ibid
30. Milan 78
31. Gregory
32. Ibid
33. Davies
34. Milan 70
35. Milan 72
36. Mian 78
37. Milan 76
38. Milan 73
39. Milan 76
40. Milan 78
41. Milan 76
42. Gregory

## Nine: Royals in Waiting 1461–1470

1. Blacman
2. Ibid
3. Milan 120
4. Halliwell-Phillipps, James Orchard, *Letters of the Kings of England* Volume 1 Colburn 1846
5. Milan 107
6. Ibid
7. Milan 109
8. Hookham
9. Dockray
10. Hookham
11. Rotuli Parliamentorum
12. Ibid
13. Ibid
14. Milan 125
15. Ross, James *The Foremost Man of the Kingdom: John de Vere, Thirteenth Earl of Oxford* Boydell and Brewer 2015
16. Ibid
17. Prevost D'Exiles, Antoine Francois, *Histoire De Margeurite d'Anjou* Jean Catuffe, Amsterdam 1741
18. Strickland
19. Griffiths
20. Gairdner
21. Dockray
22. Gregory
23. Hookham
24. Gregory
25. Hookham
26. Ibid
27. Ibid
28. Milan 191
29. Lowe, Ben *Imagining Peace: A History of Early English Pacifist Ideas* Pennsylvania State University Press 2010
30. Griffiths
31. Ibid
32. Milan 142
33. Ibid
34. Gregory

35. Wolffe
36. Ibid
37. Blacman
38. Strickland
39. Milan 146
40. Ibid
41. Milan 150
42. Milan 150,151
43. Ibid
44. Milan 154
45. Milan 162
46. Ibid
47. Milan 174
48. Hookham

## Ten: Readeption 1470–1471

1.  Milan 183
2.  Milan 184
3.  Milan 189
4.  Milan 190
5.  Giles
6.  Ibid
7.  Milan 191
8.  Ibid
9.  Giles
10. Ibid
11. Ibid
12. Milan 194
13. Milan 196
14. Giles
15. Milan 197
16. Croyland
17. Milan 198
18. Milan 199
19. Milan 208
20. Giles
21. Ibid
22. Ibid
23. Ibid

24. Hookham
25. Giles
26. Blacman
27. Ibid
28. Ibid
29. Giles
30. Hookham
31. Milan 215
32. Giles
33. Milan 216
34. Ibid
35. Giles
36. Croyland
37. Hookham
38. Giles
39. Milan 217
40. Giles
41. Hookham
42. Vergil
43. Fabyan
44. Abbott
45. Ibid
46. Milan 218
47. Giles
48. Milan 218
49. Croyland
50. Milan 220
51. Vergil
52. Croyland
53. Davies
54. Devon, Frederick, (ed.) *Issues of the Exchequer* J. Murray 1837
55. Hope, W. H. St John, 'The Discovery of the Remains of King Henry VI in St. George's Chapel, Windsor Castle'. *Archaeologia, 1911*

## Eleven: The Prisoner 1471–1482

1. Gairdner
2. Dockray
3. Haswell
4. Ibid

5.  Strickland
6.  Ibid
7.  Blacman
8.  Hookham
9.  Scattergood
10. Hookham
11. Ibid
12. Scattergood
13. Scattergood

# Bibliography

Abbott, Jacob, *History of Margaret of Anjou, Queen of Henry VI of England* Harper and Brothers 1861

Allmand, Christopher, *Henry V* Yale University Press 2014

Anjou, René d', *The Book of the Love-Smitten Heart* (1457) Routledge 2011

B. L. Egerton MS 1070

Blacman, John, *Henry the Sixth: A Reprint of John Blacman's Memoir* Cambridge University Press 1919

Brooke, C. N. L and V. Ortenberg, 'The Birth of Margaret of Anjou' *Journal of Historical Research* Volume 61 Issue 146 p357-8 October 1998

Calendar of Patent Rolls 1422–29 Henry VI, Volume 1

Capgrave, John, *Chronicle of England* (trans F.G Hingeston) Longman, Brown, Green, Longmans and Roberts, London, 1858.

Chancery Patent Rolls 1452–61

"Chronicle of Normandy" in *Gesta Henrici Quinti* Sumptimus Societatis 1853

Craig, Lee Ann, 'Royalty, Virtue and Adversity: The Cult of Henry VI' *Albion: A Quarterly Journal Concerned with British Studies*. Vol 35, No 2 (Summer 2003), 187-209

Davies, John Silvester, (ed.) *An English Chronicle of the Reigns of Richard II, Henry IV, Henry V and Henry VI* Camden Society, London 1856

Devon, Frederick, (ed.) *Issues of the Exchequer* J. Murray 1837

Dockray, Keith, *Henry VI, Margaret of Anjou and the Wars of the Roses* Fonthill 2000

Dodd, Gwilim, (ed.) *Henry V: New Interpretations* Boydell and Brewer 2013

Dryden, Daisy Dean, *Margaret of Anjou and her Relation to the Wars of the Roses*, MA Thesis, University of Illinois 1916

Fabyan, Robert, *The New Chronicles of England and France in two Parts*. (ed. Henry Ellis) F. C. and J. Rivington, London 1811

Gairdner, James, (ed.) *Gregory's Chronicle: The Historical Collections of a Citizen of London in the Fifteenth Century* Camden Society, London, 1876

Gairdner, James, *Paston Letters* Cambridge University Press 1898

Gifford, John, *The History of France, from the Earliest Times to the Accession of Louis XVI* C. Lowndes, London 1793

Giles, John Allen, *The Chronicles of the White Rose of York* J. Bohn 1845

Griffiths, R. A., *The Reign of King Henry VI* Ernest Benn 1981

Hall, Edward, *Hall's Chronicle of England* (ed. Grafton, Richard) J. Johnson et al, London 1809

Halliwell-Phipps, James Orchard, *Letters of the Kings of England, Volume 1* H. Colbourn 1846

Haswell, Jock, *The Ardent Queen: Margaret of Anjou and the Lancastrian Heritage* Peter Davies 1976

Holford Hodson, Margaret, *Margaret of Anjou: A Poem in ten Cantos* John Murray 1816

Hookham, Mary Ann, The Life and Times of Margaret of Anjou, Queen of England 1872

Hope, W. H. St John, 'The Discovery of the Remains of King Henry VI in St. George's Chapel, Windsor Castle.' *Archaeologia, 1911*

Johnson, P.A., *Duke Richard of York 1411–1460* Oxford Historical Monographs, Clarendon Press 1988

Kekewich, M, *The Good King: René of Anjou and Fifteenth Century Europe* Palgrave Macmillan 2008

Kehler, Dorothea, *Shakespeare's Widows* Palgrave Macmillan 2003

Kendall, Paul Murray, *Louis XI* Sphere Books 1974

Kendall, Paul Murray, *Richard III* (1955) W W Norton 2002

Kingford, Charles Lethbridge, (ed.) *Chronicles of London* Clarendon Press 1905

Knox, Ronald (trans.) *The Miracles of King Henry VI: Being an Account and Translation of Twenty-three Miracles taken from the Manuscript in the British Museum* (Royal 13 c. viii) with Introductions by Father Ronald Konx and Shane Leslie. Cambridge University Press, 1923

Lancelott, Francis, *Queens of England and their Times* D Appleton and Co, New York, 1859

Leland, John, *De Rebus Britannicis Collectaena*, ed. Thomas Hearne, vol. IV London, 1977

Lewis, Katherine, *Kingship and Masculinity in Late Medieval England* Routlege 2013

Lowe, Ben, *Imagining Peace: A History of Early English Pacifist Ideas* Pennsylvania State University Press 2010

McKenna, J. W., 'Piety and Propaganda in the Cult of Henry VI' in Rowland, B (ed.) *Chaucer and Middle English Studies in honour of Rossell Hope Robbins* London: George Allen & Unwin Ltd, 1974

Matusiak, John, *Henry V* Routledge 2012

Maurer, Helen E., *Margaret of Anjou: Queenship and Power in Late Medieval England* Boydell Press 2003

Monro, Cecil, (ed.) *Letters of Queen Margaret of Anjou and Bishop Beckington and Others* Camden Society 1863

Monstrelet, Engerrand de, (trans Thomas Johnes) *The Chronicle of Enguerrand de Monstrelet* Henry G Bohn, London 1853

Mortimer, Ian, *1415: Henry V's Year of Glory* Bodley Head 2009

Myers, A. R., *Crown, Household and Parliament in Fifteenth Century England* Continuum 1985

Platts, Beryl, *A History of Greenwich* Procter Press, London 1973

Prevost D'Exiles, Antoine Francois, *Histoire De Margeurite d'Anjou* Jean Catuffe, Amsterdam 1741

Rohr, Zita Eva, *Yolande of Aragon 1382–1443 Family and Power: The Reverse of the Tapestry* Palgrave Macmillan 2016

Ross, James, *The Foremost Man of the Kingdom: John de Vere, Thirteenth Earl of Oxford* Boydell and Brewer 2015

*Rotuli Parliamentorum* Volume 5, London 1783

Rymer, Thomas, *Feodera* London 1739-45

Ross, James, *Henry VI: A Good, Simple and Innocent Man* Penguin, 2016

Scattergood, V. J., *Politics and Poetry in the Fifteenth Century* Blandford Press, London 1971

Seward, Desmond, *The Hundred Years' War* Constable and Company 1978

Stowe, John, (ed.) Three Fifteenth Century Chronicles with Historical Memoranda Camden Society, London 1880

Staley, Edgcumbe *King René d'Anjou and his Seven Queens* John Long, London 1912

Storey, R. L., *The End of the House of Lancaster* Barrie and Rockliff 1966

Strickland, Agnes, *Queens of England,* Volume 1 Estes and Lariat, Boston 1894

Thomson, Richard, *Chronicles of London Bridge* Smith, Elder and Co, 1827.

1 Urlanis, BTS *Rost naseleniiav Evrope: opyt ischisleniia* Population Growth in Europe (in Russian). 1941 Moscow: OGIZ-Gospolitizdat

Vergil, Polydore, *The History of England* 1534

Watts, John, *Henry VI and the Politics of Kingship* Cambridge University Press 1999

Weir, Alison, *Lancaster and York: The Wars of the Roses.* Vintage 2009

Wolffe, Bertram, *Henry VI* Yale University Press, 1991

# Acknowledgements

My gratitude and thanks go to Claire Hopkins for commissioning this book, to my editor Karyn Burnham, and to Janet Brookes and the team at Pen and Sword. I have been particularly blessed to have some wonderful friends: thank you to Anne Marie Bouchard, Sharon Bennett Connolly and my godmother, 'Lady' Susan Priestley, for being my tireless champions, and to all the others whose friendship and encouragement have helped keep me sane. Thanks also to all my family, to my husband Tom and my sons Rufus and Robin, to Paul Fairbrass, Sue and John Hunt and Pascale Rose. Most of all, it is for my mother for her invaluable proof-reading skills and for my father for his enthusiasm and open mind: this is the result of the books they read to me, the museums they took me to as a child and the love and imagination with which they encouraged me.